D1083390

GEORG LUKÁCS
AND HIS GENERATION
1900-1918

GEORG LUKÁCS

AND HIS
GENERATION
1900-1918

MARY GLUCK

HARVARD UNIVERSITY PRESS
Cambridge, Massachusetts
and London, England
1985

Library of Congress Cataloging in Publication Data

Gluck, Mary.
Georg Lukács and his generation, 1900–1918.

Bibliography: p.
Includes index.
1.   Lukács, György, 1885–1971.
2.   Philosophy, Hungarian—20th century.
3.   Philosophers—Hungary.
I. Title.
B4815.L84G58   1985   199′.439   85-905
ISBN 0-674-34865-6 (alk. paper)

Designed by Gwen Frankfeldt

To
George,
Sandra,
and Warren

ACKNOWLEDGMENTS

The questions which motivated me to write this book preceded my acquaintance with Lukács. They stem from an interest in the historical problem of modernist culture, first kindled by Jacques Barzun, to whose broad scholarship and early guidance and encouragement I am most indebted. Péter Hanák introduced me to the writers and scholarship of fin de siècle Hungary and helped me to begin to understand this world from within.

Perhaps more than most, this study is based on the work of other scholars who, during the past decade, have made available for researchers in Hungary an increasingly rich body of primary sources on Lukács and his early circle. Éva Fekete and Éva Karádi's collection of Lukács' early letters, Éva Karádi and Erzsébet Vezér's anthology on the Sunday Circle, and Árpád Timár's collection of Lukács' early articles made my own task infinitely easier and smoother than it would otherwise have been.

On my different trips to Budapest, Erzsébet Vezér has been most helpful in both theoretical and practical ways: her expertise—which ranges from modern Hungarian literature, to the ins and outs of Budapest

vii

archives and libraries, to the secret of baking perfect *pogácsa*—was invaluable. György Litván, Tibor Hajdú, and Miklós Szabó spent many hours discussing with me the ideas of Jászi and Hungarian radicalism and politics at the turn of the century; even when we disagreed, these discussions were immensely helpful and enjoyable. I am most particularly grateful to Éva Karádi for her generosity in sharing with me both her ideas and her sources on Lukács, and for the friendship and hospitality she and Gábor Varró extended to me while I was in Budapest.

The actual writing of a book is a solitary enterprise, yet it cannot be done alone. Chapters in progress were read and commented upon by John Toews, Nancy Rosenblum, Naomi Lamoreaux, and James Patterson, whose sound criticisms much improved the structure and style of the book. David Sorkin read the entire manuscript at the end and made valuable suggestions about the introduction and the closing. The comments of Joan Scott and the Pembroke Seminar at Brown University on a talk I presented on sexual polarity in the Sunday Circle helped focus my attention on the collective presence of the women in the group and directly contributed to the formulation of the first chapter. John Komlos kindly obtained photographs and written permission for citation from the Lukács Archives on a brief trip to Budapest when he was already pressed for time. I owe a more fundamental and general debt of gratitude to Paul Breines, who has been more than generous with his time and interest and whose enthusiasm helped reassure me in moments of doubt. Finally, my deepest thanks go to Abbott Gleason, who read and commented on the manuscript in its various forms over the years and whose support and friendship have been invaluable for the completion of the book.

I received a travel fellowship from the Canada Council in the summer of 1977 for archival research. In 1980–81, combined grants from the American Council of Learned Societies and the American Association of University Women allowed me to write a good part of the manuscript. And in the fall of 1983 a sabbatical leave from Brown University enabled me to complete the book. Karen Mota and Lori D'Acunto have been most patient in typing and retyping this manuscript, a task which involved dealing with incomprehensible Hungarian words, indecipherable handwriting, and impossible deadlines.

Acknowledgments

I am fortunate in having family who are friends and friends who are family. In particular, Sandra and George Gluck, Ann and Paul Pitel, and Jan Goldstein have been not only good readers and listeners but unfailingly loyal and involved participants in this project.

CONTENTS

ILLUSTRATIONS

The illustrations were obtained from Éva Karádi, who with Éva Fekete has compiled them in a book of photographs, *György Lukács: His Life in Pictures and Documents* (Budapest: Corvina, 1981).

Following page 160

What are you really doing, erecting an ideal
or knocking one down? I may perhaps be asked.
But have you ever asked yourself sufficiently
how much the erection of every ideal on earth
has cost? If a temple is to be erected,
a temple must be destroyed: that is the law—
let anyone who can show me a case
in which it is not fulfilled.

Friedrich Nietzsche

To be a stranger is . . . a very positive relation:
it is a specific form of interaction.

Georg Simmel

INTRODUCTION

I attempt in the following pages to trace the early experiences of a small circle of radical artists and intellectuals who came of age within the world of fin de siècle Budapest, and who lived through the destruction of this world with the outbreak of the First World War, the collapse of the Austro-Hungarian monarchy, and the eruption of revolutions in Hungary between 1918 and 1919.

Technically these young people belonged to what has come to be known in European history as the "Generation of 1914."[1] Their formative years spanned the first decade and a half of the twentieth century, and their lives were irrevocably transformed and reoriented by the cataclysms of war, political collapse, and military upheaval. Yet these were also East European intellectuals, slightly out of step with Western developments, and their formative cultural experiences were not exactly parallel to those of their European contemporaries. They experienced almost simultaneously both the self-consciously negative, anti-bourgeois impulses commonly associated with the aesthetes of the 1880s and the affirmative, utopian hopes for cultural renewal more characteristic of the artistic generation of the immediate prewar years. From the prism of their unique perspective emerged some of the most interesting and sophisticated discussions about the nature of the modernist impulse and sensibility in prewar Europe.

The Sunday Circle, as the group was informally called during its heyday, dispersed after the war, and most of its members emigrated to Germany, the Soviet Union, Italy, France, England, and the United States, where they began entirely new lives and new careers. Several, like Georg Lukács, Karl Mannheim, and Arnold Hauser, were to establish important scholarly careers during those years, and have in fact become far more closely associated with their postwar achievements than with their early beginnings in prewar Budapest.[2] In resurrecting the history of their youthful circle in Hungary, I have consciously attempted to avoid the fallacy of historical hindsight by emphasizing the importance of individuals as they appeared at the time, rather than as they seem to us in retrospect. This has meant that well-known figures like Mannheim and Hauser appear fairly infrequently in my account, since they were too young to play a central role in the group before 1915, whereas individuals relatively unknown in the West, like Béla Balázs and Anna Lesznai, assume a much more dominant role in the story. My goal throughout has been to draw a collective portrait of a generational group rather than sketches of discrete individuals, no matter how interesting they may have been in and of themselves.

The role of Georg Lukács in this generational portrait is a particularly complex one which needs a few words of comment and explanation. Lukács was not only the most talented but also the single most dominant member of the Sunday Circle, which was sometimes simply referred to as the "Lukács Circle," in recognition of the budding philosopher's growing reputation and influence. Not surprisingly, Lukács has assumed a pivotal role in my account, which is often structured around the young thinker's emotional and philosophic evolution during these years. Yet my interest in the intimate nuances of Lukács' work and personality has almost always been informed by more general concerns which transcend Lukács' unique development as an individual. He was, as such Lukács scholars as Michael Löwy have remarked, an unusually passionate thinker, the very radicalism of whose life illustrates some of the quintessential dilemmas of avant-garde intellectuals in the early years of this century.

The presentation of Lukács as in some ways a representative figure for the generation of 1914 is strongly supported by contemporary evidence as well. Beginning in 1907, when Lukács officially commenced his career as a literary critic—or more accurately, as a philosopher of literary forms—he consistently thought of his life and work as indissolubly fused with and inseparable from what he perceived to be the deep-seated cultural crisis of his age. Nevertheless, it must be admitted that this particular approach to the young Lukács is based on certain implicit assumptions about the nature of his pre-Marxist career which should be spelled out somewhat more explicitly.

Such clarification is especially appropriate in this case, since Lukács is a controversial, if elusive figure, whose work remains pivotal for contemporary discussions of modernism, Marxism, Stalinism, and several other "isms" of the twentieth century. As the Polish philosopher Leszek Kolakowski accurately pointed out, "Lukács' personality and his role in the history of Marxism are, and no doubt will continue to be for a long time, a matter of lively controversy."[3] Over the past decade, a growing body of Lukács scholarship has drawn ever more subtle distinctions between the "mature Lukács" of the *Ontology* and the "young Lukács" who wrote *History and Class Consciousness* in the 1920s. In these discussions, the "young Lukács" has clearly received the more persistent and favorable scrutiny, though the "mature Lukács" has also found defenders, particularly among Italian scholars, who, following Lucien Goldmann's lead, have noted interesting parallels between the *Ontology* and Heidegger's existentialism.

My own analysis of Lukács falls somewhat outside the parameters of this debate, dealing as it does neither with the "mature Lukács" nor with the "young Lukács," but rather with a pre-Marxist Lukács anchored within the literary and intellectual world of fin de siècle Budapest. That this early phase of Lukács' life has remained essentially unknown, or at best shadowy, until recently has several interesting causes. The first is that the Marxist Lukács consistently reinterpreted his early career, obscuring and underplaying its literary and artistic dimensions. The second is that the documents which would have supplied a more nuanced and accurate picture of the early life are mostly in Hungarian, a language inaccessible to the majority of Lukács scholars, and lay hidden in a Heidelberg safe until 1972, a year after Lukács' death. (Lukács had deposited these early letters, diaries, notations for articles, and fragmentary works for safekeeping with a Heidelberg bank in 1917, shortly before his return to Budapest, and had never reclaimed them or discussed their existence with friends and students afterward.)

Based on this extraordinarily rich archival discovery, several interesting new interpretations of the pre-Marxist Lukács have appeared in recent years and, I expect, will continue to appear for some time to come. Perhaps the earliest attempts to reinterpret Lukács' biography in light of his early works came from Lukács' own students in Budapest—Ágnes Heller, Ferenc Fehér, György Márkus, and Mihály Vajda—whose subtle articles have now been translated into English and published in a collection edited by Ágnes Heller, *Lukács Reappraised*. Western scholars soon followed suit. Michael Löwy's book *Georg Lukács—From Romanticism to Bolshevism*, shows the young Lukács' early rebellion against capitalism to be inextricably connected to his later Marxist philosophy. Lee Congdon, in a more recent book entitled *The Young Lukács*, draws a slightly more critical portrait of Lukács' eventual conversion to Marxism, stressing his indebtedness to Dostoevsky and the fateful influence the concept of terror was to have on his later political and ideological development. J. M. Bernstein, in *The Philosophy of the Novel: Lukács, Marxism, and the Dialectics of Form*, focuses even more closely on the juncture between his Marxist and pre-Marxist careers and points to the essential continuities between works like *The Theory of the Novel* and *History and Class Consciousness*.

Different as these interpretations of the young Lukács are, they all share to some extent the older Lukács' characterization of his pre-Marxist career. This view implies that the years before Lukács officially joined the Communist party of Hungary in late 1918 were a time of unfocused personal radicalism and painful ideological quest, whose essential meaning derives from, and is illuminated by, the final Marxist outcome, posited as a necessary given at the end of the quest. Though the elements of continuity between Lukács' pre-Marxist and Marxist careers are undeniably strong and certainly fascinating, I do not feel that Marxism was the inevitable or even characteristic culmination of the kind of cultural radicalism that the young Lukács embodied to such a perfect degree before 1918. As the later histories of members of the Sunday Circle illustrate, revolutionary socialism was only one among several options that they might have pursued in the changed ideological climate of the postwar years. I have, in fact, focused very little on Lukács' transition to Marxism in the 1920s, feeling that this problem has already been ably dealt with by scholars like Michael Löwy, Paul Brienes, Andrew Arato,[4] and Lee Congdon.

My own reading of Lukács' early life and work tends to invest his so-called romantic anticapitalist period before 1918 with far more weight, autonomy, and philosophic seriousness than the Marxist Lukács would have felt warranted or justified. I feel not only that it was a particularly creative phase of Lukács' life but that, more important, it had a cultural coherence of its own which parallels and illuminates the inner strivings of the early modernists before the outbreak of the First World War. Given Lukács' well-known and passionate repudiation of all forms of artistic and philosophic modernism in later life, there may exist a certain paradox in this assertion, but the paradox is only superficial. It exists only if we regard Lukács' career, as well as the history of the modernist movement, as an undifferentiated monolith with no internal tensions or philosophic discontinuities, and this is certainly not the case.

Within Lukács' pre-Marxist career itself, there occurred around 1910–11 an important and infrequently analyzed crisis as a result of which he definitively rejected Impressionism and aestheticism in art and set out to formulate a new aesthetic philosophy of his own which he hoped would form the basis of a novel and revolutionary cultural synthesis in the future. This significant shift of emphasis in Lukács' early development was paralleled in the lives of most of his friends, who began around the same time to express similar longings for unity, affirmation, inner truthfulness, and simplicity, after what they perceived as the excessively negative, cerebral, and individualistic temper of the late nineteenth century. D. H. Lawrence expressed their common attitude well in a review of 1913: "The nihilists, the intellectual, hopeless people—Ibsen, Flaubert, Hardy—represent the dream we are awakening from."[5]

This mood of hopefulness verging on messianic expectation, which was shared by most young experimental artists and writers of the early twentieth century, has often been commented upon but rarely analyzed with sufficient detail and attention. Yet most historians of the modern movement in the arts have agreed that early modernism represented something more than an aesthetic event. It was also, argued Renato Poggioli, the manifestation of a "common psychological condition" and of a "unique ideological fact."[6] The nature of this "ideological fact," however, has proven to be elusive. Part of the problem is that artistic manifestoes, which have formed our major source of insight into the broader philosophic strivings of the early modernists, are too diffuse, emotional, and apocalyptic in tone to offer satisfactory definitions. But an even greater difficulty lies in the fact that modernism is not readily comprehensible within any of our established philosophic or ideological categories. When looked at closely, it seems to encompass many different, apparently contradictory elements, held together by a passionate, almost eschatological mood of hope, despair, and elation.

Manifestations of strikingly heterogeneous ideological and philosophic impulses are evident in almost any realm of modernist endeavor one chooses to focus on. The early modernists were, as several observers have pointed out, remarkably sensitive to religious and spiritual states and often defined their personal and artistic goals within the symbolic framework of a religious quest, a search for salvation or metaphysical truth. Yet they remained, in the early days at any rate, markedly hostile or indifferent to established religions. They were aggressively secular, even pagan in spirit, and they abhorred the other-worldly, instinct-denying aspects of traditional Christianity. Rejecting any kind of dualism between body and soul, they attempted not to transcend physical life but rather to integrate the physical and the spiritual in a life-affirming totality. As one commentator put it, they were looking for "ways to express their conviction that we can be religious about life itself."[7]

The early modernists' attitude toward historic traditions was as ambiguous as their approach to religion. Like traditionalists and reactionaries, they responded to the materialistic, utilitarian civilization of the late nineteenth century with passionate hatred, feeling that "the dubious material gains of progress have been made at the price of stupendous spiritual loss." They shared with conservatives an intense and nostalgic awareness of "life as it was, and is not, and should be."[8] Unlike conservatives, however, the modernists made no attempt to recapture the traditions of bygone ages. They seemed to possess a deeper, more tragic sense of separation from the past, and sensed that its forms and conventions were irretrievable and probably inappropriate for modern man. For them the past became an instrument of criticism against the present, as well as a model of integrity and synthesis for the future. Their feeling was, as Stephen Spender put it, that "the hankering for the past is merely archaic unless it can be expressed in a single, contemporary idiom. The past has to be absorbed into the struggle that goes on within the present, the sense of it re-invented." Thus, they actually transformed their temperamental traditionalism into a radical posture, creating revolutionary artistic and philosophic forms through which to express their allegiance to the values of the past. They invented a new cultural attitude which Spender has aptly described as "revolutionary traditionalism."[9]

This complex relationship to history was paralleled in interesting ways in the early modernists' appropriation of primitive and native folk traditions. They were essentially cosmopolites, closely associated with the urban landscape and cut off "from local origins, class allegiances, the specific obligations and duties of those with an assigned role in a cohesive culture."[10] And yet at the same time they were fascinated by primitivism and folk cultures. In primitive African masks and sculptures, in preclassical Greek artifacts, in Chinese paintings, and in the still unspoiled folk music and poetry of the Irish, East European, and Russian peasantry, they thought to have discovered the sense of personal wholeness and communal rootedness they so bitterly lacked in the modern world. But for reasons analogous to their rejection of traditional Western cultural forms, they made no attempt to transcribe literally into their own work those primitive art forms or nativist folk elements they so admired in their pristine original. Such attempts, wrote Bartók of his own relationship to Hungarian and Slavic folk music, "would have resulted in mere copy work and would never have led to a new, unified stylistic solution."[11] Instead, they adapted these exotic forms for their own needs, radically stylizing or transforming them to become integral parts of a modern artistic idiom.

Such seemingly paradoxical attitudes toward the religious and the pagan, toward tradition and innovation, toward the past and the future make it virtually impossible to label the early modernists as being on either the left or the right, as conservatives or revolutionaries, as idealists or materialists. Their posture has unmistakable parallels in contemporary neoconservative ideologies which also consist of an "ideological collage,"[12] containing elements from opposing poles of the political spectrum thrown together with apparent disregard for reality or practicality.

But this is only one interpretation, colored by the disenchantment of the postwar years, which failed to bring about the cultural rebirth the early modernists were striving for. Looked at from the perspective of the prewar years, their ideological heterodoxy was perfectly natural. After all, they had no desire to find affinity with any existing ideological or political position, no matter how radical it may have seemed. They were attempting to transcend all possible existing schools in the hope of creating a cultural synthesis that had never existed before. Their art and theorizing were ideological in the literal sense of the word, for they viewed these activities as the core of the creative affirmation out of which the new culture was to emerge. Many were convinced that from the sum total of their individual acts, they would somehow conjure up those new values and truths that would allow modern man to live once again in a harmonious and integrated culture.

This astonishingly grandiose enterprise represented both the symptom and the attempted resolution of an unprecedented religious and philosophic crisis in modern Western culture. Lukács and the small band of kindred spirits that began to coalesce around him after 1910 were unusually well situated to understand it, for they were a marginalized and dislocated group, more thoroughly disenchanted with the present and more passionately invested in the future than even their West European counterparts. As East Europeans they were invariably somewhat outside West European developments; as assimilated Jews they were almost completely alienated from their Jewish past; and as Hungarian nationals they were increasingly shut out of an inward-looking and increasingly anti-Semitic national community.

They self-consciously accepted and even welcomed this situation, feeling that it gave them special insights into and sensitivities toward the dilemmas of their age. They were convinced that they were living through a period of cultural rebirth, destined to give rise to a new, synthetic culture of the twentieth century, equal in splendor to the age of the Renaissance, the high Middle Ages, or classical Greece. And they deliberately set themselves up as spokesmen of this new age, whose embryonic forms they believed themselves to be already witnessing in the experimental postimpressionist and expressionist art, literature, and music of the early twentieth century. They were mistaken in their sanguine prognosis for the future, but not in many of their perceptions about the philosophic and cultural tendencies of their age. Their writings and speculations on subjects as diverse as fairy tales, Impressionism, and modern mysticism provide some of the most interesting and revealing insights into this period of transition and transformation out of which the full-blown modernist culture of the postwar period was to emerge.

Neither Lukács nor his friends were willing or able to make the transition to the newer avant-garde of the twenties, embodied in such movements as activism, Dadaism, surrealism, and postwar expressionism. The aesthetic goals, the philosophic vision, the inner sensibility of the younger generation of artists that emerged from the trenches of the First World War remained alien and deeply uncongenial to them. The erstwhile radicals and iconoclasts began to feel like "yesterday's people"[13] in the changed cultural ethos of the postwar world.

To be sure, one can no longer speak of the Sunday Circle as a "group" after 1919. The political pressures in Hungary during 1918–19 polarized them toward either explicitly liberal or Marxist positions and eventually scattered them to the four corners of the earth during the twenties and thirties. Yet whether they ended up as liberals or Marxists, the former Sunday members retained not only abiding ties of affection for one another but also a common ground for discourse and communication. In subtle but important ways, none of them entirely abandoned those formative values and aspirations that had linked them as a generation before the war. Whatever their final political and ideological destination, they remained embedded in a common matrix of assumptions about the existence of objective truths that was instinctively hostile to relativism, existentialism, or pragmatism in any of its modern varieties. Despite their initial iconoclasm and their avowed intention to repudiate the nineteenth century in all its cultural forms, they never fully succeeded, or wished to succeed, in transcending nineteenth-century rational values and breaking through to a genuinely modernist, avant-garde position.

It is, of course, no novelty to point to the elements of continuity between Lukács' Marxist and pre-Marxist careers. Yet the common assumption has been that it was the radical, subversive impulses of the young Lukács that found incarnation within the more organized framework of his mature Marxist philosophy. It is, however, equally valid to argue that Marxism, which was after all a nineteenth-century ideology, also made possible for Lukács the continuation of those rational, classicist tendencies which were equally present, though not always fully articulated, in his prewar cultural rebellion.[14]

When Lukács and roughly half the Sunday Circle joined the Bolsheviks in late 1918, they were convinced that they were throwing in their lot with the forces of the future, destined to sweep mankind to a higher stage of development. Politically this was a plausible assumption in Central Europe in 1918–19. Aesthetically and philosophically, however, it was not. Lukács' turn to Marxism in late 1918 represented a way of remaining faithful to the values of the past, rather than moving forward into the future. Lukács and most of his youthful friends and associates remained what Wyndham Lewis was to call twenty years later "the first men of a future that has not materialized."[15]

1

THE SUNDAY
CIRCLE:
AN OVERVIEW

In 1922, the future sociologist, Karl Mannheim, recently forced into emigration by the political turmoil in his native Hungary, wrote the following assessment of the German cultural scene from Heidelberg:

> The majority of cultivated Germans today are disguised sectarians, supporters of isolated movements, who view the world through the blinkers of some form of "ism" and attempt to orient themselves amidst the chaos surrounding them by means of a few not very sharply defined principles . . . Everywhere, people are awaiting a messiah, and the air is laden with the promises of large and small prophets . . . All is only useless struggle today, and yet, for all that, we find ourselves sadly sympathetic to this indiscriminate enthusiasm, for we all share the same fate: we carry within us more love, and above all more longing than today's society is able to satisfy. We have all ripened for something, and there is no one to harvest the fruit, and we are very much afraid that our spirits are fated to useless decay.[1]

The passage, with its curious blend of empathy and ambivalence, betrays as much about Mannheim as about the cultural and political tendencies of Weimar Germany in the early twenties. Mannheim himself had experienced the "hunger for wholeness"[2] that he noted among German intellectuals after the war, and had in fact been intellectually formed by the same spirit of cultural pessimism that characterized so much of European high culture in the twenties. Yet the note of skepticism and ultimately of stoic resignation in his account is also worth stressing. It betrays an essentially different sensibility, a different kind of philosophic formation from that of the followers of the sectarian movements he was describing, marking him, despite his inner sympathy, an outsider in their midst.

Mannheim belonged to a generation of European intellectuals born in the 1880s and coming to maturity during the first decade of the twentieth century, who, as he himself put it in a manifesto of 1918, "had left behind the positivism of the nineteenth century and had once again turned toward metaphysical idealism."[3] The revolt against positivism was, in fact, only one rather specialized aspect of a broader current of thought and feeling which united a whole generation of radical young intellectuals in the decade before the war.[4] Whether they expressed their views through art, music, philosophy, or even politics, they all shared a common longing for affirmation, for synthesis and community, after what they perceived as the sterile skepticism and fragmented individualism of the previous generation. They felt themselves to be, wrote Mannheim, the prototypes of a "novel type of European intellectual still in the process of evolving . . . [who] substitutes the problem of transcendence for outworn materialism; the universal validity of principles for an anarchic world view."[5]

The hopes for cultural rebirth and integration which intellectuals like Mannheim proclaimed so passionately in the years before the First World War were not to be realized—not, at any rate, in the form they had envisioned. The cultural temper of the generation that came to maturity during and immediately after the war was markedly different from that of its somewhat older predecessors. Despite obvious elements of continuity in the outward expression of philosophic and artistic concerns, the sensibilities and implicit assumptions of these younger innovators had radically changed, and they did not constitute the cultural heirs the prewar generation had hoped for.

It is, of course, a commonplace to talk of the First World War as a watershed in European history, marking a catastrophic break from the stable world of nineteenth-century hopes and verities. Yet it is far less easy to analyze precisely the nature and structure of this change and its broader philosophic and political implications. The usual accounts about the increased pessimism, disenchantment, and alienation of the Lost Generation of the twenties, though undoubtedly true, nevertheless remain inadequate explanations for what in retrospect clearly constituted a major cultural and philosophic reorientation in European history. Part of the difficulty of going beyond impressionistic generalizations lies in the fact that most West European artists and intellectuals experienced the phenomenon as a general shift in mood and ambiance rather than as a clearly marked philosophic or political event that could be identified and analyzed.

There were exceptions to this, however, especially in Eastern Europe and Russia, where the experience of discontinuity for artists and intellectuals tended to be far more catastrophic than for their counterparts in the West. Here the war brought not only cultural but also political and economic dislocations of such magnitude that no illusion of continuity with the prewar world could be maintained. The experiences of such non-Western intellectuals—and Mannheim himself was one of them—are illuminating in their very extremism, shedding unexpected light on the larger process of cultural reorientation taking place around that time.

—

Karl Mannheim had been part of the small and little-known intellectual group in prewar Hungary which has come to be known as the Sunday Circle or the Lukács Circle in the reminiscences of its participants. As the latter title indicates, and as I have mentioned, the most prominent figure in the group was the philosopher Georg Lukács, who began his career as an essayist and literary critic, and became one of the best-known and still controversial Marxist philosophers of the twentieth century.[6] But Lukács was not the only member of the group to achieve international fame in the years after the war. Mannheim[7] himself was destined to play a significant role in the world of German academic sociology during the interwar years. Other talented members included the future art historian Arnold Hauser,[8] whose *Social History of Art*, published in 1950, is still a classic; Charles de Tolnay,[9] who was to distinguish himself as an expert in Renaissance art; and Antal Frigyes,[10] who became internationally known for his work on Hogarth. But just as influential within the group were individuals who remain entirely unknown outside Hungary today. The poet Béla Balázs,[11] a close friend both of Lukács and of musicians such as Zoltán Kodály and Béla Bartók, was a key figure and an important transmitter of modernist artistic currents to the group. Lajos Fülep,[12] an art historian and art critic who had lived extensively in Italy, was also a seminal figure whose influence on Hauser, Tolnay, and Frigyes was second only to that of Lukács.

The Sunday Circle did not come into official existence until the First World War, when Lukács, Balázs, Fülep, Mannheim, Hauser, and a few other young intellectuals decided to meet informally on Sunday afternoons in order to discuss various philosophic and artistic problems that happened to interest them at the moment. For many of the friends and acquaintances who gathered in Balázs' elegantly furnished Buda apartment in the autumn of 1915, the war had come as a serious disruption in the midst of artistic and academic careers just on the verge of becoming established. Several in fact had been living abroad when hostilities broke out, and the necessity of returning to Budapest seemed a temporary and regrettable exile to be shortly terminated by the resumption of peace. Lukács had come back from Heidelberg, where he was working on a dissertation on aesthetic philosophy, in order to fulfill his military duty; Fülep had returned from Florence, where he had been studying and writing about Italian art; and Mannheim and Hauser arrived from Paris, where they happened to be visiting when the war broke out.

With the exception of Lukács, none of these aspiring artists, writers, or philosophers was particularly wealthy, but frequent travel and extended sojourns in various European universities and cultural capitals had become a way of life for them. Though their parents could not in most cases be depended upon to finance these trips, life in student and artist quarters was cheap before the war, and scholarships, government stipends, and fees from articles for papers back home in Hungary could be relied upon to cover their modest expenses. Theirs had been the carefree, semi-Bohemian, essentially cosmopolitan existence characteristic of many prewar students and artists. They not only spoke several languages fluently but had established a fairly wide network of friendships and academic contacts outside Hungary.

Though the Sunday gatherings were spontaneous and informal at first, they very quickly assumed a rather deliberate, even self-conscious character. As early as December 1915, Balázs jubilantly noted in his diary how unexpectedly successful the group had become as an intellectual forum where important ideas could be discussed and clarified. "We suddenly realized with joy," he recorded, "that our group stands for something; it represents a genuine achievement and is a document of our age and of our generation."[13]

The exact content of the Sunday afternoon discussions, which were to continue regularly throughout the war and the early twenties, is not easy to reconstruct over the distance of the intervening years, revolutions, and wars which destroyed most of the written records of the participants. Lukács' and Balázs' repeated wishes to have the discussions formally recorded were never carried out, and we can gain only passing glimpses into the proceedings of the group from diary fragments, fictional accounts, letters, and reminiscences of surviving members.[14]

The gatherings usually consisted of not more than fifteen or twenty people, most of whom were around thirty, well educated, and almost exclusively from the assimilated Jewish middle classes. Their discussions, centering on philosophic, aesthetic, and ethical questions, were highly abstract and even a little esoteric for noninitiates in philosophy. But there were lighter moments too, when members played games, read excerpts from novels, essays, or poems they were working on, or when musician friends dropped by to provide performances of works in progress. One of the most unforgettable afternoons, one participant recalled, took place when "Béla Bartók, still young but already completely white, came and played 'The Wooden Prince' on the piano . . . He said very little and smiled sweetly at what probably appeared to him to be our incomprehensible conversations."[15]

Nevertheless, the overall tone of the Sunday meetings must have been a little forbidding to outsiders, one of whom later described the participants as "dry, impractical, cerebral people whose aesthetic sensibilities lacked all spontaneity or genuineness."[16] Those who were regular members, however, found in the circle a spiritual and intellectual home to which they referred with nostalgia until the end of their lives. "Life has granted me many unhoped-for gifts," Mannheim confided to Balázs in 1930, almost a decade after the group had dispersed, "but what it has never been able to replace are the old kinds of friendships."[17] Tolnay, too, testified much later that his Budapest circle had been the essential matrix which provided him with all the intellectual tools for his future career as an art historian.[18] Ironically enough, only Lukács, the key member of the Sunday Circle, was in later life to express skepticism about the group, feeling that its visibility was due more to the prominence achieved by some of its original members than to any kind of intrinsic unity or philosophic coherence within it.[19] Lukács' ambivalence was, however, not restricted to the Sunday Circle but pervaded his assessment of his entire pre-Marxist career. His later attitudes were inevitably colored by the depth of the break that occurred in his life around 1918–19 and do not accurately reflect his actual feelings at the time.

Though the war was rarely if ever mentioned, the increasing anxieties and physical hardships could not help but act as an invisible but ever-present backdrop to the Sunday discussions. Occasionally, but very rarely, these hardships broke through into some of the diaries and letters of the members. Edit Hajós, for example, who was married to Balázs at the time, wrote to Lukács in Heidelberg to give an account of the activities of "the Sundays," as they called themselves, adding as an afterthought: "Everything causes so much worry these days, the smallest things have to be separately considered, worried over: clothing, shoes, shortening, bread, and sugar. One is constantly forced to be preoccupied by such things."[20] Balázs himself, deeply immersed in writing a novel, and at the same time choreographing the ballet for the premier of Bartók's "Wooden Prince" at the Budapest Opera, remarked at one point on the seeming incongruity between his artistic and intellectual preoccupations and the growing precariousness of physical existence. He and his friends were busy with abstractions, he mused, "today of all times, when the world is turned topsy turvy . . . when there is nothing to eat, nothing to heat with, when we have no idea what tomorrow will bring, and the Spanish influenza rages among us like the plague."[21]

Yet it was precisely this atmosphere of physical insecurity and political disintegration that lent a feverish intensity to all the activities of the Sundays. The discussions, from all accounts, were passionate and occasionally extended throughout the night well into the following morning. "It was always impossible to terminate the discussions," remembered Edit Rényi, the future psychoanalyst,[22] and the younger members of the group used to continue their interminable arguments even after the meetings had dispersed, walking through the deserted streets or sitting in one of the all-night cafés of Budapest. There was one Sunday, she recounted, during the Soviet Republic of 1919, "when we met on Sunday afternoon and continued debating nonstop until Monday morning."[23]

The war was undoubtedly a catalyst in the formation of the Sunday Circle, but it would be wrong to attribute the group's sudden and in many respects surprising vitality merely to the pressure of external events. The core of the members who formed the discussion society had been friends for well over a decade, during which time a sense of cultural and temperamental affinity had been steadily growing among them, and from at least 1910 on, they had been making repeated, if not very successful, attempts to organize as a group. Their efforts frequently focused on the notion of establishing a journal or periodical of their own which was to reflect, in Balázs' words, "a new program, a new literary style, and a new generation of writers."[24]

The most nearly successful of these early plans was the philosophic journal *A Szellem* (The spirit), which Lukács and Fülep coedited briefly in 1911. Fülep, who wrote the opening editorial, declared in strident tones that the venture was not to be regarded as "simply the result of a fortuitous meeting of a handful of individuals" but rather as a "cultural historical necessity" which was bound to usher in a new age in philosophy.[25] Despite such ambitious declarations, they had few illusions about the long-term viability of *A Szellem*. They evidently intended it to be more a symbolic gesture than a practical enterprise with a wide appeal to the educated public. As Fülep wrote to Lukács in late 1910, already anticipating the demise of the journal, "Whether we ultimately fail or not is not at all the point and does not interest me. Only one thing is important: that our *existence* find clear and unambiguous expression. Even if we exist only for a moment, that moment must be more memorable and more enduring than the years of others."[26]

Their prognosis for *A Szellem* proved to be correct; it quietly expired for lack of support in December 1911 after only two issues. Yet their sense of solidarity did not diminish in the following years. In 1912, for instance, Balázs noted in his diary that they should formally organize into some kind of clique or party, "because our cause is not a literary debate but a general social crisis. During the summer we have to come up with a few well-constructed slogans which will polarize people and allow everyone to recognize the camp into which he was born. (For I feel one has to be born into this: we are a different race) . . . There is a war coming for which we must prepare, but realistically, not just with doctrines."[27] It was during this period that Balázs confessed to Lukács that he was beginning to feel "as if you and I had been stranded in a common boat and that every statement of principle that I make is made in your name as well . . . I now have to concentrate my energies on my literary work. Since I have begun to feel that we share a common cause, I have somehow abandoned its theoretical expression to you, and I occupy myself with philosophy less and less."[28] Lukács, for his part, accepted this division of labor in the interest of a common cause. Increasingly, he wrote his close friend Leo Popper, his choice of friends was being determined by whether an individual was "in some way a comrade in arms in the struggle which will from now on occupy my life. The principle of selection is stricter and (from the personal viewpoint) more uncompromising than ever before."[29]

Despite their strong and unambiguous sense of mission, Lukács and his friends did not find it easy to define, then or later, the exact nature of the bonds that drew them together as a group. They issued, it is true, numerous philosophic and artistic manifestoes, and these expressed fairly concisely the general direction of their concerns. They were opposed to the mechanistic, materialistic tendencies of nineteenth-century positivism and awaited a "new metaphysics" and a new "age of devotion."[30] They wished, wrote Mannheim, "to disseminate and systematically examine the truths of the new spiritualism and idealism."[31] Though they used the words *soul* and *spirit* constantly, they had nothing to do, warned Fülep, "with spiritualism, theosophy, occultism, and other such things. Quite simply, we are the seekers of a higher, spiritual world outlook, and we are not to be confused with any sects."[32] The emphasis in this, as in all their declarations, was on the quest, not the goal, on the act of clarifying, not on consolidating or systematizing. They were attempting to work out, wrote Béla Fogarasi, the paths leading "from systems to the point of transcendence, from the critique of the leading philosophic tendencies of the age toward the possibility of the positive deed."[33] The artists in the group expressed the same impulse in slightly different terms. The road to contemporary art, Leo Popper wrote in 1909, led "out of the stylistic chaos of Impressionism toward the solidity of still life, which, no matter what form it takes, will be related to architecture: it will bear the mark of the same inner certitude and simplicity of which architecture is the embodiment. And through secret paths there is returning again a bygone harmony: the sacred harmony . . . of the Greeks and the Orient."[34]

These often eloquent summations of goals and principles do not, however, fully convey the breadth and complexity of the ties that bound the group together during these years. Theirs was, as Emma Ritoók perceptively remarked, not strictly speaking a philosophic society but one whose unity was based on a certain "spiritual affinity." Many of them, it is true, were training for careers as professional philosophers, yet it is worth stressing that artists and writers were equally at home in the Sunday discussions. Balázs felt this fact to be significant enough to comment upon. It was amazing, he mused in his diary, that he could communicate so easily with professionally trained philosophers like Lukács and Mannheim, "that they are interested and excited by what I have to say, and that I understand as a matter of course all their remarks, even though I have never studied philosophy in a serious way."[35]

Their collective attitude toward professional philosophy was, in fact, pervaded by a deep and complicated kind of ambivalence which surfaced unmistakably at certain crucial points. When discussing plans for *A Szellem*, for instance, they unanimously rejected affiliation with the Berlin-based neo-Kantian journal *Logos*, even though it shared their general antipositivist, antimaterialist orientation in philosophy. Fülep explained the reason for his opposition: "When I contemplate the prospect of having to exchange our youthful manifestoes for a professional style . . . my hair stands on end; . . . we, at least right now, are incompatible with *Logos*. What would we do with the cautious tone of *Logos*, which refuses to make waves, disturbing no one and nothing? . . . Let us not be in such a hurry to grow old and gray; it will come all by itself in any case."[36]

Mannheim was particularly self-conscious about this distrust of professional philosophy, and he attempted repeatedly to clarify its causes. The problem was, he wrote in a review of Ernst Block's *Geist der Utopie* (Spirit of Utopia) in 1919, that professional philosophers refused to entertain those ultimate questions of human life which were essentially mystical in origin and had to do with the nature of the universe and the meaning of human life. In place of the crucial if ultimately unanswerable questions, he complained, philosophers substituted ones which "can be answered or which already have an answer. Thus, logic and epistemology replace that sense of elemental wonder [which was the origin of philosophy]. And philosophers suppress the ultimate meaning of their questions just so they can show off with their already existing answers. They make us forget our anxious searchings for God and ourselves and replace them with mere knowledge of the world and of things."[37]

Their cultural models were invariably anchored in less specialized ages, when, as Balázs put it, "philosophy was not such an *Einzelwisszenschaft*"(isolated discipline unto itself).[38] They liked to compare the Sunday afternoon gatherings to the philosophic academies of ancient Greece, or even more tellingly to the salons of the early romanticists, to whose spirit and goals, if not methods, they felt instinctively related. Lukács suggested, for instance, that their conversations should be recorded, "if for no other reason than that people should look back on us a hundred years from now with the same envy and nostalgia that we feel when we look back at the old groups in Weimar."[39] Another contemporary, Sándor Hevesi, wrote to Lukács that he considered *A Szellem* a phenomenon "unique since the age of romanticism, a forum where the meeting of minds and individuals gave rise to a new movement."[40]

In these oblique references to the romanticists, Lukács and his friends were instinctively establishing their kinship with that pan-European movement of cultural rebellion and renewal which had begun to be felt throughout Western Europe from the 1880s on. It was during these decades that a younger generation of artists and intellectuals launched what turned out to be an ever-deepening rebellion against the moral pieties and intellectual orthodoxies of late-Victorian culture, which they began to experience as a strait jacket shackling genuine feeling and knowledge. The impulse of cultural rebellion, with its highly charged generational overtones, had unmistakable resemblances to romanticism, something which did not escape perceptive observers even at the time. They were witnessing, wrote a French literary critic of the 1880s, a "second *mal de siècle*" which produced novels "as despairing as the masterpieces of Senancourt and poems as bitter as the sonnets of Joseph Delormes."[41]

Like their romanticist predecessors, the cultural radicals of the late nineteenth century felt themselves to be victims of liberal society, and they loudly proclaimed their hatred for industrial capitalism and bourgeois individualism. Their sense of pervasive malaise found a great variety of expressions ranging from the deeply serious to the utterly trivial. Certainly by the early twentieth century the theme of alienation from the world of the philistine bourgeois was not only common but rapidly becoming something of a cliché among the more radical segments of the younger generation. For this reason Leo Popper humorously warned Lukács to avoid the subject for a while: "Don't write a word about 'isolation' for six months. I say this because it is dangerous: the theme is becoming *popular* among the prigs who within a year may be discoursing on the 'Margaret-Islandization of human life.' "[42]

The advice was well taken, but it could not change the fact that alienation did indeed constitute the central dilemma of their lives, fatefully shaping their vision of the world, defining their artistic and theoretical interests. And, dangerous or not, they talked incessantly about the subject. They were particularly indebted in these discussions to Georg Simmel's original distinction between "objective and subjective cultures,"[43] which tended to form the starting point of their collective definition of their cultural plight. "By objective culture," wrote Mannheim in one of the most compact and elegant essays on the subject, "we mean all those objectifications of the human spirit which in the course of historical evolution have become the inheritance of the human race; we mean by this religion, science, art, the state, forms of life. We can speak of subjective culture, furthermore, when—as Simmel very correctly pointed out—the subjective self seeks fulfillment and self-realization not through its own resources, by turning inward, but rather precisely through the detour of culture, by making it its own to a certain extent."[44]

They were emphatic on the point that pure inner life without the stabilizing force of culture was unimaginable. It was through the mediation of language, art, customs—in other words, cultural forms—that the self acquired reality and the potential to become known to itself and to others. This fundamental reliance on culture, which Lukács at one point called an almost biological need, constituted the "most characteristic aspect of our humanity." It was also the potential source of alienation, however. For culture, though initially linked to the individuals who created it, tended to become formalized, acquiring a finality and rigidity alien to the human spirit. In such ages, culture ceased to be a mirror of the human soul and became an autonomous reality confronting the self "like a huge Leviathan that has become independent of us."[45] Like the romanticists, Lukács and his friends saw the ideal of nonalienated culture somewhere in the past, usually in the Middle Ages, when individuals supposedly still felt that their inner selves were adequately reflected by the cultural world around them. Since then, they concluded, the sense of separation between self and the world had been steadily growing until it culminated in the modern period, which Mannheim quite explicitly saw beginning with the late eighteenth century. "Perhaps the earliest spokesman of alienation," he wrote, "was Rousseau, and there is a direct line that leads from him . . . to Schiller, whose concept of sentiment, and to Schlegel, whose notion of irony, signal the identical fact from different sides."[46]

This emphatically tragic view of modern culture was never a widespread sentiment among educated men and women at the turn of the century. Despite the antibourgeois pose of many young artists and intellectuals, serious cultural criticism remained the preserve of a small minority of radically disaffected or dislocated individuals. And yet both friendly and hostile critics of the tendency admitted that it was a significant phenomenon which had the gift of "covering over the surface of society as a little oil extends over the surface of the sea."[47] These cultural malcontents, wrote another critic, included "some of our finest intellects; our future poets, novelists, and men of letters. Indirectly through them, some of the psychological peculiarities of the time will diffuse to a much larger public; and it is of such diffusions and interpenetrations that the moral climate of an age is made up."[48]

If the tradition of cultural criticism was restricted to a small if influential minority in Western Europe, it was positively exotic in the Hungary of the early twentieth century. Members of the Sunday Circle felt, both individually and collectively, almost completely isolated in their own country, and their sense of radical homelessness forms a constant refrain in their letters, essays, and novels. "It is only now," wrote Balázs to Lukács in a not untypical confession, "that I have fully awakened to the bitter realization of how aggressively, unmistakably, continuously alone and alien I feel in my milieu . . . But this can and does have advantages. A reversed tragedy: everything on the outside collapses, and therefore I am forced to return home into myself."[49]

Lukács and his friends were correct to see themselves radically out of touch with the cultural realities of Hungary, where the majority of the population still lived in conditions of rural backwardness, insulated from the benefits, as well as the discontents, of modernity. But they were almost equally estranged from the progressive artistic and intellectual circles of Budapest, which were too closely associated with a complacent liberalism and a superficial eclecticism to constitute a congenial intellectual world for them. It is not surprising that they erected a whole private mythology about the difficulties of serious artistic and intellectual endeavors in Hungary, lacking as it did a receptive social milieu or a viable cultural tradition to which they could attach themselves. "For in this country," wrote Balázs in his autobiographical novel, *Impossible People,*

> all minds that are alive resemble trailing plants in a dark cellar. They have to creep up to the dizzying heights of a tower in order to attain even a little life-giving sunshine. What is more, they themselves have to build their own towers for this purpose. And if they are incapable of this task, they are doomed to rot away. And once on their tower tops, they grow stems that are too long and make them unfit for any kind of normal garden or flower pot . . . Thus, faced with the choice of escaping into apathy or madness, those who can seek asylum abroad for a period. For among strangers it is easier to bear being strangers than—at home.[50]

They invariably looked with envy at what they perceived to be the more favorable circumstances of West European cultural innovators. In Germany, Mannheim wrote in 1922, "the individual still finds himself in the flood tide of a great cultural tradition and can from time to time forget the chaos yawning at the pit of human existence and the self." In Hungary no such external supports existed for the radical artist. Here, he continued, "the lone self that is truly alive faces life unaided and has to do everything for himself without being able to tarry long at any one task. In our country, one is able to form ties only between disembodied souls, and one can love individuals only one at a time (hence the heightened importance of the erotic struggle)."[51]

Given the sense of infinite distance and separation they felt from the world around them, it is hardly surprising that members of the Sunday Circle could not translate their discontents into the conventional language of radical politics. It is true that they had real sympathies with the political left and were at times ready to accept common cause with such groups. But as Anna Lesznai remembered, "It would be more accurate to stress how apolitical most of us were . . . In reality, our group had a closer resemblance to a religious gathering than to a political club: the get-togethers had a ritualistic, quasireligious tone, and the participants were obliged to tell the complete truth about everything."[52] Their relative indifference to politics was ultimately anchored in the deep conviction that political action could change only the outer perimeters of human existence, whereas they were interested in the qualitative transformation of inner life. Thus Balázs remarked that socialism was incapable of bringing about the changes they desired, for they were preparing for "a moral revolution, more urgently needed than all the social revolutions in the world."[53] Lukács too seemed certain at this point that his cultural critique held a more truly radical potential then direct political plans could have. "What could be more practical than to say: return into yourselves!" he wrote the German writer Paul Ernst in 1911. "The external world is unchangeable; let us create a new and different world from that which is possible! This is what my article had said—and it was infinitely more practical than all the proposals about 'garden cities' and planned settlements which the dilettante nationalist philosophers put forth as a 'solution' to the problem of art."[54]

Their critique of society was powered not so much by rage at social or economic injustices (though they were not blind to these) as by a sense of despair at the isolation of the individual in modern society. They repudiated social conventions because they perceived them as unbridgeable barriers to true communion, as insurmountable walls locking each person into the solitude of his or her private universe. "The inhumanity of individualistic, capitalist society—I am not saying cruelty, because until now, all forms of social organization have been based on cruelty—the inhumanity of this kind of society stems from the fact that its individual members are solitary atoms whose vital relationships are not with other men, nor with nature, but with abstract institutions," remarked Anna Lesznai.[55]

They were obsessed by the solitude of the self in modern capitalism, and the need to transcend this solitude became the focal point of all their artistic and theoretical experiments. Their marked and enduring interest in fairy tales, dreams, and folk legends was due in large part to their conviction that under existing conditions only these realms could symbolize true liberation and fulfillment for the individual. They were, of course, not unaware of Freud's theories on these matters, but they remained remarkably cool toward all purely psychological explanations. "The Freudians," wrote Anna Lesznai in an important essay on the theoretical implications of fairy tales, "have, it is true, long ago established the decisive importance of *Wünscher-*

füllung in fairy tales, but they have, through a crude oversimplification, insisted that the true 'meaning' of every fairy tale is sexual fulfillment." She conceded that sexual symbolism is pervasive in fairy tales, but behind these "erotic ornaments" she perceived a more, primary motivation, the longing to transcend individuality:

> Sex itself is only a symbol. The fact that fairy tales, our dreams, our everyday language . . . even our aesthetic forms contain the unmistakable imprint of sexual imagery simply means that the sexual experience, with all its emotional components, represents the most suggestive, the most clearly palpable, the most intelligible symbol of fulfillment and self-abandonment . . . In place of the Freudians' "fulfillment of unshackled sexual wishes" *I would put the fulfillment of the longing to be without boundaries* as the essence of the fairy tale.[56]

The future members of the Sunday Circle did not confine their rebellion against social forms to the realm of theory alone. There was in their unconventionality none of the flamboyant desire to shock the bourgeoisie so characteristic of some of the West European cultural rebels of the late nineteenth and early twentieth centuries. Theirs was not so much open rebellion as utter detachment from social conventions, something they perceived as a precondition for honesty and true communication. In 1907, for example, Balázs proudly recorded a telling incident in his diary which illustrates well this trait of social innocence. An acquaintance, it seems, had remarked to Balázs that there was something raw and primitive in his manner: "It disarms people—or rather, it causes them to drop their customary social masks and forces them to be equally primitive. And this, in turn, creates a closeness and openness that the other person had never thought possible until then. Soon, they don't even recognize themselves." Balázs responded to this observation: "May it be true. May it be true in my art. I want it to turn people inside out and to destroy their masks and barricades so that they may stand facing each other, naked and astonished."[57]

It was in the fictional world of Dostoevsky that they saw the purest embodiment of their particular kind of social estrangement, and they felt unanimous and unqualified enthusiasm for the Russian novelist. Mannheim, in fact, undertook plans to write a biography of Dostoevsky in 1912, and Lukács actually began one in 1915. Dostoevsky was important for him, Mannheim confided to Lukács, "not only because I feel that I can best pose my problems, questions through him, but also because I feel that an understanding of his life offers solutions for us. For I feel that his life, his world, is extremely similar to ours, with all its contradictions, disharmonies, and distortions."[58] Predictably, what appealed to them in Dostoevsky's heroes and heroines was their innocence of life's practical difficulties, their ability to triumph over sociological barriers by simply ignoring them.

The Dostoevskian gesture of uncompromising innocence stood directly opposed in their minds to the petty calculations and compromises required by social existence. Their attitude toward this issue is neatly illustrated by a dinner party conversation that apparently took place between Lukács, Balázs, Lesznai, and Oszkár Jászi, a prominent left-wing intellectual who was married to Lesznai at the time. The discussion centered on the question whether a lie told out of kindness or social duty could ever be justified. The more worldly and practical Jászi argued that such lies were permissible, while Balázs and Lukács passionately denied the point. The soul, insisted Balázs, needs "a simple and unambiguous attitude, otherwise it dissolves into chaos and formlessness. The individual must not allow himself to change his behavior to fit each new situation." The question came up, reported Balázs, whether social life is possible at all in the atmosphere of "pure truth." That certainly represented a "sociological problem," admitted Balázs, but from their perspective it was irrelevant. The important point was that "lies mean eternal estrangement between individual souls. The enforced lies of social life cause every desired truth to rot at its roots."[59]

Such attitudes toward society and all that is taken to be worldly wisdom made Lukács and his friends remarkably doctrinaire, intransigent, and uncompromising as a group. They had, declared Lukács in a characteristic statement, no tolerance for the tolerance of their liberal elders. They hated all "ambiguous situations," and they recognized only two kinds of relationships: total intimacy and total estrangement. Whatever lay in between was simply a mixture which leaned toward one or the other of the two poles.[60]

—

It is impossible not to note in these statements and attitudes a residue of adolescence. They are characteristic of men and women who were young and very much "in transit," both personally and professionally, as well as culturally. The personal and cultural factors were, of course, intimately connected. It was precisely because they were young and therefore relatively free from social and professional attachments that they could afford to see existing culture with such single-minded intransigence; and it was precisely because existing culture was in crisis, rapidly losing its inner vitality and self-confidence, that they chose to remain outside social and professional commitments for so long. Balázs, as usual, expressed their collective sense of incompleteness eloquently. "I feel as if I am reaching a critical turning point," he wrote Lukács in 1915, "as if I am about to shed my last skin which is not yet myself . . . And though I do not yet possess my final self, I already feel its scent, its reassuring promise, its security . . . Generally, we are at a turning point. Strange that I should put it this way, in the plural, but *I do not feel my path to be unique or solitary.*"[61]

Balázs' assessment was, it is true, only partially applicable to Lukács by 1915. Lukács had already reached by this point a certain preeminence, not only in Hungarian but also in German intellectual circles, such as Max and Marianne Weber's in Heidelberg and Georg Simmel's in Berlin. Moreover, his personality had already assumed an impressive external poise and inner authority which made him the natural and undisputed leader of the Sunday afternoon gatherings. From all accounts, he possessed a virtually charismatic power over his friends and acquaintances. "Your departure," Balázs wrote his friend in 1916, "had a powerful effect on me (and it seems on others as well). It is as if we had become accustomed to regularly consume morphine and it was suddenly withdrawn from us. The Sundays are, somehow, not *sincere* without you."[62] The sheer force and magnetism of Lukács' intellect dazzled those about him, making them feel inexplicably that they were "in the presence of a great man." "Gyuri's presence," elaborated Balázs, "gives us a sense of security in our theoretical quandaries the way the presence of the schoolmaster reassures little boys . . . There is something monumental in the superior assurance of his brain . . . And yet, his judgment is not firm—his taste is unformed, easily influenced, like a child's."[63]

Balázs, who was probably Lukács' closest friend during the war years, had no way of knowing that Lukács' impressive self-possession had been bought at the price of long and hard-won struggles and were, in fact, closely linked to years of crisis during which he had virtually created himself anew for his intellectual task. Lukács' early youth was marked by a deep need, as well as an abnormal fear, of intimacy. "My inner warmth," he speculated in his diary in 1910, "is surrounded by layers and layers of ice, and no matter how easily I talk and get into superficial intimacy with people, I am almost impossible to approach."[64]

This was not entirely true, for there were, during these early years, three people who had miraculously found their way to the center of his life: his adolescent comrade László Bánóczy, his later and much-loved friend Leo Popper, and perhaps most important of all, his first romantic love, Irma Seidler. All of these had been extreme and passionate friendships in which the young Lukács gladly—some said even abjectly—subordinated himself to the object of his affection. Lukács' concerned and sensible father warned his son against his impetuous infatuations and the inevitable disappointment they would lead to: "At first it was Laczi Bánóczy compared to whom you felt yourself to be small and a nonentity . . . Now, you insist on placing Leo on a divine pedestal way above yourself. May God grant you not to be as deeply deceived here as you were with Laczi . . . What I wish for you . . . is that you should maintain with your friends as well that calm and at times cruelly unyielding objectivity that you know how to manifest so perfectly toward your environment."[65]

As was often the case with the elder Lukács' genuinely well meaning warnings, this one, too, missed the point almost entirely. It was precisely because Lukács was incapable of weighing and calculating consequences that these early friendships were so exhilarating, releasing him for a time from the almost pathological reserve that was his nature. And he repaid these privileged guests in his life with extravagant, poignant gratitude. "Beyond all moods, beyond all knowledge and ignorance," he wrote Popper in 1910, following his near engagement to Irma,

"I feel the affairs of the two of us to be solid—the only solid thing that exists in my life. (A mediocre English verse haunts my brain: 'Others leave me. All things leave me. You remain') . . . How one could thank the other for this is not something one can decently discuss in words. Indeed, let us not speak of it."[66]

Lukács' emotions, however, were never so overwhelming as to entirely silence his critical intellect or his powers of dispassionate observation. On some level he was perfectly aware of the fact that his friends were not his intellectual equals and that he needed them precisely for this reason. His most productive relationships, he confessed in his diary, were not with strong and original minds like Simmel, Bloch, or Weber but rather with artistic, intuitive friends like Popper and Seidler, who

> were deep enough to sense exactly where my train of thought was leading, but not strong enough to derail it into their own direction once they had begun to travel with me. At the same time, their inner life is more sensual and mercurial than mine, which means that they find, or make me find, things along the way which my essentially asensual, asexual, rational thinking would never have discovered on its own. This is why everything with them was so fruitful, why it is barren with everyone else.[67]

Not surprisingly, it was Irma Seidler who had the most powerful influence over Lukács, acting as the vital catalyst in the maturing of his early literary essays. Such intellectual-emotional partnerships between men and women, Lukács wrote in his diary, were essentially an irrational phenomenon which could not be explained in terms of rational concepts:

> Those philologists who try to make a goddess of Frau Stein in order to make her influence on Goethe comprehensible are laughable. But the psychologists who minutely discuss how utterly she did not understand Goethe are even more laughable. Of course she didn't understand him: Fr. Schlegel understood him and W. von Humbolt—but out of her incomprehension was born *Iphigenia*, out of their comprehension, nothing. What is at issue here is not a mythical thing; it is the ability to believe the miraculous in someone; the ability to unravel (slowly and naturally) the un-

conscious until it becomes conscious; it is the ability to give form to the other's emotions. And somehow I feel: one can have a true marriage only with such a woman, because only from such a woman can a man have a child: in such cases, the man also has a child: a child that is the objectification of his great longing to win form for his thoughts, rather than just the fortuitous fruit of an intoxicated hour.[68]

The almost perfect friendship with Irma did not, in fact, develop into marriage. Placing such absolute power in the hands of another must have implied a degree of vulnerability difficult for someone of Lukács' temperament to tolerate. Moreover, with his customary lucidity, Lukács must have suspected that no friendship or love affair could sustain for long the weight of the expectations he invested in these relationships. Whatever mixture of conscious and unconscious motivation may have been at work, he gradually began to disentangle himself from these intense early friendships, first by breaking with Irma and then by partially distancing himself even from Popper.

The emotional cost of regaining his autonomy was inordinately high, however, and Lukács was unusually self-conscious about, and even fascinated by, the process. He subjected himself to merciless and meticulous self-scrutiny, discovering in his own emotional inadequacies an unmistakably "Lukácsian" family trait. "We are all," he confided in his diary, "dreamers without fantasy; utterly impractical people who are at the same time earthbound; realists out of a sense of necessity without a sense of reality. It is astonishing how closely Mama and Papa resemble each other in this. I am the only one who is self-conscious among them; I have trained myself to see clearly—but this has not granted me the missing sense of reality, and there can be no question of substitution."[69] An integral element in Lukács' new self-definition was to involve the acceptance of this flawed "sense of reality" which made him feel disconnected from everyday life. It meant the realization that his real home was to be in the realm of abstractions rather than in concrete life. "I am finally at home," he wrote to Popper in the midst of these struggles, "in a land where I know the roads and travel with assurance. In the other—I feel with serious and contrite shame—I am not at home and never shall be. Starting from the simplest shopping expedition, all the way to those serious, human situations where one is expected to be serious and human. In these I am only serious—but helpless."[70]

This dramatic reorientation in Lukács' life, which took place sometime between 1909 and 1911, involved an extremely complicated kind of inner denial and an asceticism which, at the same time, had none of the external appearance of asceticism. In fact Lukács' social life began to expand around this time, which saw the formation of many of those friendships and acquaintances which were to blossom into the Sunday Circle in 1915. Yet these were new kinds of friendships, consciously circumscribed and limited by common goals and professional objectives. "Everything has moved far from me," Lukács wrote to Popper. "What has remained is my polite façade with people of intelligence. But behind it, the emphasis has changed. I have become truly patient with people. I put up with them . . . I know that feelings like this can give rise to friendships, and that is what happened with Herbert [Balázs] and a little with Paul Ernst. But these are different. What is at their base is the common cause, and if our roads were to diverge—then the people would part as well."[71]

Lukács was not discounting the possibility of marriage, either, it seems. "Women, possibly even marriage, are perfectly compatible with my new state of mind," he wrote Popper in late 1910. "The only difference is that the value of everything has completely shifted from what it used to be . . . Formerly, I was *unglücklich* [unhappy]; now I am *jenseits von Glück und Unglück* [beyond happiness and unhappiness]. I am on the way toward my own center, and I now know that no one can 'share' this with me . . . and that no one can 'help' here . . . And the only road is through work."[72]

Two years later, while vacationing with Balázs and his wife, Lukács met the woman who was to become his first wife. Ljena Grabenko, a radical Russian student living in Paris at the time, was a fascinating, unconventional figure who disarmed not only Lukács but also Balázs and their entire circle. She appeared to them a Dostoevskian heroine, the living incarnation of those literary ideals they cherished in the Russian novelist. "All her anecdotes, ideas, feelings could have come out of the most fanciful of Dostoevsky's chapters," wrote Balázs. "She had been a terrorist, had spent years in jail, had ruined her nerves, her stomach, her lungs in the terrible labor. She is now ill and tired. She fears death and still wants something for herself out of life— to learn, to acquire culture . . . She is a sad, beautiful, deep, and wise human soul. And she has wonderful anecdotes." One of these anecdotes, which Balázs recounted with relish, illustrated perfectly in their mind those qualities of social innocence and personal goodness they so admired in her. While in Paris, at one point Grabenko apparently found herself totally without money. After two days of fasting she had sadly resigned herself to pawning her cherished watch, when an unknown fellow Russian knocked on her door, asking for money. With tears in her eyes, Grabenko told the stranger that she herself was destitute and just on the point of selling her watch, but that she would gladly give it to him instead. The next day the stranger returned with the watch. Afterwards she learned that he was a notorious swindler who had already defrauded half the Russian émigré community of Paris.[73]

Not all of Lukács' friends, it is true, were equally taken with the unconventional Ljena. Hilda Bauer, Balázs' sister, herself romantically interested in Lukács, was somewhat more skeptical about the Russian student. She unwisely confided these mixed feelings to Lukács. "She is not clever," Hilda wrote him,

> but has strange flashes of insight. And then, she is a heroine out of a Russian novel, from which I can't tell how much is pose, how much reality . . . She is a hundred, no a thousand times better, more self-sacrificing than me, there is no comparison— she is a million times better. And yet, all the same, she seems such a sadly incomplete person! She is a painter! Herbert [Balázs] and the other unfortunates have discovered her! She is only beginning, without any transition from being a revolutionary. She only wants to live for art, and if she can't produce something great, she will kill herself. She will do it, too, and not just say it . . . The only problem is that she does absolutely no work, but is "Russian," in Paris—which means that she "makes friends," is "good," and sometimes draws something, just like that without any "school" or "system." I think she is better suited for the role of a revolutionary.[74]

In the long run, Hilda Bauer's skepticism, clouded though it was by feminine jealousy, turned out to be not entirely unfounded. Ljena was profoundly unstable, subject to wide oscillations of mood and behavior, and perhaps even worse suited for the career of marriage than of painting. Shortly after her marriage to Lukács, she fell madly in love with a young musician, himself unstable to the point of needing institutionalization, and the Lukács household in Heidelberg turned into a bizarre ménage à trois in which Ljena was afraid to leave her lover for fear he might commit suicide, and Lukács was afraid to leave Ljena for fear the musician might hurt her. Balázs described the situation in his diary: "There exists a terrible, unimaginable hell down there in Heidelberg, and Gyuri speaks quite seriously of one day all three of them being found dead—at the hand of the insane musician. And yet he stays with them, because it is safer for Ljena this way. Gyuri is the greatest martyr of decency." "But," Balázs could not help adding, "there is also intermingled here a certain inability to act, even cowardice—the assumption that it is better to put up with, or postpone all disasters in life rather than get up from one's desk, even when one cannot really work at it. And yet, in spite of all, Gyuri has managed to write three large chapters of his aesthetic during all this. Around three hundred printed pages. Unbelievable!"[75]

It seems, however, that even Lukács' complicated sense of love, duty, and indifference had limits. By 1918 he had definitively broken with Ljena "and that unspeakable life in trio they had been leading in Heidelberg. New plans, new confidence, the energy to begin all over again are beginning to awaken in him. But at the price of great resignation. 'If I had been truly good, I would have stuck it out with Ljena,' "[76] reported Balázs. With the disintegration of his marriage, Lukács decided to move back to Budapest for an unspecified length of time, resuming full time the leadership of their little circle, which had invariably devolved on Balázs during his absences.

Balázs was, in many respects, the polar opposite of Lukács: a man of great warmth, charm, and intuitive insight whose inner life was disturbed by none of those complicated inhibitions which paralyzed Lukács. If Lukács decisively influenced the intellectual and philosophic direction of the Sunday Circle, Balázs certainly defined its aesthetic and emotional tone. As Hauser recalled years later, "What could be called sensibility—responsiveness to aesthetic experience and artistic quality—existed to a far greater degree in him [Balázs] than in Lukács . . . Lukács had absolutely no aesthetic sense at all, and being a man capable of considerable objectivity about himself, he was the first to acknowledge this."[77]

Balázs had other admirable qualities as well. He was adventurous and unconventional, possessing a genius, if not exactly for friendship, at least for good fellowship and the creation of an exceedingly varied and colorful social life. His circle of acquaintances extended into layers of artistic Bohemia where the more sober Lukács would have felt out of place and ill at ease. (Lukács recounted late in life that at one point a friend had taken him to visit the much-admired symbolist poet Endre Ady, who usually held court in a disreputable tavern called the Három Holló. Lukács apparently was so repelled by the rowdy company surrounding the poet that he left without even attempting to speak to him.) In contrast to Lukács, Balázs had an interest in people that was unforced and insatiable, and his diaries are filled with sharply-etched, if not always charitable, character sketches which are little masterpieces of the genre.

He was particularly at home in the company of musicians, "in that good old quiet, eccentric, and elegant musical environment"[78] to which his friend Zoltán Kodály had introduced him early in their university days. Through Kodály he had come to know Bartók as well, and he occasionally accompanied the young musicians on their folkloric expeditions into the Hungarian countryside. "We spent a week together collecting folksongs," Balázs recalled in 1905. He found Bartók

> naive and awkward. A twenty-five-or-odd-year-old child prodigy. And yet there exists in him an incredibly quiet tenacity. He is a weak, puny, sickly little man, and yet I was already more than exhausted when he was still urging us on, to collect some more . . . He is inquisitive, impatient, unable to keep still, but he seems to be searching for something whose reality he already senses . . . He is modest like a little girl—but also vain. And outside of his music, I am able to enjoy almost nothing about him. His naiveté is not fresh enough, and his irony (for that exists too) is without force. And yet his face is sometimes very beautiful. Perhaps he is, after all, more than a grown up *Wunderkind*.[79]

Balázs' judgments were remarkably consistent, and six years later he was no more enthusiastic about Bartók as a person, though he was now ready to grant him greatness as a musician: "There is a wonderful paradox about his appearance. His figure, his face, his movements resemble those of a rococo prince, and yet there is also a kind of titanic majesty about him. A thirty-two-year-old, deadly serious *Wunderkind.*"[80]

There is in these assessments of Balázs' a sureness of insight, coupled with a pervasive ambivalence which was deeply characteristic of the man, for despite his great vitality and natural gifts, Balázs was secretly haunted by a sense of his own lack of accomplishments. "I fear," he admitted in 1915, "that Gyuri no longer believes in me, and I feel left behind when compared to his enormous growth. I am jealous of him, whereas formerly I did not even know what that emotion meant."[81] Yet he seemed invariably drawn to friends who surpassed him in talent, drive, and self-discipline. In 1918, partly as a result of his realization that his friendship with Lukács would never develop into an intimate one, he made an effort to get to know Mannheim more closely. By this time it had become clear that next to Lukács, Mannheim was probably the most able theoretician among them, the one who showed signs of becoming "a first-rate and significant future philosopher."[82]

Mannheim belonged to a slightly younger generation than Lukács and Balázs, both of whom already enjoyed reputations in Budapest when Mannheim was still in high school, just beginning to orient himself culturally. In 1911 the barely eighteen-year-old philosophy student had approached Lukács in writing, explaining his philosophic plans and asking for Lukács' continuing guidance and good will. In the following years a polite if formal correspondence developed between the two men, but their contacts did not gain real substance until 1915, when Mannheim joined the Sunday discussions as an already fully formed thinker. Though temperamentally Mannheim was more akin to Lukács than to the mercurial Balázs, he was not insensible of Balázs' flamboyant, freewheeling style. Mannheim confided to Balázs at one point that he envied the older man's freedom from convention and the "courage to make mistakes. I am sometimes afraid to even budge for fear of making the wrong move."[83] For his part too, Balázs felt the difference of temperament, and after a concerted effort decided that, much as he and Mannheim liked each other, they were not destined to become intimate friends.

"The difference of generations stands in the way," he concluded, "some kind of temperamental difference. There is lacking in him simplicity, passion, the talent for exultation. I sense in all his doings a kind of weakness, small-mindedness, anemia: a lack of courage and an eternally mistrustful analysis . . . It is wonderful to see such clear differentiation of the generational types. They are epigones. But whose epigones? We have not yet accomplished anything."[84]

If Balázs' male friendships were difficult, his contacts with women seemed more successful. In any case, there was a seemingly unending procession of women moving in and out of his life during these years. It was through the energetic Balázs that some of the more interesting and unconventional women members of the Sunday Circle were recruited, many of whom were his friends, lovers, wives, or former wives.

In almost none of the contemporary accounts or later reminiscences of the Sunday Circle did anyone make a specific issue of the fact that there was a remarkably large number of talented women participating in these discussions. Yet the integration of women into serious intellectual and philosophic enterprises was hardly common practice in prewar Hungary. Only in the Sunday Circle, recalled one woman participant at the time, could she "freely debate all kinds of philosophic and artistic questions without feeling the condescension of the male intellectual toward the woman."[85]

The women of the group, it is true, were rather unconventional themselves and rarely fit the stereotype of contented domesticity and passive gentility which still dominated the ethos of late nineteenth-century middle-class life. The University of Budapest had only recently opened its doors to women, and several of them, like Juliska Láng,[86] had been part of the little pioneering band that first took advantage of the new opportunities. Others, like Edit Hajós[87] and Emma Ritoók,[88] had studied abroad, attending classes in Paris, Switzerland, Leipzig, and Berlin. Still others, like Anna Lesznai,[89] were simply born nonconformists. (Lesznai had achieved considerable renown by the war years as a poet, artist, and embroiderer of stylized folk motifs characteristic of her native region in northern Hungary.) Whatever the individual circumstances that forced these women outside the well-defined boundaries of womanly existence, most were breaking new ground, struggling to establish themselves independently as painters, writers, philosophers, doctors. They seemed at the same time strikingly unself-conscious about the novelty of their experiences as women, and even less concerned about articulating new identities, new self-images appropriate to their aspirations.

Certainly the feminist movement, which was fairly well established in Budapest by the turn of the century, had fewer attractions for them than one would have expected in the circumstances. Anna Lesznai actually raised the question of feminism briefly but revealingly in her autobiographical novel *Kezdetben volt a kert* (In the beginning was the garden), where she recounted the details of her "brief debut into respectable middle-class life" and conventional marriage. After a pampered and unrestrained girlhood, spent under the doting eyes of a somewhat eccentric father, she was shocked to find that her new husband actually expected to exercise his authority over her. He disapproved of her writing and threatened, at one point, to throw her writing desk out. Her short-lived and disastrous excursion into matrimony left her, according to her later account, with two unexpected prizes: a child and the status of a divorced woman, which gave her the freedom (much envied by her unmarried women friends) to do as she pleased without much fear of social censure. The experience also left her with a sense of rage and a new sympathy for the peasantry of her still primarily agrarian homeland, "for at the side of my husband, I also felt like the oppressed. After my marriage, I was never angry when they [the peasants] cursed the gentlefolk, and I even understood it when a drunken young peasant once tried to attack me." In fact, as she confided to a sympathetic male listener, her experience of marriage had been so dreadful that, "though I am not a feminist, I almost became one then." The response of her companion, himself a renegade from middle-class respectability, is revealing. She was, he retorted angrily, "a good-looking, healthy, and clever woman," and therefore, by definition, had nothing to seek among the feminists.[90]

Their collective reluctance even to enter into serious dialogue with the woman's movement, as it was then called, had complicated roots which cannot entirely be explained as a residual traditionalism, though that was present too, no doubt. More important, however, they distrusted organized feminism for the same reason they distrusted socialism or any other radical political movement of the time: such movements appeared to them crudely materialistic, excessively focused on externals, and therefore impervious to the really important issues, which concerned the inner life of instincts and emotions.

The fact that they were not feminists does not mean that they were not intensely preoccupied with questions of gender or that they did not incessantly debate the unique attributes of femininity and masculinity. These discussions were permeated by the notion of sexual polarity, popular among radical artists at the turn of the century, and rearticulated in Otto Weininger's best-selling book on the subject, *Sex and Character*, published in Vienna in 1903. Despite appearances, Weininger's notions of sexual polarity were not simply extensions of Victorian stereotypes; they represented an attempt to replace those by what he regarded as new, more truthful, and radical insights into the nature of male and female character. Lukács and his friends did not follow Weininger on all points, but they did subscribe to Weininger's basic premise that women were not the equals of men but rather their polar opposites, personifying the dark, irrational, subversive forces of instinct, in opposition to the male's moral, rational, culture-creating capacities. Unlike Weininger, Lukács and his friends invested these supposedly feminine, nonrational qualities with a positive valuation, arguing that women had privileged access to realms of insight and sensibility which the men were just in the process of discovering for themselves and which they, as a generation, hoped to actualize in art and society. Thus, Balázs became convinced that women in general were more receptive to modernist art and poetry such as his own, because "they are spiritually fresher than men, ethically more restless, expectant, and prepared for something new. They are still evolving, and for this reason, they do not take for granted or consider useless the serious discussion of spiritual problems."[91]

The variations on the theme, once sounded, were endless and sometimes actually contradictory. Women could at times embody men's most cherished aspirations, their most radical hopes. "Ljena is the incarnation of Gyuri's ethics," Balázs wrote in his diary. "Anna [his own wife] is the incarnation of that new spiritual realm which I strive after . . . Gyuri says that . . . the fact that Ljena is the way he would wish himself to be liberates him and reconciles him to the unchangeable. Because someone has realized in actual life the idea that he only conceived in thought, it is no longer an empty abstraction, it no longer hangs in mid-air."[92] The same "feminine" qualities, however, could at other times take on a more fearsome aspect and find an overtly contemptuous, even slightly sadistic interpretation. Balázs was actually planning to rework the "Strindbergian theme" of the tragedy of the sexes, and jotted down the following sketch for the work:

> Woman is stupid, but she possesses a deep-rooted instinct in opposition to man's rootless intellect . . . Woman's security is vegetative and unconscious; she is strong, tenacious, never doubts or hesitates, because her attitude has nothing to do with the certitude of judgment, and therefore alternate possibilities don't even occur to her. She is a force of nature. And for this reason, it is precisely those men who lack the security of instinct who are most entrapped by her wiles . . . [Such men] are truly impressed by this first taste of absolute instinct which they see and venerate and fear in these women and know they can never match. They feel themselves to be lost children by their side.[93]

What is striking about these visions of the feminine, as about notions of sexual polarity generally, is the almost total absence of the women's own voices in them. They seem to have abdicated any active role in the elaboration of these psychological and cultural constructs, which nevertheless purported to define them so intimately and minutely. There is no evidence, it is true, that the women disagreed with them or considered them inaccurate, but there is ample evidence to suggest that they never actively embraced these definitions of femininity as the basis of their own vision of themselves. Indeed, they could not have even if they had wanted to, for these were not viable cultural roles or genuine identities, forged by real people to meet real situations, but rather projections reflecting men's needs, hopes, and fears once their own moorings from the relative safety of external, purely socially defined identities had been cut.

The women, for their part, remained oblivious to the need to define themselves actively in terms that were distinct from the general cultural definitions of their generation. They made no attempt to crystallize for themselves specifically feminine identities which would have given them, individually and collectively, a separate presence within the radical grouping where they had found shelter from the world of their parents. Their reluctance to do so is understandable. They did not feel that creativity, intellectual and cultural accomplishment, were gender bound, and they saw themselves as individuals freely participating in "the sexless sphere of disinterested intelligence."[94] They had no desire to emphasize the differences between themselves and the men and thus relegate themselves to a subgroup within a subgroup. To become radical women intellectuals, rather than radical intellectuals, was too reminiscent of the culture of their parents to be appealing.

The difficulty was that the women's early experiences, social training, and cultural reflexes were, in fact, significantly different from those of the men, and whether they wished to admit it or not, they *were* a subgroup within a subgroup, a marginalized minority within a marginalized minority. Whereas for the men such self-definitions of marginality became, ultimately, the source of enormous creativity and radical insight into the nature of culture, for the women no such truly appropriate identities developed. That is perhaps the reason why so few of these talented and adventurous women managed to realize even a fraction of their early promise. Their collective achievements remain strikingly flawed and incomplete, especially when compared to those of their equally talented male contemporaries. Emma Ritoók, who had a genuine flair for abstract philosophy, unfortunately "took two years to finish an article,"[95] as Lukács could not help pointing out, and she spent most of her time translating other people's articles into German rather than writing her own. Juliska Láng, Mannheim's future wife, wrote a subtle review of Mannheim's "Soul and Culture" in 1918,[96] and was never heard of again in print. Edit Hajós, Balázs' first wife, could never fully resign herself to practicing medicine, and spent a good part of the war years playing with fantasies of becoming a professional gardener or possibly even a carpenter. Perhaps the greatest disappointment was Anna Lesznai, who never managed to concentrate her multifaceted talents in any one direction where she could have realized a significant achievement.

The men in the group were not entirely unaware of the problem, which Balázs at one point called "the woman's tragedy."[97] Fülep actively protested against it in the case of Lesznai. After the war, when Fülep ordered a recent collection of Lesznai's poems, he was so bitterly disappointed in them that he did not know, as he wrote to a friend,

> whether to laugh or cry, because both emotions are appropriate. I love Mali dearly, and think the world of her. That is why it hurts to see her fritter herself away to the point of demoralization. Mali is more than talented, she has genius! And circumstances and the environment still have such an effect on her. I am convinced that if our old circle had stayed together, she would not have ended up like this. I still feel that if once I could have a serious, heart-to-heart talk with her, I could shake her up. But she won't come to visit me. She has a bad conscience.[98]

It is difficult to know for certain whether the continued existence of the Sunday Circle would have provided those necessary supports within which a talent such as Lesznai's could have unfolded and matured. The chances are that the women would eventually have found ways of contributing actively to the ethos of the group and thus helping to generate definitions of feminine identity more compatible with reality and their needs than the men could do alone. But their accomplishments, like those of their entire circle, were destined to remain incomplete, or to become radically reoriented by the force of external events. The political collapse of Hungary in 1918–19 also destroyed the social and cultural world that had nurtured them, and most were forced into emigration and the necessity of commencing entirely new lives. Nevertheless, in their youthful, often immature and incomplete works, they have left behind a legacy of achievement which gives some idea of what they would have achieved had they been given the chance to complete their task.

2

THE HISTORICAL
FORMATION
OF A GENERATION

In their groping efforts at self-definition,
Lukács and his friends often spoke of generation as the unifying force linking them
as a group. They could not escape the feeling that their "generation or sect or whatever more appropriate name it might have,
possesses a common fate," as well as a
common idea, that was destined "to be
continued by the next generation."[1] The
notion of generation as a source of collective identity was pervasive at the turn of
the century, but it was not until the postwar years that the phenomenon found more
precise definition among sociologists and
cultural historians. And it is deeply appropriate that one of the classic formulations
of the generational phenomenon should
have come from Karl Mannheim himself,
who had a distinct talent for transforming
his early cultural experiences into important sociological insights and generalizations.

The forces that mold a group of similarly aged individuals into a self-conscious generational unit, he wrote in 1927,[2] are in some ways analogous to those which create class unity. Both realities are based on a similarity of location within the social and economic hierarchy, which makes it possible for a group of individuals to share common historical experiences and therefore similar structures to sensibility. In order to belong to the same generation, individuals must be about the same age, so that their formative cultural experiences take place at roughly the same stage of life. They must, furthermore, be located within similar social and historical milieus so that they are in a position to experience roughly analogous events, problems, and challenges. (To take a far-fetched example, a youth born in China and one born in Germany at the same time would not necessarily be part of the same generation, since their formative historical experiences would be so utterly different.) And finally, the culture within which the individuals find themselves must have undergone "dynamic destabilization" so that the cultural inheritance of the young differs significantly from that of the previous generation.

In the case of the Sunday Circle, these criteria for generational unity were clearly present. Almost all the members of the group were born between 1885 and 1895,[3] and all, with the notable exception of Lajos Fülep and Emma Ritoók, came from the ranks of the assimilated Jewish middle classes.[4] Most significant, their formative years occurred during the 1890s and the early years of the twentieth century, which witnessed the end of a quarter century of liberal hegemony and relative political stability in the Austro-Hungarian monarchy and the beginning of ever-worsening constitutional, political, and social conflicts which would eventually cause the collapse of the monarchy itself in 1918.

The assimilated Jewish middle class of Hungary, to which Lukács and most of his friends belonged, was a fairly heterogeneous group which, by the late nineteenth century, contained within it significant differences of wealth, rank, occupation, and styles of life. These differences were clearly reflected in the backgrounds of the Sunday group and well illustrated by the family histories of three of its central figures: Georg Lukács, his comrade in arms Béla Balázs, and their friend Anna Lesznai.

Lukács' father was a self-made man who, during the Gründerzeit of the 1860s and 1870s, rose to become a wealthy and influential banker in Budapest.[5] His mother, who it seems had a strong influence in the family, was a worldly, clever woman, preoccupied by the anxious desire of the newly rich for respectability and social legitimacy. The sensitive and precocious young Lukács was raised in an atmosphere of comfort, indulgence, and privilege, but he was never able fully to forget, or forgive, the traces of social pretension and vulgarity he sensed in his early environment. Even in advanced old age he was to recount with sardonic irony the details of his early years in the Lipótváros.[6] There were, he remembered, trips to Paris and London as a very young child, where he was dragged through museums and art galleries, despite his clearly stated preference for the zoo.[7] There were dance lessons in the Budapest apartment of the Lukács family, where the children of the Jewish elite were taught to dance, and also, through Lukács' subversive influence, to satirize the world of the grownups.[8] There were music lessons from the unknown young musician Béla Bartók, who eventually became a family friend. Later, as a high school graduation present, there was a trip to Scandinavia to visit his literary idol, Henrik Ibsen. Above all, there was the constant and unstinting financial support from the elder Lukács, which made possible years of study abroad, the purchase of books and paintings (Lukács was one of the first purchasers of the Hungarian postimpressionists known as "The Eight"—"Nyolcak"), and generous aid to poorer friends. All this, however, was provided with the unstated expectation of literary and scholarly success, which in his upwardly mobile parents' eyes was synonymous with social advancement.

Balázs, in sharp contrast to Lukács, came from the narrow, somewhat claustrophobic world of the provincial intelligentsia. His father was a high school teacher, who had the misfortune to combine in his character both scholarly and worldly ambitions and high, unyielding moral principles. Early in his career he ran afoul of his superiors by standing up for the rights of a student against the school authorities and then refusing to apologize for his action. With this heroic and fateful gesture, he closed forever all doors to academic promotion and condemned himself to the straitened existence of a provincial schoolteacher. Balázs' early childhood was spent in a family atmosphere of genteel poverty and disappointed hopes, which became, it seems, even more pronounced after his father's untimely death. Yet precisely be-

45

cause his family was able to offer so little by way of financial support or cultural sustenance, the young Balázs was better able to cut the umbilical cord tying him to respectable society than were most of his Sunday Circle friends. From the time of his arrival in Budapest to continue his studies at the university, Balázs lived the free and marginal existence of the Bohemian intellectual. He accompanied Bartók on his village expeditions to record folk melodies; he briefly attended Simmel's private seminars in Berlin; he traveled to North Africa with Kodály and Bartók; and he apparently felt equally at home in all these environments.[9]

Anna Lesznai's background differed too from that of her friends. She came from a wealthy landowning family which, fairly atypically for the Jewish middle classes, had internalized the values and way of life of the Hungarian landed nobility. Her grandfather, Mór Moskovitz, a successful doctor, had become the family physician and trusted friend of the powerful Andrássy family at the time of the cholera epidemic of 1831. Gyula Andrássy's friendship secured for the Jewish doctor not only entry into the society of the landed nobility but also a title of nobility in 1867, when Count Andrássy became the foreign minister of the newly established Austro-Hungarian monarchy. Lesznai's father already belonged, if not by birth certainly by instinct and upbringing, to the anachronistic but still seemingly intact world of the Hungarian landed nobility. He hunted, took an active part in local politics, kept a lavish open house, and squandered money on mistresses in Budapest.[10]

The early memories of his daughter were anchored in the rather idyllic life of their baroque country house in northern Hungary, which was surrounded by an enormous garden, beyond which unfolded the colorful, alien world of the Slovak peasantry. Most of them still lived in virtually medieval conditions and regarded the Moskovitz family rather as feudal overlords.[11] Many years later she was to summarize this early environment in the following words: "If I allow my imagination free reign, I would say that my beginnings were somewhere in the Middle Ages, in a backward Slovak village, and what is more, in a charming old house which was called a castle, and which, even then, resembled an enchanted fairy tale dwelling amidst a forest of illusions. The road from there to the present traverses at least three centuries, for the calendar says it is 1959 and my address is New York City, U.S.A."[12]

The tremendous diversity of wealth, status, and ways of life so strikingly illustrated in the backgrounds of Lukács, Balázs, and Lesznai did not imply, oddly enough, an equal diversity in ideological positions among their parents. The wealthy banker, the struggling schoolteacher, and the extravagant landowner were closer to each other in their basic philosophic premises and political orientations than the surface of their lives would indicate. They were, after all, the children, or at most the grandchildren, of humble Jewish peddlers, artisans, shopkeepers, and merchants; and memories of their common past were not entirely erased from their consciousness. Even more significant, however, they were all the products of late nineteenth-century Hungarian liberalism, whose ideals and assumptions they wholeheartedly accepted and welded into a common world outlook. In philosophy they subscribed to the tolerant, individualistic, essentially optimistic creed of laissez-faire liberalism which had its flowering in Hungary during the 1860s and 1870s. They believed firmly in the power of reason, culture, and individual effort to overcome obstacles, and they looked forward with unclouded optimism to increasing economic and political progress in Hungary.

Curiously enough, their thoroughgoing secular rationalism did not often result in a total break with Judaism. Most assimilated Jews, like Lukács' and Balázs' fathers, had a rather easygoing, untroubled attitude toward their religion, whose rituals they observed on special occasions such as weddings, funerals, and once a year on Yom Kippur (the Jewish Day of Atonement), more out of social obligation than genuine religious or spiritual need. Judaism, wrote Lukács in his autobiography, "episodically intruded into the life of the child as *protocol:* its essence consisted of social obligation to take part in the weddings and funerals of acquaintances . . . For this reason, the learning of Hebrew was totally neglected."[13]

The final, and certainly the most powerful component of the parents' world view was their strong, unequivocal Hungarian nationalism. They firmly believed that it was possible and desirable for Jews living in Hungary to become fully integrated into the Hungarian nation, and they eagerly accepted its language, customs, and attitudes. In his dying words the elder Balázs instructed his young son "to root himself firmly within the soil of the Hungarian homeland."[14]

If it was not yet possible for most Hungarian Jews to feel completely "rooted" in the Hungarian soil they certainly felt tolerably comfortable in it. Budapest, which in the 1880s and 1890s was just in the process of being transformed into a cosmopolitan, sophisticated city consciously imitating Paris and Vienna, offered a way of life and a kind of sociability in which most assimilated Jews took conscious pleasure and pride. In later years Lukács was to refer to his father's Hungarian patriotism in the curt words, "My father was 'Jewish ambassador' in Budapest."[15] The epithet "Jewish ambassador" came from a well-known contemporary joke illustrating the attitude of newly assimilated Jews toward their adopted nation. The joke asks, "Why does Cohn want the establishment of a Jewish state in Palestine?" Answer: "So he can be the Jewish ambassador in Budapest."

This amalgam of beliefs and loyalties, consisting of secular rationalism, Jewish religious observance, and Hungarian nationalism, was the characteristic offshoot of late nineteenth-century Hungarian liberalism. It provided a coherent world view and an avenue for relatively harmonious social integration for the liberal generation that came to maturity sometime in the 1860s and 1870s. It was, however, a rather fragile phenomenon whose existence was directly tied to a particular set of social, political, and economic conditions which obtained in Hungary between 1867 and 1890.

This period, which is often called the Age of Dualism, saw the brief but spectacular flowering of a particular kind of liberalism in the Austro-Hungarian Empire, whose roots were anchored in the Compromise of 1867. The Compromise provided a new dualistic constitution for the lands of the Hapsburg monarchy, thus ending fifteen years of constitutional experimentation which followed the abortive revolutions of 1848. The new constitution was, admittedly, hardly the model of liberal constitutionalism that midcentury reformers and radicals had dreamed about. It was a solution imposed from above, and represented a division of power among the three strongest political forces of the monarchy: the Austro-German bourgeoisie, backed by the

landed aristocracy; the Hungarian landed nobility, also repre-
senting the interests of the rather small Hungarian bourgeoisie;
and finally the imperial army and bureaucracy, headed by the
Emperor Francis Joseph. [16] Not surprisingly, given the nature
of its origins, the dualistic constitution was oligarchic, its social
base narrow, and its policy toward the non-German and non-
Hungarian nationalities repressive and intolerant.

At the same time, however, the commitment of the architects
of Dualism to those liberal reforms that did not interfere directly
with their political hegemony was quite genuine. As Antal Csengery, one of the Hungarian founders and defenders of Dualism,
put it in an electoral speech of 1872, the goal of Dualism was to
create in Hungary a modern, liberal nation-state as well as a
"Kulturstaat," and a "Rechtstaat." In its attempt to achieve these
goals, he pointed out, Dualism had already succeeded in "dis-
solving the remaining vestiges of the feudal past in Hungary
and in completely liberating the land, as well as the working
hands on this land, from the shackles of the Middle Ages."[17]
Csengery's optimism was not entirely unjustified: the quarter
century following the Compromise of 1867 did indeed prove to
be the golden age of Hungarian liberalism. The new liberal government was especially successful in two general areas of reform:
in guaranteeing basic civil liberties and in fostering the modernization of the economy.

In 1867, for the first time in Hungary, freedom of the press,
of speech, assembly, and religion were constitutionally guaranteed and, what is more, genuinely respected. In the 1870s
separation of the judicial from the administrative branch of government was accomplished, the independence of judges guaranteed, and equality before the law, regardless of religion and
nationality, granted. In the 1890s the liberal government passed
the highly controversial secularization laws, which separated
church and state and declared Judaism a religion equal to all
others in Hungary.

In the realm of economic modernization too the actions of the
liberal government were significant and effective. Not only did
it guarantee a favorable legal and political climate for the ex-
pansion of railways, credit institutions, and infant industries,
but it also extended direct aid to them in the form of state loans,
subsidies, and tax exemptions. As a consequence of these meas-

ures, the transformation of the Hungarian economy during the last quarter of the nineteenth century was rapid and more thorough than was the case generally in Eastern Europe. During the so-called Gründerzeit of the 1860s and 1870s, an industrial base consisting mostly of food processing such as flour mills, sugar refineries, distilleries, and breweries was developed; and both agriculture and industry experienced an unprecedented boom. By the 1890s the economy was ready for its second stage of development, which consisted of the consolidation of existing iron and coal-mining industries and the development of new enterprises such as the machine industry, textile production, and smaller electrical, chemical, and pharmaceutical industries.[18]

The atmosphere of civic equality, religious tolerance, and economic dynamism which accompanied the Hungarian Gründerzeit of the 1860s proved to be an ideal environment for the rational, tolerant, and optimistic liberalism characteristic of the parents of Lukács' generation. However, their sincere, often fervent Hungarian nationalism cannot fully be accounted for by these economic and political factors alone. For, as Anna Lesznai was to write under the vastly changed conditions of the 1930s, "it always depends on the host community what kind of guest privileges are extended to another community living in their midst."[19] During the 1860s and 1870s the "guest privileges" extended to foreign nationalities by Hungarians were decidedly generous, and were offered willingly.[20]

This generosity was, of course, not without a healthy dose of self-interest. As late as the turn of the twentieth century, ethnic Hungarians made up less than half the population of Hungary; the other half comprised Germans, Slovaks, Romanians, Ruthenians, Serbians, Croats, and Jews. Yet despite the clearly multinational composition of the Hungarian state, the Hungarian political leadership insisted on governing it as a centralized, unitary nation-state, within which all citizens were extended equal political rights but not ethnic or national autonomy. The necessity for Hungarian dominance within the state was considered axiomatic in Hungarian liberal circles. The fate of progress and enlightenment in the Danube Basin, so the argument ran, depended directly and exclusively on Hungarian political and cultural hegemony over the more backward, less politically developed nationalities of the area. In the succinct words of a leading Hungarian journalist of the time, "Hungarian supremacy is based on the economic, political, and cultural superiority of the Hungarians."[21]

Given the ethnic composition and the political structure of Hungary, it was clearly in Hungarian interests to encourage assimilation among the non-Hungarian elements of the state. As a contemporary liberal politician bluntly put it, "Our self-interest requires that we attach to ourselves with ever stronger ties all those elements on whom we can count in the midst of our great struggles."[22] The problem was that most ethnic groups in Hungary defined *their* self-interests in terms that clashed directly with those of the Hungarians. By the turn of the century it had become amply clear that, despite policies of forced Magyarization in the schools, the non-Hungarian ethnic groups had resisted assimilation and were in fact becoming increasingly militant and politically conscious from the 1890s on.

One of the few exceptions to this general tendency was the case of the Jews in Hungary, who not only did not resist but eagerly welcomed the privileges of Hungarian nationality and contributed the largest and most significant group to Hungarian assimilation. (Between 1880 and 1910, 80 percent of Hungarian assimilants came from the ranks of the Jewish population.)[23] Under the circumstances, liberal Hungarians pointed with pride and gratitude to their new converts, whom they perceived as welcome allies in the otherwise hostile environment of ethnic Hungary. As one of these liberal politicians, Miklós Zay, put it as late as 1903, "It is my strong belief that Jewish assimilation can only strengthen us . . . Only those who have struggled for the Hungarian state ideal over many years can know the invaluable service Jewish citizens render us in those non-Hungarian areas of the country where, outside of one or two state officials, they are the sole representatives of the Hungarian nation."[24]

———

By 1903, when Zay wrote the article defending Jewish assimilation in Hungary, his point of view, and the entire national-liberal ideology on which it was based, was rapidly becoming an anachronistic holdover from an earlier age. The new political atmosphere was registered by sensitive observers like the poet Endre Ady as early as 1901, when he lamented that Hungarian liberalism had been eclipsed "by a cloak of black reaction [which] was preparing to cast its shadow over us."[25] Six years later the liberal Ady, still faithful to the ideal of the past, expressed his sense of radical discontinuity and dislocation in the following words: "I have an odd relationship with the few representatives of the liberal generation of the 1860s still alive today. I feel myself to be both their heir and their contemporary and sometimes wonder if the devil had not sneaked two newer generations between us."[26] During the 1890s a radical realignment of political and ideological forces took place, not only in Hungary but within the entire Dualistic monarchy, which resulted in the defeat of Austro-Hungarian liberalism and in the growing political and constitutional instability of the dualistic structure itself.

The Austro-Hungarian monarchy, as it was conceived of in 1867, had been based on, and its continuing stability depended upon, three major political and economic preconditions: the predominance of narrowly based, essentially elitist liberal parties within the Austrian and Hungarian half of the monarchy; the dominance of Germans and Hungarians within these parties; and finally, the cooperation of agrarian and mercantile interests both within Austria and Hungary and between the two halves of the monarchy. By the 1890s all these preconditions for stability were beginning to break down. The narrow German- and Hungarian-dominated liberal parties began to be challenged by the increasingly powerful forces of democracy and Slavic nationalism, which until then had been more or less held in check by the repressive apparatus of the state. Of equal significance was the breakdown of the alliance between business and agrarian interests in the monarchy, which resulted in the emergence of new right-radical, integral nationalist, often anti-Semitic mass movements which were as hostile to the rule of Austro-Hungarian liberalism as were the forces of Slavic nationalism.

After the widening of the franchise in Austria in 1882 and 1896, these antiliberal, radical, nationalist political forces made their voices heard with increasing frequency in the Austrian Reichstag. Parliamentary life, which until the 1880s had been based on carefully balanced coalitions, was ever more frequently disrupted by the growing violence of nationality conflicts, especially between the Czechs and the Germans. By the 1890s these conflicts had become so severe that the Austrian parliamentary process was virtually paralyzed, and government was kept functioning by emergency executive decrees, invested in the emperor by paragraph fourteen of the constitution. (Between 1895 and 1900 paragraph fourteen was used forty-three times—that is, in effect, for all important decisions that came before the Reichstag.)

It is this increasingly troubled period of Austrian political life that formed the basis of the novelist Robert Musil's affectionate satire of the political practices of "Kakania," the "vanished monarchy":

> By its constitution, it was liberal, but its system of government was clerical, but the general attitude to life was liberal. Before the law, all citizens were equal, but not everyone, of course, was a citizen. There was a parliament, which made such vigorous use of its liberty that it was usually kept shut; but there was also an emergency powers act by means of which it was possible to manage without a parliament, and everytime everyone was just beginning to rejoice in absolutism, the crown decreed that there must not again be a return to parliamentary government.[27]

On the Hungarian side too, from 1890 on the growing disintegration of liberalism and the dualistic system that was based upon it became increasingly evident. Here, however, the political crisis manifested itself in different forms. In sharp contrast to the Viennese Reichstag, the Hungarian parliament continued to function relatively efficiently throughout the 1890s and into the early twentieth century.[28] As one journalist wryly observed in 1908, "The Hungarian parliament compares to the Viennese Reichstag the way the ceremony of high mass compares to the chaos of the stock exchange."[29] The relative decorousness was due chiefly to its restricted social and ethnic composition. Unlike its Austrian counterpart, the Hungarian nobility had not extended the vote in the late nineteenth century, and therefore it continued to exert virtually complete control over the political and administrative apparatus of the state. The working classes and peasantry never had the vote, and the number of non-Hungarian ethnic representatives in parliament between 1875 and 1887 declined from twenty-five to one. The same situation obtained in the administrative and judicial systems at the turn of the century. Though Hungarians made up only about half the population of the state, 93 percent of the bureaucracy was Hungarian, 97 percent of the judges, and 92 percent of high school and university teachers.

The artificial homogeneity and ideological consensus which characterized the Hungarian parliament and officialdom in general could only mask, but not eliminate, those deep-rooted social, economic, and nationality tensions which began to make themselves felt in the 1890s. Chronic discontent among the poor, landless peasantry of the southeast erupted into violent agrarian strikes and disorders, which served to remind the Hungarian ruling classes of the precarious nature of their hold over the country. The nationalities too began to organize and to assert in increasingly visible forms their discontent with Hungarian rule.

Most significant in terms of its impact on young Hungarian intellectuals growing up in this period, was the emergence and growing influence of new conservative, nationalist, and anti-Semitic tendencies within the social and political fabric of the country. The new conservative ideological forces made their appearance partly in the form of ephemeral political groupings like the Nemzeti Párt (National party) of 1892 and the Néppárt (People's party) of 1895 and partly in the form of a large-scale agrarian pressure group whose formal organizational framework was the Hungarian Association of Agriculturalists (Magyar Gazda Szövetség), founded in 1896. The membership of these new conservative political groups or pressure organizations, overlapped with and was recruited from all those elements of Hungarian society who found their traditional ways of life and status increasingly threatened by the new commercial enterprises and business practices which had emerged during the Gründerzeit of the 1860s and 1870s.

The liberal political leadership of the 1860s had, of course, been aware of the potential conflict between the newer industrial and mercantile interests, which were just beginning to make their weight felt, and the traditional, overwhelmingly agrarian interests of the lower and middle nobility, which had always been the backbone of the Hungarian nation. They had optimistically hoped, however, that these potentially antagonistic tendencies could somehow be united and harmonized in the future.[30] Specifically, they had trusted that the Hungarian nobility would modernize and would thus help form the core of a new, truly bourgeois middle class, which would bring about the transformation of backward, agrarian Hungary without a major break from national traditions. This hope, implicit within the Hungarian liberal ideology of the 1860s, never materialized. By the 1890s it was becoming clear not only that the interests of the new industrial-mercantile sector and the traditional agrarian sector of the nobility were diverging, but also that the newer forces were gaining superiority in the Hungarian economy.

The middle nobility, once the proud spokesmen of Hungarian national consciousness, proved to be the hardest hit by, and the least able to adapt to, the new competitive market conditions of the latter half of the nineteenth century. Their estates rapidly slipped out of their grasp into the hands of other, often Jewish, elements, who proved more adaptable to the novel world of capitalist enterprise. The vast majority of the middle nobility, which began in the 1880s to be called the gentry, was irretrievably undermined by the new economic conditions of the late nineteenth century, and was forced to leave the land and find employment within the national and county bureaucracies that came into existence after the Compromise of 1867. It was this déclassé Hungarian gentry, eking out a meager living in government offices, embittered by the contrast between its poverty and the obvious affluence of the newer bourgeois classes, that became the core of, and the most radical element in, the new conservative, antiliberal movements of the 1890s.[31]

They were joined by other social groups whose way of life and livelihood had proven equally vulnerable to the new tendencies and techniques of a modernized economy: the lower-middle-class artisans threatened by factory production and large department stores; the poor, landless peasantry, whose plight was worsening rather than improving; the Catholic lower clergy, resentful of the secularizing laws of the liberal government which took key functions such as marriage, divorce, and the registry of births and deaths out of its hands; and finally some members of the landed aristocracy who, though not threatened economically, deeply resented the fact that economic and social supremacy was clearly slipping into the hands of the new commercial bourgeoisie.

In fact the leadership of these forces tended to come from the ranks of the aristocracy, who traveled widely in Europe and were thoroughly familiar with the conservative ideologies that were just then emerging in Western Europe as well. Men like Albert Apponyi, for example, the leader of the Nemzeti Párt, had spent time in Germany and was deeply influenced by German Catholic social reformers like Bishop Ketteler, while Sándor Károlyi, the leader of the agrarian movement, looked to the French new conservatives and to the sociologist Frederic Le Play for example and inspiration.

The general ideological orientation of the Hungarian new conservatives was fairly similar to that of their West European counterparts. They too rejected the individualistic, competitive ethos of laissez-faire liberalism and postulated in its place the communal ideal of medieval corporatism, with its concrete, personal social bonds and its stable, hierarchical political organization. In many ways they were simply reviving the ideas of early nineteenth-century conservatives like Joseph de Maistre, Louis de Bonald, Samuel Taylor Coleridge, Robert Southey, Adam Müller, and others who had opposed from the first the abstract, fragmenting tendencies of the French Revolution and the modern economy, and held up against it an idealized portrait of the communal and religious Middle Ages.

The late nineteenth-century new conservatives, however, went far beyond their philosophic predecessors, born in theory and in practice. Unlike them, the new conservatives could hardly be called nostalgic reactionaries ineffectually dreaming of a long-lost past. The Middle Ages for the new conservatives represented simply a social ideal to be emulated in a radical future reconstruction that would create a brand-new social order to take the place of failed liberal society. They opposed the reigning liberal regime with an ideology that was revolutionary, and with political techniques that were modern and particularly well adapted to mobilize and manipulate large mass audiences, which for the first time were becoming a political force in Central Europe.[32]

Unlike the liberals, who still operated as an elite political club, the new conservatives became adept at the technique of mass political organization, a skill that, ironically, they had learned from the Social Democrats. They realized that if they were to organize and influence large, often poorly educated masses of the population, they would need a permanent and far-flung network of local organization that would be in touch with the daily lives of people. In Hungary the already existing parish organization of the Catholic church proved to be an ideal basis for political organization. They also realized early that the ideological requirements of democratic mass politics differed considerably from those of elitist liberal electioneering. Issues had to be simplified, and made to have broad emotional appeal that could bind large numbers of people, often with diverging economic interests, into a cohesive group.[33]

Nationalism proved to be one of these broad, loosely defined causes which could cement internal divergences and generate a mood of emotional fervor and exultation among large masses of people. It is true that throughout most of the nineteenth century Hungarian nationalism had been closely associated with the political left, it being held axiomatic as late as 1880 that nationalism, liberalism, and constitutionalism were inseparable ideals. One of the most significant accomplishments of the new conservative movement in Hungary was to reformulate Hungarian nationalism and create for it a new ideological context based on conservative rather than liberal assumptions. New conservative theorists repudiated the ethic of modern capitalism and individualism, arguing that the new tendencies were alien to the Hungarian character and destructive of national traditions. What is more, they also repudiated all the political goals and accomplishments of Hungarian liberalism and argued that not only the Compromise of 1867 but even the popular revolution of 1848 had been a great mistake and a tragic divergence from Hungary's genuine national path. The revolution of 1848, wrote one of the leading conservative pamphleteers of the time, "has brought to ruin a thousand-year-old building, has destroyed a thousand-year-old community, without creating anything in its place . . . Who will bring back to us the ruined Hungarian estates, the Hungarian gold which has been transformed into Jewish mobile capital; who will give us back the moral clarity of our nation; who will bring back to us our vanished middle classes?"[34]

The other crucial element of the new right-radical nationalist ideology was anti-Semitism, which also provided a powerful emotional rallying point for a mass audience with diverse economic and social grievances. Within the East European context, it is not difficult to understand how the painful dislocations caused by the rapid transformation of a traditional economy and social structure would find expression in virulent anti-Semitism. Jews did in fact play a disproportionately large role in the modernization of Hungary, which lacked an indigenous bourgeoisie.[35] By the late nineteenth century, Jews made up 5 percent of the total population of Hungary but supplied 12.5 percent of the industrialists, 54 percent of the businessmen, 43 percent of the bankers and moneylenders, 45 percent of the lawyers, and 49 percent of the doctors.[36]

Thus, in the eyes of much of the population, Jews inevitably became the symbolic representatives of capitalism, and the living embodiment of all the alien, destructive tendencies of the modern world. The peasant's anger at high interest rates was inevitably directed against the local Jewish tavern keeper, who often functioned as a moneylender as well. The urban artisan's frustration at competition from factories and large department stores found expression in hostility toward Jews, who often owned these enterprises. And perhaps most intense was the déclassé gentry's desperation over the loss of its traditional social and economic dominance in Hungary to the new Jewish middle classes, who seemed to profit from the very tendencies which had destroyed its former way of life.

The close interconnection between anti-Semitism and anti-modernism in new conservative doctrines was well illustrated by a pamphlet of the Catholic People's party entitled "Hungary and the Jews," which was published in 1899. "The settlement and resolution of the Jewish question," wrote the author, "has become a virtual life and death issue in Hungary, because something has to happen . . . We either helplessly give up everything to the Jews . . . or we finally stand up on our feet and we gain back what has always been our own, a Christian Hungary."[37] Such pamphlets and convictions were undoubtedly characteristic of only the more radical elements of the population, and they never became official government policy under Dualism. They did however penetrate, gradually and in milder forms, into all layers of the population, so that from the first decade of the twentieth century they expressed a fairly widespread attitude in Hungary.[38]

The growing importance of this new anti-Semitic, conservative mood is easily observed in the periodical literature between 1900 and 1918. In 1900 the problem of anti-Semitism, or as it was then called the "Jewish question," was still a taboo subject that caused considerable embarrassment in liberal Hungarian circles. Thus, when Ady inadvertently raised the issue in 1901, claiming that though there was naturally no trace of anti-Semitism in the public forum, "social anti-Semitism still existed because it was perpetuated by the women,"[39] he was sharply reprimanded by a reader for lack of tact. "To speak of anti-Semitism," wrote the irate reader in a letter to the editor, "is to create it. It is like the honor of a woman. Once one begins to wonder about it, doubt and suspicion are inevitably generated."[40]

However much liberal Hungarians wished it, the embarrassing topic would not go away, and by the second decade of the century it had become a question of common, frequently recurring concern. As the radical journalist Dezsö Szabó put it in 1914, "The historical problem of Hungarian Jewry can no longer be separated from the historical problems of Hungarians. Their spiritual and economic existence has become such an integral part of Hungarian life that the question of their future, their development, and their social role has become one of the vital and integral problems of Hungary."[41] By the war years, the "Jewish question" had become such a pressing and pervasive issue that the radical sociological journal *Huszadik Század* (Twentieth century) actually initiated in 1917 a questionnaire entitled "Is There a Jewish Question in Hungary?" which was sent to the leading literary and political personalities of the country; their diverse answers and opinions were published in early 1918. Half the respondents thought there was a definite "Jewish problem" in Hungary, while the other half felt that it was a question of passing importance.[42]

Perhaps nowhere was the newly radicalized ideological climate more in evidence than at the University of Budapest, where the student population provided fertile soil for the more extreme political impulses of the time. The liberal Ady, who followed with great concern the unmistakable trend, wrote in 1901, "The ever-growing clerical reaction has caught in its trap the not quite fully grown youth of today . . . It has enticed them out into the forum, put weapons into the children's hands . . . and now, the troupe of underaged, poor, blinded children have confusedly begun to move, to restore the nation, to conserve morality, to save Christianity, and to kick the Jews."[43]

The new right-radical ideological tendencies were especially in evidence in certain sections of the university, such as the faculty of law, which was dominated mostly by students of noble Hungarian background. The highly charged atmosphere, which saw an increasing polarization between conservative and radical students, did not require much to erupt into open conflict. In the spring of 1900, just a year and half before Lukács and many of his friends were to enter the university, a new building was to be officially opened. The night before the ceremony was to take place, the cross from the Hungarian coat of arms decorating the corridor was broken by an unknown perpetrator. When the mutilated crest was discovered next morning, the conservative students assumed that a Jewish student was responsible and proceeded to make a universitywide issue out of it. In fact, some decided to go beyond the university, and wrote an appeal to a right-radical political leader, asking for outside help in the matter. The letter, which was read in parliament, recounted the incident of the crest and went on: "If this were not the most serious symptom of the growing pan-Judaism . . . we would not react with such fear to this deed; but given its symbolic significance, the villainous deed assumes real importance. In the name of the fatherland and of our beloved religion, I ask that you make a public issue of this in your newspaper. It is time that we finally wake up from our lethargy and teach a well-deserved lesson to the Jews who have grown on our necks."[44]

The issue of the broken cross did not result in the nationwide debate that the right-wing students had hoped for, but it did succeed in polarizing and radicalizing the student body. The next spring, in 1901, the whole question was reopened, this time by the demand of the right-wing students to have crosses hung in the university classrooms. The administration and the faculty, loyal to the liberal creed of separation between church and state, refused the request of the students. These in turn took the issue into their own hands and marched through the university, hanging crosses in each of the classrooms. The administration reacted by promptly suspending classes, removing the crosses from the classrooms, and reprimanding the conservative students. Once again the symbolic significance of the conflict was more important than the actual issues or their outcome. The conservative students had, strictly speaking, lost their battle with the liberal administration, but they had succeeded in airing their point of view, and in generating considerable support throughout the country. "Behind the university students," claimed the conservative paper *A Hazánk* (The fatherland), "stands an entire multitude."[45]

That almost any issue could inflame the tinderbox atmosphere of the university is illustrated by another somewhat different conflict which erupted in 1907 around a progressive professor of legal history, Gyula Pikler.[46] Pikler, a philosophic liberal and a positivist, explained the evolution of social hierarchies and privileges on the basis of economic differentiation. Right-wing students protested vigorously against such an explanation, claiming that Pikler was undermining the philosophic basis of noble privilege and that he was spreading subversive doctrines against the fatherland. Not satisfied with verbal protests to the school authorities, they showed up in Pikler's class to heckle him and make it impossible for him to deliver his lectures. Pikler, however, had supporters of his own, who organized for weeks, occupying every seat in the lecture hall and thus keeping the right-wing hecklers out. Although the lectures took place with a certain amount of decorum, the corridor outside Pikler's lecture hall became the scene of violent fistfights between supporters and opponents of the controversial professor.

"The Pikler affair," as it came to be known, though symptomatic of the deep political tensions within Hungarian society, was, once again, not particularly conclusive in itself. The radical right-wing students, though better organized and more militant than the rest of the student body, did not form a majority at the university even in 1907, and certainly could not prevail upon the administration to suspend Pikler. But the affair hit a raw nerve in the nation and received considerable attention and coverage from the national press. Even Emperor Francis Joseph, it seems, followed the events with close attention and concern.

Perhaps nothing illustrates more graphically the sudden disintegration of the old national-liberal consensus than the marked student unrest of the first decade of the twentieth century. As late as 1895 liberal causes such as the separation between church and state had still been able to rally the student body,[47] but by

1910 few traces of such attitudes remained. In 1911 the official cultural organ of the still liberally inclined government, *Magyar Figyelö* (Hungarian observer), deplored the extremist tendencies of the university students and looked back with nostalgia to the national-liberal student generations of the past, who had still felt convinced that "it was their responsibility to express strong nationalist attitudes and equally strong liberal convictions. Thus, whenever one or the other principle became a public issue, the university students also made their voices heard."[48]

During the first decade of the twentieth century, when Lukács and his friends were attending the University of Budapest, the atmosphere of the university, and, to a lesser extent, of the entire country, had become so radicalized that maintaining a moderate posture based on the old national-liberal ideology had become a practical impossibility for most young Hungarian intellectuals. The question, thus, was not whether Lukács and his friends would become radicalized but rather what form their radicalism would assume.

Contrary to one's expectations, they joined the ranks of neither the conservative nor the radical students. In fact we find in their letters, diaries, and later reminiscences almost no mention of university politics and the student disorders which characterized institutions of higher learning during those years. What we do find in the way of public activity among them is involvement in an experimental, avant-garde theater group called the Thália.

The idea for the Thália emerged among Lukács and a few of his university friends who were deeply dissatisfied with the repertoire of the established theaters in Budapest. As Marcell Benedek, a close childhood friend of Lukács', and one of the cofounders of the Thália, wrote in his diary at this time, "We all feel that the Nemzeti Szinház [National theater] has been arrested somewhere in 1850 and the Vígszinház [Comic theater] somewhere in 1880. In the former, a kind of stylized dramatic declamation holds sway, while in the latter a form of naturalism which turns out every play with the identical 'naturalist style' whether it is appropriate or not."[49]

It was, it seems, Lukács' idea to take steps to remedy the situation and attempt to establish a theater company which would give performances of the modern European avant-garde plays that he and his friends liked to read. At the first organizational meeting, which took place at the Lukács' home in January 1904, there were around thirty young people—mostly beginning teachers, students, and writers—including some subsequent close friends like Béla Balázs and Zoltán Kodály. The key organizers were Lukács and two friends, Marcell Benedek and Lászlo Bánoczi; but the person who was to be of crucial importance to the success of the theatrical venture was Sándor Hevesi, the assistant director of the Nemzeti Szinház, who brought not merely enthusiasm but also considerable professional expertise to the company.

The Thália opened its doors on November 23, 1904, with scenes from Goethe, Courteline, Brandes, and Mongre. In the course of the next few years, the young company brought to Budapest such controversial modernist playwrights as Strindberg, Hebbel, Gorki, Wedekind, and Ibsen. The Thália, wrote Lukács in 1908, expressed in its productions the essential meaning of modern dramatic literature in the lives of his generation. It gave voice "to the tragic fate which recognizes the futility of everything; the necessary imperfection of all knowledge; the eternal estrangement of people from one another."[50]

In 1906, a year that represented the golden age of the Thália, the organizers took a significant step to broaden the activities and preoccupations of the theater by including working-class audiences in their venture. In February 1906 they made an agreement with the Social Democratic party to perfrom plays by Hebbel, Ibsen, Wedekind, and Gorki specifically for workers. Lukács wrote, "In enabling the working classes of Budapest to be exposed, for the price of a minimal entry fee, to some of the finest examples of dramatic literature . . . the Thália has established a new precedent among the large metropolitan centers of Europe."[51] Marcell Benedek too placed great importance on these working-class performances. The Thália, he wrote in his journal, introduced Budapest to the modern drama and created "a new style of direction that was free from empty conventions and able to adapt to the style of the play itself. But the historical significance of the Thália lies in its worker performances, in which it proved that even simple people with uncorrupted taste can enjoy the highest manifestations of art."[52]

The Thália did not prove to be long-lived; by 1908 it had been forced to close its doors. (It seems that its demise was due partly to the defection of talented young actors and actresses, who, once discovered by the Thália, were often enticed away by the established theater companies; and partly to official harassment because of its cooperation with the Social Democrats.) Nevertheless, the significance of the Thália experience in the lives of Lukács and a few others was lasting, and not inconsiderable. "The Thália," wrote Lukács in his autobiography "showed a way out of the half-childish experimentations of adolescence,"[53] and allowed him to clarify certain personal and professional options. He realized during this period of theatrical activity that he had no talent for directing, nor for creative writing, and at the age of eighteen he resolutely destroyed all his earlier attempts at literary production, never to be tempted in that direction again. The realization that his professional path was to lead through literary criticism and philosophy, and not creative literature, was in many ways a painful renunciation and an admission of personal limitations, whose echo can be found even in his last autobiographical account shortly before his death: "Not an artist! Only a philosopher! Only abstractions."[54]

Important as the Thália experience was for Lukács as his earliest venture into cultural politics, it was by no means his first encounter with modernism. He had already discovered the modernists at the age of fifteen, ironically through his father's copy of Max Nordau's *Degeneration,* a provocative and well-known polemic against modernism written in 1893. From there, as Lukács put it, he had only to make a 180 degree turn to discover such authors as Baudelaire, Verlaine, Swinburne, Zola, Ibsen, and Tolstoy, all of whom had been denounced by the severe Nordau as cultural and moral degenerates.

These literary discoveries provided the young Lukács with the first appropriate expression of his deep-rooted inner rebellion against his early environment. As he was later to express it, for him and his friends the "attempt at inner liberation from the spiritual crisis of official Hungary took the form of extolling European modernism."[55] Modernism implied for them a form of cultural radicalism which appeared not only more congenial but more fundamental than the political radicalism of socialists and other oppositional groups in the country. In contrast to their merely "external," "superficial" radicalism, explained Lukács, the modernists stood for an "inner revolution" whose intention was to transform the internal life and the consciousness of individuals, not merely their external power relationships in the social and political world.[56]

Why modernism and not some other "ism" of the age proved to be the congenial channel for their radical impulses is a question that falls on the borderline between individual psychology and general history. In the case of individuals, the choice can best be explained through an innate psychological and temperamental predilection toward introspection and emotional nuances. In the case of entire generational units or cultural formations, however, it is reasonable to assume that more general historical and sociological forces were in operation as well, which channeled individuals with diverse emotional make-ups toward common cultural perceptions and choices.

Looking at the spotty records available to us of the childhood experiences of Lukács and his friends, we find in them expressions of extreme estrangement from the world of their parents. As Lukács was to stress over and over again in later life, he had grown up with an unadulterated hatred for "the remnants of Hungarian feudalism and for the capitalism which grew upon this soil."[57] In the eyes of the young Lukács, the common perceptions and expectations of the adult world—embodied in parents, teachers, and authority figures in general—seem to have taken on an air of unreality and unreliability. The young child increasingly seemed to have found the moral and intellectual guideposts of adults untrustworthy, and he concluded at an early age that "there are no general public highways to reality; only uniquely individual and personal paths."[58] He began by systematically rejecting the customary reading material of boys his age, which consisted mostly of heroic tales of Hungarian knights fighting the Turkish invaders. "The daring of the heroes of the Turkish wars," he wrote revealingly, "reminded me too much of the social condescension of the real-life ladies and gentlemen who visited my parents."[59] Instead of the conventional heroism of the Hungarian stories, the nine-year-old Lukács

65

turned to Fenimore Cooper's *Last of the Mohicans* and a year later to Mark Twain's *Tom Sawyer* and *Huckleberry Finn*, whose marginal characters all embodied values and attitudes directly opposed to those of his conventional, success-oriented parents. Cooper especially proved to the boy that "the conquered is morally right and [is] the real conquerer, as opposed to the merely external, socially accepted conquerer."[60]

Lukács' deep-seated distrust of the conventions of the adult world was echoed by Balázs as well, who claimed that the most fundamental experience of his childhood was the "deep inner suspicion with which I observed the adults of my environment." As a young child he was convinced that "nothing was really what it seemed," that behind the appearance of everyday reality there lurked a different secret sphere of life in which "all objects and people are totally different from those here, and are connected to each other in totally different ways."[61] The young Balázs' attitude toward reality was essentially magical and supernatural and totally at odds with the empiricist, matter-of-fact approach of adults. Not surprisingly, the child was extremely receptive to the world of dreams, nightmares, fantasies, and fairy tales as well, which apparently played as important a role in his early life as did real events. In fact, Balázs began his account with the memory not of actual happenings but of two extremely vivid nightmares, whose influence defined his early years. "In the beginning was the dream," he wrote. "At my beginning it was there in the absolutely literal sense of the word, for my earliest memory consists of two dreams."[62]

By a curious coincidence, Anna Lesznai began her own autobiography on an almost identical note. "In the beginning was the garden," she wrote, "wonderful colors and tastes—and fear." Her basic childhood experience too was defined by distrust of surface appearances and empirical reality. "It slowly became evident to the little girl," she wrote about herself, "that absolutely nothing could be trusted, because everything is different from what it appears."[63] What the world of dreams and fairy tales was for Balázs, the huge park surrounding her house became for the young Lesznai. The garden embodied a separate universe where the ordinary rules of reality did not apply: trees talked here, flowers had feelings, and the natural elements had mysterious powers. Her attitude toward the garden of her early childhood was that of a primitive nature worshiper who invests the inanimate world around her with sentient human characteristics. "In the garden of Liszka," she wrote in her novel,

only such trees and flowers bloom which intervene directly in one's life . . . From the kitchen a row of linden trees lead to the barnyard. The linden trees are demanding. One has to sacrifice to them as on the altar of the gods. If no one sacrifices under them (something that can't happen because there are always lovers), perhaps they could not even bloom. But farther up on the hill, the scent of tuberoses fixes the lovers to the earth, just like in the old fairy tales. At such times the lovers can't even move, and stiffly face each other until a wind starts up and wafts the scent from them . . . The wild chestnut tree can tell fortunes. It hums differently when it expects good tidings and differently when unhappiness threatens. Then there are paths in the garden which lead to a different place every day. If a storm is about to break, every bush and every plant becomes stiff, lights up like a torch, and stands apart in its glory.[64]

What is at once striking in these autobiographical accounts of Lukács, Balázs, and Lesznai is the fact that many of the childhood attitudes and intuitions described in them were eventually to form the focus of their mature intellectual and cultural investigations. The figure of the child, with its independence of social authority and its intuition into prelogical and preconceptual experiences, was to become for them the compelling symbol of a more primary, more authentic reality which receded as one approached adulthood. As Anna Lesznai put it in 1921, "Man falls out of the world at birth—that is when he becomes homeless.—And all subsequent experiences of life draw a veil between him and authentic and intensive truth. From the time of childhood, there is a distancing from nature and from our true selves."[65]

Their intellectual passion to get behind the mere appearance of things, to experience an essential reality that is perceived directly without the intermediary of rational concepts and inherited cultural typographies, was once again directly related to their early childhood experiences. In fact Lajos Fülep stated explicitly in one of his early essays on modernist art that the child's capacity for a direct, nonconceptual relationship with reality was the source of all artistic creativity: "Precisely because its mind absorbs impressions separately and sharply, and does not hook them together into concepts, it [the child] has a need to give form to these impressions . . . This is why the child draws and sculpts, not for others but for himself, not for mere beauty but out of a life instinct."[66]

The culturally significant factor in these childhood accounts of Lukács and his friends is not that they expressed rebellion against parental authority or shared magical, preconceptual intuitions about reality; that is characteristic of most young children. What is noteworthy is that they carried over these impulses and intuitions into adult life; that they chose these particular details as the defining characteristics of their early worlds and as the measuring rods of their mature cultural strivings. In other words, the process of selectivity operating in the adult writer, not the actual experience of the child, is what takes on special significance.

In the normal process of socialization, children very early learn to repress the preconceptual, nonrational elements of their personalities and gradually replace these with the culturally acceptable truths of their society. These objective cultural forms, of which language is the most important, make it possible for individuals to communicate with one another and to deal efficiently with the outside world. Eventually the internalized norms and assumptions of society become automatic, spontaneous, totally axiomatic reflexes which leave in the adult few traces of the earlier, more primitive cognitive development of the child.[67] In the case of the Lukács group, however, the normal process of socialization seems to have been interrupted or reversed. The moral and cultural norms of the larger social world either were not internalized fully or came to be rejected, so that the irrational, magical attributes of childhood retained their existence and their intellectual validity in the adult mind. That this is what happened is made quite explicit by Balázs, who recounted that his disenchantment with the social world around him had become so complete and devasting by his high school days that

all standards of value and measure, order and law, that existed around me began to wobble and crash . . . A violent defiance erupted within me, even before I knew exactly against what. I denied something without being sure what I was denying. There awakened within me a deep and never-to-be extinguished suspicion against every manifestation of bourgeois respectability. This was the lifelong longing for inner independence and freedom . . . The moral concepts of society which surrounded me and held me in their grip had lost their authority.[68]

The cultural and historical roots of this attitude, which was echoed in different forms by other members of the Lukács circle, are not hard to find. In an age of growing anti-Semitism and intransigent conservative nationalism, the children of the assimilated Jewish middle classes became the social group most vulnerable to marginalization and social dislocation. The ideological and cultural heritage of the liberal parents, with their comfortable adherence to a ritualized Judaism and their enthusiastic assimilation of Hungarian nationalism, became increasingly inappropriate in the changed political world of the turn of the century. For the children of the liberal generation, both their Jewish and their Hungarian heritage began to appear deeply problematic and paradoxical; eventually they found themselves estranged from both communities. This social marginality was to be the chief determining influence in the choice of their later cultural and intellectual paths. "The fact that I was excluded from one community," wrote Balázs in his reminiscences, "without belonging to another; the fact that from early childhood on, I stood outside all communities, isolated as a solitary individual, had determined my fate and conduct for life. Whether this has been fortunate or not will be determined by the events of the rest of my life. But if, ultimately (as I believe), it has been fortunate, then I have paid for the privilege with the greatest of human sufferings: with loneliness."[69]

Their estrangement from the particular kind of Judaism practiced by their liberal, assimilated parents was extreme and self-conscious. After all, even for the liberal fathers, Judaism had largely ceased to be the source of spiritual and cultural meaning which could be integrated into their everyday life and conduct. The parents nevertheless continued a formal allegiance to Jewish practices, partly because these had not yet been emptied of all emotional significance for them. The rituals were obscurely connected with memories of a living Jewish community to which, if not they, certainly their fathers had belonged. For the children, however, no traces of such communal memories and experiences remained, and the rituals contracted into mere formalities and empty gestures. "My father," recounted Balázs about his contact with Judaism,

> who otherwise never went to temple and certainly never prayed, once a year took me to some secret ceremony . . . There were only men there whom I did not know and with whom my parents did not socialize. With white sheets on their shoulders, they wailed and beat their breasts. But what was really frightening for me was that my father too donned such a white sheet, which was edged with black stripes, and dressed like them, he joined and entered this alien and secret alliance . . . I heard that this was Yom Kippur and our most holy day of the year, because we are Jewish. Why are we Jewish? This I did not quite understand . . . Otherwise, during the rest of the year no detail of our life gave me the sense that we were Jewish. In the Protestant high school which I attended there was no instruction about Judaism, and my father, who was a passionate freethinker and Freemason, never considered instruction in Hebrew necessary.[70]

This generation's attitude toward Judaism was even more complicated than such accounts of estrangement from religious practices would indicate. By the first decade of the twentieth century, in a political atmosphere of growing anti-Semitism and latent violence, the total renunciation of Judaism became morally and socially difficult, if not impossible, for many young Jewish intellectuals. In 1910, for example, when Balázs found that gaining a permanent job as a high school teacher was hindered by his religion, he wrote to Lukács, "It is a pity that I am Jewish or that I did not convert long ago, because at this point a causeless but nevertheless insurmountable defiance, self-respect, and shame would make such a step totally inconceivable."[71]

In sharp contrast to the strong assimilative impulse of the parents, the children's generation began to show an unmistakable tendency to dissimilate and to assume, or search out, some form of Jewish identification that would prove more meaningful than the ritual-bound inheritance of the parents. Lukács, for example, became interested in the Jewish mystical traditions of Chassidism, and not only reviewed the writings of Martin Buber on the subject but also carried on a fairly prolonged correspondence with Buber in the years immediately before the war.[72] Such gropings toward an intellectually and emotionally more viable Jewish identity remained on the whole marginal to the concerns of the future Sunday Circle, however. At the root of their tenuous Jewish identification was a moral defiance against an increasingly hostile external world, rather than genuine spiritual or religious affinity. As Anna Lesznai was to write in a revealing diary entry in 1923, her spontaneous sympathy for the Catholic rituals of her beloved native village had become morally difficult in the wake of Jewish persecutions:

> A few years ago, I—converted Calvinist with no religious affiliation—have still been able to tearfully pray along with [these Catholic peasant women]. But today my soul walks on different paths, and their religious rapture can no longer lift me into their community. No childhood memories tie me here. I become separate, even though I also accept . . . Christ as the ultimate ethical manifestation of humanity—what is more, as the ultimate metaphysical embodiment of man's soul . . . and still I cannot pray along with them. A thousand things draw me away from here . . . I cannot stay with them because I am Jewish. Do I have the right to sit here in a Catholic church when fanatics are killing my people in the name of Christianity? . . . Today, Jesus himself would go to the synagogue, not to pray with them but to be stoned along with them. So I have no right to sit in a Catholic church but should be in the synagogue along with my people. My people, to whose faith, language, traditions, culture—probably even racial stock—I have no binding connections, but who are, nevertheless, I know today, my people, whom I choose above all others (but not against all others).[73]

If the group's relationship to Judaism had been rendered deeply problematic by the social and political conflicts of the age, their relationship to Hungarian nationalism had become equally paradoxical. For their assimilationist fathers, Hungarian nationalism had opened up vistas of personal liberation and had made possible the transition from the confinements of the ghetto into a larger, secular European culture. For the children of the assimilationist generation, however, Hungarian nationalism, with its increasing stridency and xenophobia, had shrunk into a constricting, provincial ideology which had to be transcended in order to find a way to the larger, more universal philosophic questions of the age. It is not at all accidental that so many of the Sunday Circle were bilingual (usually in Hungarian and German, but in the case of Fülep, Hungarian and Italian) and that their scholarly and artistic work almost always appeared simultaneously in both Hungarian and German. In the case of Lukács, his alienation from Hungarian culture was so complete that after publishing his first volume of essays, *Soul and Forms* (1910), he actually stopped writing in Hungarian and switched exclusively to German.

Lukács and his friends had become cosmopolites, in the fullest sense of the word; they felt at home in most of the major cities of Europe, and tended to have well-developed social and professional contacts in many of them as well. (Lukács' close relationship with the Weber circle in Heidelberg is only one, if the most obvious, example of such contacts.) They traveled constantly and extensively, not in the spirit of tourists, as their parents had done, but as spiritual émigrés, seeking a deeper, more authentic intellectual and cultural experience than was possible in their native land. "Without art and ever-changing impressions," wrote Fülep to a friend, "I am unable to live; my soul suffers from malnutrition, it is always hungry . . . I detest Budapest, but at least I recognize my malnutrition here and intend to leave this year for Italy to saturate myself with art."[74]

Fülep, like so many of his circle, was constantly toying with the idea of permanent emigration, and certainly always left Budapest in that state of mind. "In about three or four weeks," he wrote a friend in 1906, "I am leaving for Paris with the fixed intention that only the most abject poverty will drive me back home. As long as there is a roof over my head and a piece of bread to stuff in my belly, I am staying. I have a strong feeling that I shall never again see the soil of our glorious fatherland. May it be true. Away from here . . . I can no longer endure the filth and the stench of rotting here . . . I feel I shall be ruined here within a short time. Are you not coming?"[75]

Constricting as most of them found early twentieth-century Hungary, their frequent references to permanent emigration were not fully serious, for the rather pragmatic reason that they were not financially feasible, unless, as in the case of Lukács, there existed a large personal income to support such plans.[76] But they were also not serious for the more complicated reason that their often negative comments about Hungary masked strong feelings of ambivalence and frustration, not just outright hostility. After all, this generation had been raised as patriotic Hungarians; many of them, like Balázs, has been instructed by their parent to "grow roots in the Hungarian homeland." Their inability to find genuine roots in the stony soil of turn-of-the-century Hungary produced in many not detachment but a strong nostalgia for the possibility of a community that kept eluding them. As Balázs wrote, his response to his father's dying words was to "set out immediately to search for the Hungarian people and their inner essence. For I had a vague spatial and objective image of it; it appeared as some sort of sectarian community, which exists in a definite place and waits for me to enter ceremonially into it."[77] That he never found this mythical community left in the boy a sense of nostalgia and a negative homesickness which was itself, as he later pondered, a not inconsiderable cultural inheritance. Before leaving his hometown forever, he realized that he suffered from an inner pain "which led in a definite direction. It led toward the landscape of the Tisza . . . where the huge red disk of the sun drowns in the glowing evening mist. In that existed what did not exist. In that existed the . . . song that I did not catch, and the landscape that I recognized, but whose 'open sesame' I never found so that its gates might open to me. I will, after all, have a homesickness. I will long after a pain, I will long for a longing. Perhaps that is not even so little."[78]

As one might expect, the full emotional and cultural implications of their radically marginalized social position did not become apparent to members of the Sunday Circle all at once. However, it is clear that by around 1916–17 some of them at least had not only become fully conscious of their outsider status in postliberal Hungarian society but were also in the process of constructing a new cultural identity based on their very marginality. One of the first indications of this process can be seen in the context of a very interesting misunderstanding between Fülep and Balázs over the meaning of one of Balázs' poems. "We were talking about a poem of mine entitled 'I Have to Die Here,' " recounted Balázs in 1916 in his diary.

> The question was, to whom was I referring in the phrase "the forgotten ancestors." Both Fülep and Emma Ritoók . . . thought they had discovered there a reference to my Jewish ancestors.

73

Nothing was further from my mind. I feel my determining roots, but not there . . . I know who my brothers are too, but Hebbel, Kierkegaard, and Dostoevsky were not Jews. I am the descendant of a spiritual type which has never appeared in history as a separate race of people, of whom only theosophy gives occasional glimpses, and which has sent only isolated, individual messengers like myself into the world, who even in their isolation and orphaned state recognize their own kind.[79]

Members of the Sunday Circle came to see their very Jewishness as the source of a new, more universal cultural identity: that of the marginal artist and intellectual who transcends all social groups and accepted conventions and is therefore freer and more critical than other, more anchored individuals. In Anna Lesznai's words, "The Jew is a born émigré, and every person is Jewish to a certain extent: I would say to the extent of his disaffection with what exists."[80]

The value of marginality for this generation lay primarily in its sense of deepened intellectual insights and social perspective that such situations provided them. Thus when Anna Lesznai was planning her epic novel about the Hungarian turn of the century, she repeatedly emphasized in her preliminary notes the importance of her particular vantage point as both an outsider and an insider in the world she meant to immortalize. Here was the ideal situation, she noted, from which to describe the disappearing world of the Hungarian gentry and the patriarchal village, "because I lived intensely within it, and yet I also had the objectivity of the outsider. The very position of the outsider forces one to become an observer and recorder of events because one's fundamental situation is ambiguous. One is inside but is still a foreigner and thus has sharper eyes. The great writers have all become outsiders within their particular caste."[81]

It was Karl Mannheim who would explore most fully the implications of social marginality for the modern intellectual. The main outline of his famous concept of the "free-floating, unattached intellectual"[82] was more or less complete by 1918, when he delivered what amounted to a generational manifesto. As a group, wrote Mannheim, his generation has been pried loose from its social anchorage and, as outsiders, had acquired a special kind of insight into the dynamics of its cultural world:

Owing to this distancing, the inner structure of the cultural world has become transparent to us. In such ages, critical thinking becomes primary: logic, aesthetics, the philosophy of history come to the fore in scholarly works. I believe that the most valuable task of today's intellectual generation lies in this direction . . . It is on the basis of this unique intellectual perspective of ours that I would wish to indicate our particular historic mission as a generation. And if we accept this mission, the outlines of the solution already become clear.[83]

3

LIBERAL FATHERS
AND
POSTLIBERAL CHILDREN

The themes of social estrangement and cultural revolt which form the central refrain
in the youthful experiences of Lukács and
his friends were, of course, not only familiar but even fashionable subjects in the
accounts of late nineteenth- and early
twentieth-century artists and intellectuals.
Contemporary playwrights and novelists
have left searing records of what became
known as the "conflict of generations," in
which bourgeois parents, rigidly uphold-
ing the claims of Victorian morality and
respectability, were pitted against rebellious children, stridently proclaiming the
rights of individuality, spontaneity, and
nonconformity. In these accounts the bitter
confrontation between liberal parents and
radical children ultimately stems from the
irreconcilable opposition between repressive moralism and utilitarian ethics on the
one hand and the demands of instinctual
liberation and radical individualism on the
other.

The conflict of generations, however, could have many subtle variations and forms of expression, depending on family circumstances, class background, and national cultural traditions. In the case of Lukács and his friends, disenchantment with the liberal values of their fathers did not necessarily result in violent generational conflicts or hostile withdrawal from middle-class society, as was frequently the case in Western Europe. To a certain extent, the Hungarian cultural rebels continued to share the fate and aspirations of the larger middle-class society from which they hailed and with which they never completely lost their ties of loyalty and solidarity.

It is possible to distinguish at least two separate circles—which represent at the same time two distinct generations—of liberal middle-class society with which the Lukács group enjoyed close, if at times ambivalent and problematic, relationships in the decades before the outbreak of war. The first group was the liberal generation of their fathers and teachers, who, though dimly aware of the political changes taking place around them, continued to advocate the tolerant, optimistic, accommodationist ideal of nineteenth-century Hungarian liberalism. The second group consisted of a younger generation of scholars and sociologists who were committed to the goal of reformulating and rejuvenating liberal theory in Hungary with the ultimate intention of transforming the very fabric of Hungarian society.

The extensive correspondence between Georg Lukács and his father sheds an unexpectedly revealing light on the complicated, deeply ambivalent relationship that existed between the cultural radicals and their liberal fathers. József Lukács, a successful Budapest banker, was in many respects an admirable if fairly conventional representative of the liberal upper bourgeoisie of fin de siècle Hungary. Though he himself had risen to success through activity in business and commerce, he was by no means eager to have his talented son follow in his footsteps. On the contrary, he encouraged the younger Lukács' literary and academic aspirations, seeing in them a happy convergence of his own liberal convictions and his social ambitions. As he movingly declared in a letter to his son in 1909: "You yourself write that I have been liberal in your education and have left you free to choose your own inner paths and development. I did this intentionally, because I trust you completely and love you unboundedly. I would sacrifice everything in order to see you successful, recognized, and famous; I will consider it my greatest happiness if one day people remember me as Georg Lukács' father."[1]

Though József Lukács was possibly more demonstrative in his affections than most parents of the time, his unconditional support for the cultural ambitions of his son was characteristic of the upper-middle classes, not only in Hungary but throughout the Hapsburg monarchy generally. Here, as Carl Schorske has pointed out, the upper bourgeoisie had never managed fully to supplant the aristocracy as a ruling class or to fuse with it successfully as a new commercial elite. Thus, high culture often became for this bourgeoisie a means of transcending the ambiguities of its social position and of gaining access to the highest reaches of society. "If entry into the aristocracy of the genealogical table was barred to most," Schorske wrote, "the aristocracy of the spirit was open to the eager, the able, and the willing . . . Learned culture could serve . . . not only as an avenue to personal development but as a bridge from a low style of life to a high life of style."[2]

József Lukács showed his support for his son's literary and academic pursuits in the most tangible way possible: through financial support. His generosity, which was extended not only to his son but to many of his son's needy friends, as well as to their various literary projects, was both consistent and remarkably tactful. "I do not think you spend too much," he wrote reassuringly to his son, who from 1913 lived almost continuously in Heidelberg. "On the contrary, I am confirmed in my long-held opinion that with growing years, one's expectations in life also increase. And this is so natural that it does not deserve to be mentioned. You ask very little of me financially, and it is wrong that money causes you worries."[3] Béla Balázs too occasionally received a helping hand from his friend's father, who told him on one occasion that the fact that he was Georg's friend "was sufficient reason for him to stand fully at his disposal financially."[4] Even the literary projects of the Lukács Circle did not completely escape the eager attention of the elder Lukács. In 1911, when Georg Lukács and Lajos Fülep jointly undertook the editorship of the philosophic journal *A Szellem*, he actually requested permission to be allowed to contribute to it financially. "What is happening with *A Szellem*, my son?" he asked in a letter of 1911. "Have you forgotten that I have gladly offered to finance the printing and possibly the other expenses connected with it? I think it would be a mistake to allow this journal to go under. It might become successful if it is enabled to stay alive for a certain amount of time. Think it over, and listen just for once to the advice of your father."[5]

These numerous instances of love, concern, and generosity which the elder Lukács showered on his son did not, however, succeed in completely obscuring the fundamental difference that separated them. Their inner estrangement, which was to deepen rather than lessen with time, sprang not from willful ingratitude or even incompatibility on either side but rather from an essential divergence of values and sensibilities. For the elder Lukács, the artistic and academic career which he so fervently wished for his son was also synonymous with upward mobility and worldly success; his support was motivated by vicarious social ambition as well as by parental love. But for the younger Lukács the exclusive dedication to artistic and scholarly pursuits involved an implicit critique of respectable society, a contemptuous repudiation of conventional social and moral norms. Despite the surface convergence of career ambitions, there existed between the generations a tragic misapprehension about each other's ultimate cultural goals.

At no time was this deep-rooted disagreement articulated or made explicit between father and son. But the hidden conflict occasionally found indirect expression in the elder Lukács' anxious remonstrances against what he called his son's "otherworldliness," his indifference to social forms and external prestige. "I am happy to hear," he wrote for example in 1910, "that you stand by your earlier decision to place your inner peace, your personal satisfaction and self-approval ahead of the demands of the world. Here, however, we begin to differ, for I say: you feel this way only at this particular point in your life. For after all, you have to admit, my dear son, that external success, external achievements, are also very important in life, for frequently it is not even possible to draw a sharp line between external and internal success."[6]

József Lukács, solidly anchored within the humane, thoroughly civilized traditions of nineteenth-century liberal culture, still inhabited a world of unproblematic, tolerant sociability, in which the rewards of external life could be prized as meaningful symbols of personal worth. His respect for social opinion and the external signs of success did not stem from personal weakness or vanity, as his son thought, but rather from a genuine sense of solidarity with the values of his society, which he had been able to internalize completely. Nevertheless, it was precisely this sense of being "at home" in the world that blinded him to the deepening political shadows of the times, and to the serious malaise suffered not only by his son but by many of his son's generation. He was incapable of understanding the source of that steely intransigence and fanatical single-mindedness which motivated his son to reject the social rewards he wanted for him, and to strive for goals that always remained obscure and irrelevant to him.

The latent tensions and unresolved differences between father and son resulted, not surprisingly, in tragic, sometimes tragicomic misunderstandings between them, especially at major turning points in the young man's life. In the spring of 1911, for example, when Georg Lukács was living through the last chapter of his tempestuous and painful love affair with Irma Seidler, the unsuspecting and well-meaning father confided to Balázs that he was concerned about the puritanical streak in his son, especially in sexual matters. "We talked extensively, mostly about you," the faithful friend reported to Lukács. "He mentioned your 'sexual life' to me. With you, he 'does not dare' to broach the topic; and yet it causes him concern that at the age of twenty-six you do not have a mistress, that you are 'ascetic' . . . He was fearful for your health and was obviously seriously worried by the matter. I tried to reassure him as much as possible."[7]

The accumulated misunderstandings would finally explode into genuine estrangement in the spring of 1914, when the elder Lukács was informed of the fait accompli of his son's marriage to the Russian student Ljena Grabenko. "Until now," he wrote, terribly wounded, "I have always discovered the means to find the lock to the door that leads to your life, even if I did not always approve of the roads you traveled, the goals you pursued, or the people you surrounded yourself with. Yours was, at times, a foreign world to me, but at least it was accessible to my intellect. Now I find myself face to face with an incomprehensible puzzle—and truly, I can say nothing except *des Menschen [Wille] ist sein Himmelreich* (Each man fashions his own paradise)."[8] At the end of the reproachful letter, however, the ever solicitous father added that he assumed his son's household expenses had increased with his marriage, and therefore he was depositing an additional amount in the Heidelberg bank that took care of their financial transactions.

Clearly, certain important elements in this troubled, poignant relationship between József and Georg Lukács were atypical, and rooted in the particular emotional dynamics and economic realities of the Lukács household. At the same time, however, some of the general characteristics of the generational conflict in fin de siècle Budapest become apparent through this particular case. Among the Hungarian upper-middle classes, unlike in Western Europe, there did not seem to be an open breach between the generations. On the contrary, the older generation of liberal parents was frequently supportive—both psychologically and financially—of the cultural ambitions of the younger generation. The older generation generally extended itself, going more than halfway to meet the children, while the younger generation maintained an attitude of rigid intransigence and dogmatic isolation vis à vis the parents. Yet the external and formal bonds between the generations never snapped completely, nurtured as they were by financial dependence on the one side and emotional and intellectual need on the other.

This rather paradoxical relationship of outward harmony and inner estrangement between liberal parents and radical children was not simply the result of fortuitous family circumstances. The same kind of ambiguities recurred in the very different context of academic relations between the Lukács group and the liberal philosophic establishment at the University of Budapest. Since a significant number of the Lukács Circle—Lukács himself, Karl Mannheim, Arnold Hauser, Béla Fogarasi, Lajos Fülep— were graduates of the faculty of philosophy, their initial association with the academic philosophers at the university was inevitable and not at all surprising. What does appear noteworthy, however, is that these personal contacts continued even after their graduation. The young philosophy students had, of course, realized very early on that their strongly metaphysical, neoidealistic interests, anchored within a German philosophic tradition, were incompatible with the essentially eclectic French and English orientation of their teachers. Yet their social and professional contacts with the academic philosophers were never fully severed, and certain of their philosophic essays even found acceptance in *Athenaeum*, the official philosophic journal.

In 1919 *Athenaeum* actually published a brief message of greeting to the recently established lecture series through which Lukács and his friends hoped to propagate their new philosophic ideas. The official recognition extended to the efforts of the Lukács group did not, however, mean full approval, or even genuine understanding, of their intellectual goals. The very wording of the greeting betrays a barely disguised irritation with the innovative young philosophers, whose intellectual style struck the Hungarian academicians as alien and pretentious. "We would like to send our greeting to the group [the Sunday Circle]," ran the editorial. "We look forward to the development of the thesis of their program, we await with interest the progress of their work. We ask of them only one thing: that they take more care to speak clearly, in good Hungarian. Why, for example, do they always have to refer to *das Werk*? If there is no Hungarian word for the concept, it is a waste of time to philosophize about it in Hungarian."[9]

A particularly close relationship developed between Bernát Alexander, the dean of the liberal philosophic establishment in Budapest, and Lukács and Fülep, whom Alexander considered among his most talented students. Alexander began to follow Lukács' career with some interest from 1908 on, when Lukács won the coveted Kisfaludy Társaság prize[10] for his essay "History of the Development of the Modern Drama." "I am happy," wrote Alexander in his letter of congratulation to Lukács, "that by setting the theme for the competition, I have been instrumental in the birth of this excellent, far-reaching, fresh, and interesting work."[11] Though Alexander's appreciative interest in Lukács continued over the following years, his occasional comments about his protégé betray a striking lack of serious inner sympathy for the metaphysical problems Lukács was struggling with at the time. As he confided in a letter to Fülep, with whom he always had a warmer personal relationship than with the austere Lukács, "What attracted me to Lukács was his personal nobility, a certain refinement of his inner being—which for me is worth far more than all his metaphysics put together."[12] Nor could he resist a certain note of irony when reporting on Lukács' ambitious philosophic project begun in 1912: "Georg Lukács was in Budapest and visited me twice . . . He says that he is presently working on a seven-volume aesthetics, of which one volume on music will be written by his friend [Ernst] Bloch. Lukács is actually capable of doing it and writing seven volumes!"[13]

The almost unconscious condescension with which Alexander could not help viewing his talented protégés was reciprocated, on their part, by self-conscious reservations toward the older philosopher. The young generation had as little sympathy for, or patience with, the civilized urbanity and tolerant eclecticism of their liberal professor as for that of their liberal parents. Their less than total agreement with Alexander culminated in their first public venture, the appearance of their own philosophic journal, *A Szellem*, in 1911. Lukács and Fülep found themselves considerably embarrassed by Alexander's enthusiastic endorsement of their project and his offer to take part in it in any way they saw fit. Alexander's offer of help was no more welcome than József Lukács' financial backing, and he too was politely but firmly rebuffed by the young philosophers. Their reason, made explicit in their correspondence, was that they were unwilling to open their journal to tendencies they opposed; they wanted a journal that was strongly and intentionally one-sided and metaphysical.[14]

Alexander's hurt response to his exclusion from *A Szellem* was almost identical in tone to József Lukács' bewildered reaction to his exclusion from his son's marriage plans. He wrote to Fülep in the winter of 1911:

> You really do not sense the impression your letter made on me. Or do you want me to spell out the details? I had a feeling analogous to what Master Solness felt [in Ibsen's *The Master Builder*] . . . I am clearly in a different sphere from Lukács, Béla Zalai, Sándor Hevesi, and Vilmos Szilasi. I am the past! Let us not speak of gratitude. I think we both agree that gratitude is a sort of entrée, a surrogate gate. By itself it is a dreary place where one does not want to tarry for long. But if it can lead to love, trust, and understanding, then it is excellent . . . Tell me, what am I to do with your gratitude? Should I sit on it? Or should I demand

compound interest on it? . . . The devil take your gratitude. What did I do? I published your book. But the book is good . . . Let us not speak of it any further. What I did I did out of a sense of duty . . . And what you cannot prevent is my continuing to act in your interest if it is within my power. After all, I am older, and my word carries some weight; you are young and at the moment proudly autonomous because you live outside, on the fringes of society. But once you decide to reenter, you will have need of friends.[15]

These complicated bonds of mutual dependence and solidarity which, despite their clearly perceived philosophic differences, continued to exist between the liberal and modernist generations cannot be explained on purely personal and psychological grounds. This unceasing, if at times strained, cooperation was due, in part at least, to the pressures of the external political environment, which, whether consciously acknowledged or not, was becoming ever more precarious and unwelcoming for the assimilated middle class and their children. The growth of an increasingly conservative, chauvinistic, and intolerant political climate in prewar Hungary could not help but isolate the old liberal middle class and create between them and the rebellious younger generation a certain sentiment of solidarity, if not in philosophic and aesthetic matters, at least on political and ethical issues. Carl Schorske's apt generalization about the Viennese aesthetes—that they were "alienated not *from* their class, but *with* it from a society that defeated its expectations and rejected its values"[16]—applies, at least in part, to the situation in Hungary as well.

Yet the alliance between the liberal generation and their culturally disaffected children remained potential and unacknowledged on both sides of the generational divide. In the eyes of the fathers, the illusory magic of the old liberalism which had promised to unify the interests of the assimilated middle class and the Hungarian nobility under the aegis of a liberal Hungarian Rechtstaat still exerted a certain irresistible fascination. Thus they were not yet willing or able to take an explicitly oppositional stance toward official Hungary, which would have made a genuine alliance with their rebellious children plausible.

Only with the emergence of a younger, more intransigent generation of liberal thinkers was the paradoxical alliance between Hungarian modernism and liberalism to be consummated and intellectually clarified. The "radicals," as the new, militant generation of liberal thinkers came to be known, were always viewed by Lukács and his friends as firm and unconditional allies in their rebellion against the status quo in Hungary. For himself and his friends, Lukács reflected much later in an interview, it was self-evident that they belonged to the ranks of the radicals.[17] Their solidarity with the radicals was not merely passive and circumstantial, as was the case with the older liberal generation, but quite active and self-conscious. They published their writings in the scholarly and literary journals of the young radicals (named, with conscious symbolism, *Twentieth Century* and *West*); they took part in their seminars and lecture series; they participated in their debating society; they frequented the same intellectual salons. In fact, they all belonged to one large, loosely knit social circle, which gave rise to frequent informal interactions, common friendships, and in the case of Anna Lesznai and Oszkár Jászi, marriage between members of the radical movement and the Lukács Circle.

The inner core of the radical movement consisted of a small group of university-trained middle-class intellectuals like Oszkár Jászi, Bódog Somló, Ervin Szabó, Ödön Wildner, Arnold Dániel, and József Madzsar. For the most part, they came from the same kind of middle- and upper-middle-class assimilated Jewish background as Lukács and his friends, but they were somewhat older, having been born in the 1870s and attended university in the 1890s.[18] This half-generation's difference gave rise to noticeable cultural and ideological discrepancies between the two otherwise closely related Budapest intellectual circles. The radicals were, on the whole, indifferent to modernist, experimental culture, and showed not even the hint of a tendency toward Bohemian nonconformism or social irreverence. They were a high-minded and self-conscious little group who were enamored of all things West European. They liked to compare themselves to the British philosophic radicals of the 1820s and 1830s, or better still to the Fabians of the 1880s and 1890s. Despite the radicals' passionate Anglophilia and Francophilia, there was something essentially provincial in their outlook and attitude, which remained closely tied to the Hungarian cultural world and almost exclusively focused on specifically Hungarian social and political problems. The radicals traveled to Western Europe as "passionate pilgrims," who, in their eagerness to find worthy models for backward Hungary, always remained somewhat insulated from the harsher, less idyllic side of modern urban society. Unlike Lukács and his friends, the radicals had had relatively few opportunities to live abroad for extended periods of time and to get to know non-Hungarian cultures in an intimate, first-hand way.

The fundamental difference between the older radicals and the Lukács group, however, was not the extent of their familiarity with West European cultures but the nature of their exposure to Hungarian social and political life. The decade and a half which separated the groups had witnessed some of the most momentous changes in the history of modern Hungary. With the turn of the century, accelerating economic growth caused enormous social dislocations and exacerbated to the breaking point the political and ethnic tensions in the nation. During these years the liberal heritage of the past became virtually bankrupt, and the dualistic constitutional system was in constant crisis. It is highly significant that the impressionable student years of the Lukács Circle took place during the first decade of the twentieth century, by which time Hungarian liberalism had been more or less discredited, while that of the radicals took place in the 1890s, a period which had not yet seen the helplessness of the old political tradition fully revealed. (It was, for example, during the 1890s that the momentous secularizing laws were pushed through parliament by the liberal government, and it was only at the end of this decade that the mood of the student population showed definite signs of new conservative, right-wing influences.) The radical generation was, consequently, less thoroughly disenchanted with liberalism than was the younger group; their ideological strivings were defined not by the attempt to transcend liberalism but by the effort to redefine and rejuvenate it.

What the discovery of European modernism meant for Lukács and his friends, the encounter with late nineteenth-century positivist social theory signified to the radicals. *"The Principles of Ethics,"* wrote Oszkár Jászi to his friend, Bódog Somló in 1899, "enchants me daily, and I am almost afraid of the thought that a day will come when I will have exhausted the marvellous richness of his [Herbert Spencer's] kingdom. What will we read after that?"[19] The goal of the young radicals was to graft modern—by which they meant positivist—sociological theory onto the partially discredited body of Hungarian liberalism, thus rendering it both intellectually more up-to-date and politically more relevant than the old mid-nineteenth-century liberal ideology. With this end in mind, they founded in January 1900 a bimonthly sociological journal which they optimistically christened *Huszadik Század* (Twentieth century). It was to become the most prestigious and intellectually innovative scholarly publication of the decade and a half before the outbreak of the First World War.

This was only the beginning of the wide range of scholarly and pedagogical activities initiated and sponsored by the young radicals during these years. In 1901 they founded the Sociological Society (Társadalomtudományi Társaság), whose purpose was to hold bimonthly meetings at which scholarly papers could be read and debated. So successful was the idea of the Sociological Society that by 1908 four provincial branches had sprung up outside Budapest (in Szeged, Györ, Nagyvárad, and Fiume), and by 1913 the total membership of the Sociological Societies numbered 2,853, divided almost evenly between the Budapest and the provincial branches.

In 1903 the radicals also initiated a series of workers' seminars and lectures which were usually held before trade union organizations located in the various working-class suburbs on the outskirts of Budapest. The subject matter of these lectures was remarkably diverse, ranging from chemistry, law, history, and Russian literature to the "woman question," public health, venereal disease, and health care for pregnant women and infants.

Finally, in 1906 the sociologists extended their pedagogical interests to include the educated general public as well by founding the Free School for Sociology. The Hungarian school used as models both the French *universités populaires,* which specialized in short, one- to three-hour lectures and seminars on specific topics and problems, and the English university extension, which specialized in a systematic introduction to different problems through a whole series of lectures. The founders of the Hungarian Free School for Sociology made clear that they wanted to reach not only the "university-bound youth fresh out of high school" but also "the elite of every social layer, irrespective of age and sex," so that they may "become acquainted, within the framework of a well-organized institution, with the most important tenets, methods, and achievements of modern sociology."[20]

Sociology was to be the symbolic, emotion-charged banner of the young radicals, and Herbert Spencer, the English liberal social theorist, was a kind of patron saint of their movement. In fact, the opening page of the first issue of *Huszadik Század* carried a letter of greeting from the aged Spencer:

> I rejoice to hear that you propose to establish a periodical having for its special purpose the diffusion of rational ideas—that is to say, scientific ideas—concerning social affairs. All the world over, down to the present time, a society has been regarded as a manufacture and not as an evolution . . . You will doubtless find it a hard task to undeceive your fellow countrymen in this matter. I cannot, however, but applaud the attempt you are about to make, and wish that elsewhere the example you set may be followed.[21]

In the following years the radical sociologists were to diverge in significant ways from the orthodox, laissez-faire liberalism preached by Spencer. Nevertheless, Spencer's letter caught admirably the inner spirit that would animate Hungarian radicalism throughout its two decades of existence. Perhaps no attitude was more central to, and more characteristic of, the mentality of the radicals than their passionate, quasireligious faith in science. Only with the discovery of the scientific outlook, wrote Oszkár Jászi, "had the merciless power of natural forces been tamed, and, like tractable domestic animals, harnessed to the use of man." The evil to be combated, according to Jászi, was the outmoded, atavistic attitude among Hungarian political leaders and the public, which still insisted on viewing social phenomena as the result not of objective, inflexible, and invariable laws but of individual wills, or worse still, of metaphysical agents. "Are such views not as unspeakably naive," Jászi asked rhetorically "as the belief of our far-off ancestors who explained their illnesses, their successes in the hunt, their dreams, and the other events of their daily lives as the results of otherwordly, spiritual intervention?"[22] The only genuine solution for evil in the world, claimed Jászi and his associates, lay in the scientific method, which could as validly be applied to the social organism as to natural organisms. The discovery of the laws of society would finally give man the same beneficial power and control over his social world that he had already learned to wield over nature.

Not surprisingly, given their overwhelmingly theoretical orientation, the radicals diagnosed the underlying problem of Hungarian society as one of philosophic backwardness. Their task was to remedy this situation by generating disciplined, technical knowledge about the laws of social evolution and by educating public opinion and political leadership in the scientific method of approaching social phenomena. They were to become intermediaries between the realms of pure scholarship and practical politics, acting as both disinterested social scientists and politically engaged citizens.

The reconciliation of these two roles—the political and the scholarly—was to cause them immense difficulties in practice, but on the theoretical plane they found a fairly simple and ingenious solution to the problem. The radical movement, they claimed, constituted both a society for the objective, scientific discussion of social theory and a politically engaged pressure group fighting for the realization of certain ideals and values in society. They admitted that by the turn of the century these two functions were frequently differentiated in societies such as Germany; but they also stressed that just as the same individual in Germany could be a member of both the scientific Gesellschaft für Soziologie and the politically engaged Verein für Sozialpolitik, so under the less differentiated conditions in Hungary could they participate in the Sociological Society in a dual function as social scientists and political agitators.[23]

Despite their single-mindedness, the radicals were far from being dogmatic. As Jászi hastened to add at the end of his detailed outline of the scientific outlook and goals of radicalism, "On no account does the above-mentioned orientation mean to express a rigid program in the sense that evolutionary theory is the only one our journal wishes or intends to publish."[24] The radicals believed, perhaps even more passionately than in the universal validity of the scientific method, in the necessity of freedom of inquiry and discussion if truth is to emerge. So central was this ideal to the radical world outlook, and so novel a concept was it within the increasingly dogmatic Hungarian political context of the turn of the century, that the radicals found it necessary to repeat it often and in many different forms. "One of the essential conditions of the scientific spirit," said Ágost Pulszky, the first president of the Sociological Society, in his opening speech, "is the principle that one accept without anger, fear, or antipathy all scientific theories which are sincere and verifiable. We have no reason to fear truth, no matter what its sources."[25] In 1903 Jászi once again reiterated the point, in an article devoted entirely to the thesis that "it is contrary to the laws of progress to restrict in any way freedom of inquiry or the communication of the results of free inquiry."[26]

The radicals acknowledged only one extremely revealing exception to their universal endorsement of free inquiry and discussion. "The pages of *Huszadik Század*," wrote Jászi, "will remain closed to one, and only one, tendency. Every explicit or implicit, courageous or cowardly expression of the reactionary world view will be banished. And this does not contradict our strongly held belief in freedom of speech, because reactionary political theory cannot be, by definition, scientific theory."[27] With this clever if blatantly transparent qualification, Jászi revealed the strongly political role that positivist sociology would have in Hungary between 1905 and 1914. Political interests, just as decisively as scientific objectivity or even intellectual affinity, were to determine editorial policy.

From the very beginning, *Huszadik Század* was open to those newer, antipositivist, modernist currents of thought and literature which influenced Lukács and his friends so decisively. Articles by and about Georg Simmel, Friedrich Nietzsche, Rainer Maria Rilke, and August Strindberg appeared with some regularity even in the early issues. From 1910 on these tendencies became even more pronounced, as frequent and exhaustive studies of Henri Bergson, William James, Sigmund Freud and the psychoanalytic movement, and the impact of quantum physics on the philosophy of science began to make their appearance in its pages.

Not surprisingly, *Huszadik Század* and its literary counterpart *Nyugat* carried numerous works by members of the Lukács Circle as well. Almost all the essays Lukács was to publish in his first volume of essays, *Soul and Forms* (A lélek és a formák), first appeared either in *Huszadik Század* or *Nyugat*. Balázs, Lesznai, and Mannheim too were frequent contributors to these youthful, innovative publications. The solidarity among the moderns and the radicals was also evident in the strong editorial support that *Huszadik Század* gave to such modernist enterprises as the Thália theater. "Whoever keeps track of the really important happenings in our city's cultural life," wrote an enthusiastic reviewer in 1906, "cannot pass silently by the new enterprise of the Thália. This truly youthful company . . . has once again brought into our cultural life a breath of fresh air."[28] The official suspension of the Thália in 1908 also elicited a strong reaction from the editors. "Here, the question is not simply the continued existence of the Thália," thundered an editorial. "When they trample over them with Asiatic tyranny, they spit in the eye of all of us."[29]

There exists little question that during the first decade of the twentieth century the radical movement established itself as the unambiguous champion of modernism in Hungary and as the umbrella organization for most innovative political and cultural strivings among the younger generation. By 1910 Jászi could claim without exaggeration that for the future historian, *Huszadik Század* would provide a faithful mirror of all "the ideas and ideals that stirred the most radical, the most intransigent, and the most international segment of Hungarian society at the beginning of the twentieth century."[30]

What is noteworthy in this alliance between Hungarian radicalism and modernism is the fact that it was maintained with, and in spite of, full consciousness by both parties of the deep-seated philosophic and temperamental differences that separated them from each other. The radicals could never accept the validity of that fundamental pessimism about modern civilization that underlay so much of modernist philosophy and literature. For them, West European liberal societies, with their democratic political institutions, their thriving economies, and their vital intellectual life, offered not a spectacle for despair and disenchantment but rather an idealized model for emulation by "backward" Eastern Europe. A six-month stay in Paris in 1905 convinced Jászi more than ever that Hungarians were "but pale and belated echoes of the creative energies of the West,"[31] and that the road to progress could only lead along the path already traversed by the industrial and democratic West.

For the radicals, literary pessimism, subjectivism, and aestheticism, which were implicit in the early manifestations of European modernism, appeared to be nothing more serious than the emotional immaturity of adolescence, the unwillingness of hypersensitive individuals to face objectively the nature of reality. Contemporary pessimism, wrote Wildner, one of the leading radicals, was anchored "in the individual's assumption, or at least confused illusion, that he is the center of the universe, that the world is created expressly to realize his happiness, to fulfill his personal dreams and emotional needs. And, since time after time reality contradicts the extravagance of this assumption, . . . the individual becomes disenchanted and suffers, and in his suffering gives voice to his pain and hurt."[32]

Ten years later, in an article defending evolutionary theory against the relativistic implications of Durkheim's *Division of Labor,* Jászi betrayed the same incapacity to comprehend the source and nature of cultural criticism among the moderns. The complaints of the cultural pessimists appeared to him trivial and petty when compared to the gross physical sufferings and psychological deprivations still experienced by great masses of people. "One or two of our fellow human beings," he wrote in obvious parody of the modernist posture, "might conceivably experience a genuine sense of loss in the fact that there are not enough madonna-faced women in the world; or that they no longer experience the warmth of true altruism in today's society; or that the industrial towns of the modern world offend their aesthetic sensibilities, trained in the enjoyment of classical Greek art. Nevertheless, such discontents cannot even begin to compare in intensity with the tortures of hunger, lack of sleep, sexual deprivation, and unchanging servitude" which are the lot of the majority of mankind.[33]

Lukács and his modernist friends were fully aware of the fact that the radicals, with their essentially political and economic preoccupations, were more or less tone deaf to the nuances of the inner life, which formed the core of their own preoccupations. If any proof of this were needed, it was amply supplied by repeated instances in which the radicals proved monumentally insensitive to the intellectual and emotional connotations of the modernists' work. "In vain did my history of the drama raise several sociological questions; these did not command any interest among the positivist sociologists," remembered Lukács with traces of bitterness almost sixty years later.[34]

Even more striking was the complete misunderstanding by young Hungarian radicals of Lukács' first book of essays, *Soul and Forms*, which was published in Hungarian in 1910. While the German edition, published only a year later, elicited glowing responses from thinkers like Max and Marianne Weber, Georg Simmel, Martin Buber, Max Ernst, and Wilhelm Worringer, reactions among the young Hungarian liberals were ambivalent at best. Their criticisms of Lukács bore a remarkable resemblance to those leveled against the Lukács Circle a few years later by the academic philosophers in *Athenaeum*. Instead of a discussion of the substantive issues raised by the book, here too the question of Lukács' "difficult," "German," "non-Hungarian" style emerged as the central point of debate.

Perhaps the best-informed example of this kind of objection came from the well-known poet Mihály Babits, who reviewed *Soul and Forms* in the literary journal *Nyugat*. While admitting that *Soul and Forms* was "a decidedly valuable book, whose thoughts are interesting, deep, subtle, often true, and remarkably unified in world outlook," he could not help adding the seemingly irrelevant comment that "these thoughts are, in the fullest sense of the word, German . . . The author insists on using that modern, slightly affected German terminology toward which—I must confess—I feel an irrepressible antipathy . . . This kind of culture is typically German, or rather Viennese."[35]

Lukács' response to the Babits review, also published in *Nyugat*, was equally blunt and to the point. The reason his work appeared incomprehensible and "foreign" to Hungarian audiences, he wrote, was that Hungary lacked a genuine philosophic culture. "This is the reason why among us the flattest, most lifeless materialists appear as great philosophers, while the most important philosophers are avoided and labelled 'incomprehensible.' "[36] The public controversy in the pages of *Nyugat* triggered a rather polite exchange of letters between Lukács and Babits, which, however, also failed to get to the bottom of the differences between them. Babits continued to insist that what he was objecting to was not the abstract nature of Lukács' philosophic preoccupations but rather "the lack of clarity . . . in the instruments of expression, in the sentence construction."[37] Thus, even with one of the best-intentioned and most erudite members of the liberal generation, Lukács was unable to turn the discussion of his work to more substantive issues than the question of style.

Despite such obvious signs of philosophic and intellectual incompatibility, the formal alliance between the radicals and the Lukács group remained intact and, if anything, grew stronger during the last years of the war. Lukács and his friends, who were by definition more self-conscious and philosophically introspective than the radicals, were of course fully aware of the paradoxical nature of their association with the left-wing sociologists. In an interview in 1967 Lukács expressed their mutual affinity and differences in the following way: "Our [the Sunday Circle's] common standpoint was that we were absolutely opposed to the growing Hungarian reaction, and in this respect we were in complete alliance with *Huszadik Század*, but in the realm of philosophy, we were in sharp opposition to their freethinking positivism."[38] Anna Lesznai recorded an almost identical observation in a diary entry for 1926: "The left, which I fully support politically and ethically, remains alien to me intellectually . . . it appears dogmatic, materialistic, simplistic."[39]

The Hungarian modernists thus found themselves in the somewhat curious position of having simultaneous allegiances to metaphysical idealism in philosophy and to radical liberalism in politics. They could not but be aware of the internal contradictions between these two positions. The long-standing historical association between left-wing politics and philosophic materialism on the one hand and right-wing politics and philosophic idealism on the other was well known to everyone even remotely familiar with current political debate. The issue had most recently resurfaced in 1908, when Lenin passionately repudiated empirio-criticism, a form of radical empiricism advocated by the philosopher Ernst Mach, on the grounds that it was a disguised form of idealism and hence ideologically suspect to all Marxists. In *Materialism and Empirio-Criticism* Lenin had denounced those contemporary Marxists who had abandoned dialectical materialism for this more fashionable stance, and asserted that epistemology was a "partisan science" which had direct political consequences. Ultimately, claimed Lenin, all philosophic systems boiled down to two contending positions: idealism and materialism, the first standing for reaction and the

second for progress.[40] Despite the oversimplification of the problem, Lenin was, in effect, simply reiterating a position which
had been a truism of European philosophy since the early
nineteenth century. As John Stuart Mill pointed out in his
Autobiography, "Adherence to the school of intuition and that of
experience," that is, idealism and empiricism, "is not a mere
matter of abstract speculation; it is full of practical consequences
and lies at the foundation of all the greatest differences of practical opinion in an age of progress."[41]

Members of the Lukács group realized that their somewhat
unusual ideological position made them outsiders within both
the left-wing and the right-wing political camps. Balázs expressed this dilemma as early as 1911, when he wrote to Lukács:
"Whenever I read an article by a radical or even a socialist, I
always feel a violent opposition or antipathy toward their superficial enlightenment and antimetaphysical rationalism (Dostoevsky calls this *Verdauungsphilosophie*). On the other hand,
whenever I read conservative, religious writings, then I realize
that in spite of everything, I am a man of the Enlightenment;
that I find their outlook narrow, ignorant, inhumane."[42]

In the spring of 1918 Lukács and his friends finally made a
concerted common effort to clarify their ideological orientation
in general, and their relationship to Hungarian radicalism in
particular. They chose as their forum the radical Sociological
Society; their key speaker was Béla Fogarasi. In a speech entitled
"Conservative and Progressive Idealism" Fogarasi set out to dis-
prove the commonly held notion "that all forms of philosophic
idealism are allies of a conservative world outlook, while progressive movements, in direct opposition, find their justification
in a scientific world outlook based on positivism and monism."[43]
Fogarasi argued that in fact there existed no definite, unalterable
relationship between political goals and philosophic assumptions. The association between idealism and conservatism, and
between empiricism and liberalism, was due not to logic or inner
necessity but to historical circumstances prevailing in Europe
during the nineteenth century.

Fogarasi then went on the offensive, claiming that ethical idealism, far from being antithetical to progressive politics, was in
fact a necessary precondition for it, for ethical idealism simply
meant belief in an autonomous realm of values existing inde-

pendently of empirical reality. Defined in this way, all political action that went beyond mere routine or expediency clearly had to be anchored in ethical beliefs held as absolutes. Lukács reinforced this idea, stating in the course of the extensive debate that followed Fogarasi's talk, "Ethical idealism, in so far as it is directed toward politics, cannot want anything other than the creation of such institutions as correspond most closely to an ethical ideal, and the destruction of such institutions as stand in the way of the realization of such ethical ideals."[44]

This debate did not by any means lay to rest all questions that might arise about the philosophic or logical compatibility of idealism with left-wing politics. This was not its primary goal, and philosophic rigor was not its primary virtue. What the modernists were attempting to do was to make a political statement: to declare clearly and unambiguously their total solidarity with left-wing politics in spite of their unchanging opposition to the philosophic and epistemological foundations of these politics. In this goal they clearly succeeded. During the following months of political upheaval and revolution, their commitment to left-wing politics was to be tested, not just in theory but also in practice.

—

The alliance between the Lukács Circle and the radicals, which found its clearest and strongest expression in the debate on progressive and conservative idealism, presents the same paradox as the continued cooperation between the young modernists and the older liberal generation. In both cases, individuals with fundamentally different intellectual styles and cultural orientations were forced into firm, if at times uneasy, alliance by the pressures of an outside world which had become equally inhospitable to both liberal and modernist strivings.

The young modernists found that their natural inclination to remain aloof from political and ethical issues and to concentrate on predominantly cultural and aesthetic questions had become increasingly difficult to maintain in the midst of the new conservative, intolerant, and anti-individualistic political climate of prewar Hungary. They discovered, as other apolitical artists and scholars were to do in the 1930s, that political aloofness is a unique luxury made possible only by a self-confident liberal society; it is not a viable posture in face of political fanaticism and aggression. Conscious solidarity with the humanistic goals and reformist politics of Hungarian radicalism became for the Lukács Circle a matter of social and ethical responsibility whose imperatives eventually outweighed their reservations about liberal philosophy and liberal culture in general.[45] These reservations, however, remained very much alive, and if anything became sharpened and clarified in the course of their association with the radicals. Their political support for liberal, democratic reforms in Hungary was undertaken out of ethical considerations, not intellectual conviction or philosophic affinity. Their liberal politics could never obscure their abiding dislike of liberal society, or supplant their striving to transcend this society entirely through the creation of a radically new culture.

That these contradictory impulses—one ethical and the other cultural—could coexist in the minds of the Hungarian modernists was not entirely due to their high tolerance for paradox. It was also the result of the peculiar nature of Hungarian radicalism itself, which became an increasingly utopian, unrealizable enterprise during the decade of its unfolding before the First World War. By the summer of 1914 the reformist politics advocated by the radicals had become in fact what they had always been to the Lukács group: a noble if somewhat quixotic ethical gesture, entirely devoid of political reality.

In January 1900, when the radical movement was launched with the first issue of *Huszadik Század*, almost no indications of its political future had yet become visible. The initial goals of the founding members were relatively modest, and politically fairly conventional. They wished simply to continue, on a more sophisticated philosophic basis, the role that the liberal bourgeoisie had always played in Hungarian public life. Here, as generally in East Central Europe, the middle classes had never been strong enough or self-confident enough to challenge directly the political hegemony of the nobility. They had instead worked out a policy of compromise and accommodation which guaranteed them favorable economic and political conditions in exchange for their passive support of, and acquiescence in, the traditional social and political order.[46]

The young sociologists' intention to continue the cautious policies of their liberal predecessors and avoid all direct confrontation with the political establishment was made clear from the very beginning. Membership for the Sociological Society was intentionally recruited from a relatively broad cross-section of society, and included both the younger and older generations, as well as influential representatives of the higher bureaucracy, the academic establishment, and the free professions.[47] "They wanted to win over the Hungarian academic community slowly and peacefully," wrote one of the sociologists in 1912. "That is why they had asked as large a number of representatives of official scholarship to take part in the movement as possible."[48] Continuity with the past was further emphasized by the election in 1902 of the liberal politician Count Gyula Andrássy as president of the society.

The radicals were also careful to define the goals and objectives of their movement in such a way as to arouse the least possible distrust in official quarters. "What we set out to do at the beginning," recounted Bódog Somló, "was not much more than to acquaint the official political circles with our new ideas and to attempt to persuade them of the truth of these ideas."[49] In other words, the sociologists' often stated desire to become intermediaries between the realms of objective scholarship and active politics was simply the continuation of the traditional, apolitical posture of the Central European middle classes. Often, under the guise of the fashionable sociological jargon of the day, the radicals were simply giving advance notice to official circles that they would not trespass into the forbidden domain of direct political action.

It became clear within a very short time, however, that the traditional alliance between noble political leadership and liberal middle-class supporters was becoming increasingly unworkable in the highly charged political atmosphere of the early twentieth century. The first round of ammunition was fired by the conservatives, who chose to make an issue of the teaching of positivist social theory at the university by two legal scholars associated with the radical movement, Gyula Pikler and Bódog Somló.

The controversy around Somló is illustrative of the nature of these academic attacks. In 1903 Somló delivered a seemingly innocuous speech before the Sociological Society entitled "The Theory of Social Evolution and Its Practical Implications." Five of Somló's conservative colleagues responded by sending a memorandum to the minister of culture, Gyula Wlassich, requesting the dismissal of Somló from the university, where his teaching, they felt, undermined the legal foundations of the existing order and was likely to awaken disharmony in the minds of his young students. Wlassich eventually rejected the memorandum on the grounds of respect for academic and intellectual freedom, but not before the Somló case had become the subject of wide-ranging national controversy.

In the aftermath of the "Somló affair," the positivist sociology of the radicals became a suspect ideology in which conservative Hungarians began to discover nefarious and unpatriotic plots. "Behind their scholarly façade," claimed an angry representative in a parliamentary speech of 1906, "the sociologists really want to undermine the Hungarian nation. In their hands, scholarship is merely an instrument with which to attack the Hungarian state at its roots."[50] Not surprisingly, with the growing public notoriety of radical ideas, the more conservative elements of the Sociological Society, recruited in the first place to placate official distrust, began to drift away in ever growing numbers. The decisive break with the early conciliatory phase of radicalism came in 1905, when the remaining conservative segment of the Sociological Society openly seceded, leaving both the society and *Huszadik Század* solidly in the hands of the younger generation clustered around Jászi and a handful of friends.

From this point on, the tone and orientation of the radical movement underwent a notable change. It gradually abandoned its cautious, apolitical stance and began to take increasingly open positions on specific social and political questions. The change is evident in Jászi's correspondence, in which the conflict between political activism and scholarly research became the dominant theme after 1905. "The state of mind in which I have been working," recounted Jászi in the spring of 1905, "is unsuitable for scholarly achievement. To put it graphically, I have been acting as foolishly as the physicist who attempts to study the laws of acoustics in the midst of drumbeat and cannon fire. It is impossible."[51] Gradually the claims of scholarship gave way to those of politics, and by 1907 there seemed to be little doubt in Jászi's mind about the underlying political goals of radicalism. "We intend not simply to create well-written monographs," he wrote to Somló, "but to stir up the intellectual life of this dark, backward country."[52]

The change of perspective that Jászi's personal correspondence betrays surfaced in the pages of *Huszadik Század* as well. During these years, abstract theoretical articles about the nature of liberalism or the source of political rights were replaced by concrete empirical studies and sociological surveys concerned with the conditions existing in the country. "We realized with astonishment," wrote Jászi in retrospect, "that the living Hungarian social reality, which had always been the object of our theorizing and organizing, was more foreign to us than Europe or the social customs of a number of savage tribes."[53]

The nature of radical journalism also underwent a transformation after 1905. The measured, reasonable tone of scholarly discourse gave way to sharp polemics and heated political harangues which carried a simple and passionate message. All progress in Hungary, the radicals claimed, depended on two major preconditions: "the first is the transformation of the existing legal system into a pure democracy: and the second is the growth of . . . productivity through the replacement of an obsolete economic and cultural apparatus by a modern, more advanced system."[54] These general goals crystallized around two basic demands which were to remain central to all radical political action in the years before the outbreak of war: universal, secret suffrage and agrarian reform to redistribute the large noble estates that still dominated the Hungarian countryside.

Gradually radicalism became a political force of some significance, especially after 1910, when, together with the Social Democratic party and the left wing of the Independence party,[55] the radicals entered into a loose coalition for the explicit purpose of winning universal suffrage. Referring to their growing political prestige, Jászi wrote jubilantly in 1912, "The large parliamentary parties now consider it a sign of distinction if the sociologists propose some common action with them . . . What a change!"[56] In the summer of 1914 the radicals took the final logical step and established an independent political party of their own, the Bourgeois Radical party (Polgári Radikális párt).

The historical and symbolic significance of these developments cannot be overestimated. The rapid politicization of a section of the Hungarian middle class signaled a fundamental break with its traditional posture of alliance with, and dependence on, the Hungarian nobility. It signaled too the emergence of an independent, self-conscious, and militant bourgeois politics for the first time in Hungarian history. The radicals were fully conscious of these broader implications of their actions. "That section of the Hungarian bourgeoisie," wrote Jászi in 1910, "which has become class conscious no longer wants handouts but the acceleration of national productivity which may provide it with a decent living. They no longer demand aristocratic and clerical patronage but rather a political program which will make the masses into genuine economic and cultural consumers."[57]

The very existence of the radical movement acted as a catalyst in Hungarian political life, forcing the assimilated middle class into a conscious choice between the old, apolitical tradition of cooperation and accommodation, and the new, openly political attitude of confrontation and attack. Sociology became a "battle cry" during these years, remembered Jászi, and a "dividing agent which separated Hungarian middle-class society into a progressive and a reactionary section."[58]

The radicals' fiercest and bitterest reproaches were reserved for that section of the bourgeoisie which chose not to join forces with them but rather to continue the traditional alliance with the Hungarian establishment. Occasionally these reproaches flared into blatant and, since the radicals themselves were overwhelmingly Jewish, illogical anti-Semitism. The spirit of "gray compromise," wrote one radical reviewer, which had always characterized the Hungarian middle class, "is reinforced by racial characteristics too, which should never be ignored when judging Hungarian conditions. It makes a great deal of difference whether the industrial base of a society is built up by the descendants of proud Anglo-Saxon gentlemen or the descendants of a despised race . . . in whom the desire for social acceptance is so great that economic rights are often traded for social privileges."[59]

The radicals' anger and disappointment at the unwillingness of the wealthy upper bourgeoisie to join forces with them is understandable. An independent middle-class political movement in Hungary, even if embracing the entire Hungarian bourgeoisie, would still have been a relatively small, isolated group, comprising no more than 5 percent of the population.[60] But with divisions even within this tiny middle class, the radical movement stood little chance of becoming a viable political force in the country. Radicals realized this, of course, and they made self-conscious and concerted efforts to attach their movement to a mass base. "Hungarian democracy," wrote Jászi, with an eye toward the three largest mass constituencies in the country, "has three living currents: the working-class question, the peasant question, and the nationality question."[61]

Despite their acute awareness of the need for allies, the radicals never really succeeded in attaching to themselves either the working classes, the peasantry, or the nationalities. The socialists, toward whom they felt the clearest affinity and from whom they hoped for the most support, proved to be only halfhearted allies at best. It is not hard to see why the radicals, despite their almost obsessive preoccupation with socialist theory and working-class movements, were less than successful in their attempts to woo the socialists to their cause. In the final analysis, the radicals remained a fastidious intellectual elite who were, on occasion, glad to give lectures for the edification of working-class audiences; were more than ready to theorize about the "proletariat" as an abstraction; but who remained essentially ignorant of and indifferent toward the concrete, individual manifestations of working-class life. In fact, associating even with the leaders of the Social Democratic party proved uncongenial, as Jászi made clear in a letter of 1904, written to the socialist theoretician Ervin Szabó: "But these people! Believe me, dear Ervin, great historical movements are never created by such inferior leaders; for me, the present company—Comrade Csizmadia not excluded—is a virtual cultural insult whenever I happen to make contact with them."[62]

If the radicals' alliance with the Hungarian working classes was tenuous and fundamentally abstract, the same could be said, with even more truth, about their relationship to the peasantry. Notwithstanding their impassioned articles about the sufferings of the landless peasantry[63] and their well-meaning sociological studies about Hungarian village life,[64] the sociologists remained urban intellectuals, fundamentally out of touch with the realities and aspirations of peasant life. They did not even begin to grasp that the impoverished peasant masses were far more likely to listen to the Christian Socialist, anti-Semitic demagogues who explained their economic plight in terms of foreign exploitation and traditional distrust of the city than to the radicals, with their abstract, utilitarian arguments.

As for the non-Magyar nationalities, Jászi and the radicals were once again tragically unaware of the real concerns and motivations of their potential allies. Throughout the prewar years Jászi insisted that the root of the nationality problem in Hungary was essentially economic and cultural, not political. Once fundamental liberal reforms had transformed Hungary, once the nationalities were given good administration, good schools, language, and cultural rights, their demands for political autonomy would disappear. They would settle down to purposeful cooperation under the hegemony of a Hungarian democratic state, in the same way that the different nationalities of the United States had merged to form one nation. "Out of the unilingual class rule," wrote Jászi in an important book on the subject, "a multilingual democracy would emerge under the protection of the unified Hungarian state and under the peaceful hegemony of Hungarian culture."[65] In insisting that in a more socially just and democratic Hungary the nationality problem would simply dissipate, Jászi was totally ignoring the non-Magyar nationalities' very real aspirations for political autonomy, and once again projecting his own cherished desires onto the uncogenial reality.

The radicals' attempt to forge viable alliances with the masses failed unconditionally, and by the summer of 1914, when the Bourgeois Radical party was established, radicalism was already an isolated, disembodied political force in Hungary. If this was not yet apparent to Jászi and his followers, it was amply clear to the conservative opposition, who in 1914 openly pronounced the bankruptcy of radicalism. "The democratic radical movement," wrote the government's official cultural organ, *Magyar Figyelő*, "which only recently filled the whole nation with the noise of its military preparations and acted as if they could bring down the walls of thousand-year-old Hungary with the mere sound of their trumpet calls, has ceased to be a problem today."[66] The radicals, elaborated the author, underestimated the strength and vitality of traditional bonds and belief systems within the population; they had become "paper revolutionaries" without any support among the large masses of people.

The cruel truth about the total failure of their movement was to be revealed to the radicals themselves only gradually. More than twenty years later, from the distance of self-exile, Jászi himself finally admitted the ill-advised nature of the radical movement. "It was a great mistake to found a political party," he wrote a friend in 1936.

> As the leader of a purely scholarly-intellectual movement, free from political ties, I could have worked more freely and more effectively . . . It was thus a great pity that I was drawn into politics. And here, the problem of religious-racial differences also enters the picture. It has frequently occurred to me that had I come from a gentry or even a peasant background, the effectiveness of my work would have increased a thousandfold . . . Politics involves the ability to evoke symbols and emotional reactions. To understand these, one must have lived among a people over several generations. Perhaps I was more hasty and impatient than was appropriate in the given situation.[67]

The relative weakness and isolation of the Hungarian urban middle class before 1914 made a self-assertive and aggressive political posture unrealistic. Thus the earlier, more cautious phase of the radical movement, based on the premise of cooperation with the Hungarian establishment and on the practice of reasonable persuasion, was more realistic and practicable than the later, openly political, aggressively autonomous posture of radicalism. Perhaps the ultimate irony of the situation is that at precisely the point when radicalism was beginning to reformulate its program, focusing on less theoretical, more pragmatic questions and venturing into specific political and economic issues, it lost touch with the actual political and social realities of Hungary and became a hopelessly utopian venture. Perhaps the most fitting obituary for the movement as a whole was spoken by Jászi himself, recalling in 1914 the early years of radicalism:

> We were young and utopian, and we believed in the power of ideas; we believed in the limitless optimism of the theory of progress; in the invincible strength of truth; in the weakness of the debauched "ancien regime"; and above all, we believed in the importance of spreading our noble, simple, and clear principles among our fellow men. We were rationalist, anticorruptionist knights errant . . . who, with the diamond-tipped lances of our

utilitarian truths, carried on proud, solitary guerrilla warfare against the thousand-year-old bastion of feudalism and clericalism.[68]

The radicals themselves, despite their commitment to social causes, despite their passionate concern with the reform and improvement of Hungarian society, gradually came to share with the modernists the same fate of social marginalization and psychological isolation. Their common alliance in support of an ethical liberal politics could not provide them genuine anchorage within the Hungarian political world, since by 1914 liberalism itself had become a disembodied ideal rather than a genuine political possibility.

The Hungarian modernists' affinity with their Viennese counterparts becomes more apparent at this point. "The Austrian aesthetes," wrote Carl Schorske, "were neither as alienated from their society as their French soul-mates, nor as engaged in it as their English ones. They lacked the bitter anti-bourgeois spirit of the first and the warm melioristic thrust of the second. Neither *dégagé* nor *engagé*, the Austrian aesthetes were alienated not *from* their class, but *with* it from a society that defeated its expectations and rejected its values."[69]

Lukács and his friends were indeed politicized, and in this respect had certain superficial similarities to the British generation of the fin de siècle, whose members pioneered a new interventionist, socially committed liberalism. Yet the liberal politics of the Hungarians had little, if anything, in common with the self-confident optimism of the British Fabians and socialists. Liberal beliefs in Hungary represented the disembodied ideals of a marginalized and dislocated social group, not realistic alternatives to actual government policy, as in Britain. The position of the Hungarian moderns was in fact much closer to that of the Austrians, who, having lost all possible connections with the larger social world they inhabited, turned to art and culture for solace and redemption.

4

THE CRISIS
OF
AESTHETICISM

Lukács was to recall in later life that his youthful rebellion against the world of his parents and teachers had found its first concrete symbols in the works of such European modernists as Baudelaire, Verlaine, Swinburne, and Wilde, whom he had accidentally discovered through Max Nordau's polemical book *Degeneration*.[1] In the writings of these artists the fifteen-year-old Lukács encountered for the first time a radically new kind of sensibility—disenchanted, introspective, solitary, and irreverent—which unmistakably echoed his own as yet unfocused and unformulated sense of malaise.

For Lukács and his generation, the moderns still evoked powerful cultural resonances whose nuances have been virtually obliterated by the overwhelming triumph of the modernist movement during the decades after the First World War.[2] The word *modern* itself had come back into general currency in Western Europe during the

1880s and 1890s, when hundreds of books, articles, periodicals, and collections of poems appeared with some form of the words *modern* or *new* in the title.[3] To be "modern" at the turn of the century could mean a bewildering variety of things, but on the most general level it implied participation in or sympathy with artistic styles and movements such as Impressionism, Symbolism and naturalism, which were dramatically proclaiming the independence of art from the control of the salons and academies and the freedom of artists to create as they willed, unhampered by moral, political, or social conventions. The essential claims of modernity, wrote one unsympathetic observer in the 1890s, "is to assert the absolute independence of Art, and to defy any sort of convention or limit, whether of tradition, philosophy, morality, or even good sense."[4]

The well-known creed of the young innovators was "art for art's sake," or aestheticism, whose doctrines were wittily summarized by Oscar Wilde. The new philosophy of art, he explained in "The Decay of Lying," consisted of three cardinal truths: that "Art never expressed anything but itself," that "all bad Art comes from returning to Life and Nature and elevating them into ideals," and finally that "Life imitates Art far more than Art imitates Life." The ultimate result of these doctrines, he concluded in a provocative but not inaccurate summary, was that "lying, the telling of beautiful, untrue things, is the proper aim of Art."[5]

But the "modern" impulse was something more complex than the most up-to-date artistic mode. As Lukács perceptively remarked in 1909, "What is new is not necessarily modern. It is not always that. Only very rarely."[6] Beyond aesthetic innovation, modernism came to be associated for Lukács and his friends with a particular kind of sensibility, a particular form of interactions with the social world which was not necessarily restricted to the late nineteenth century. Lukács, in fact, insisted in an early article that the Elizabethan playwright John Ford had already displayed the characteristics of the modern sensibility. Ford's characters, Lukács wrote, "live only in the spirit, for . . . the external world no longer offers, no longer can offer them anything of substance . . . [They] are men of great inner stillness, refinement, and culture . . . [who] feel deeply and painfully their own solitude. They make sentimental journeys to free them-

107

selves from their inner anguish, but neither traveling nor religion nor philosophy can bring them solace. They are a breed fated for destruction. Today, undoubtedly, we would call them decadents."[7]

The passage is revealing not only for its nuanced evocation of the modern sensibility but also for its suggestion of the close links between the moderns and the decadents. The roots of the modern impulse do, in fact, reach back to the so-called decadents, to men of letters like Walter Pater, Charles Baudelaire, and the Goncourt brothers, who first made their mark on European high culture during the 1850s and 1860s. Decadence, as defined by these men, was not so much an artistic or literary movement as a distinctive personal style through which they expressed their deep disenchantment with what they considered the mediocrity of everyday life. The decadent pose that they invented was associated with exquisite refinement of clothes and manners, self-consciously cultivated eccentricity, and scathing disdain for the ordinary and the commonplace. Its essence, wrote Barbey d'Aurevilly in *Du Dandyism et de Georges Brummel* (1895), was "anti-vulgarité" and independence from the "values and pressures of a society in pursuit of money."[8] Decadence implied a particular cultural mood consisting of gentle melancholy, ironic detachment, and exquisite fatigue, which found early expression in the journals of the Goncourt brothers. "Nobody," they wrote in 1855, "has yet expressed in literature the contemporary French melancholia, not a suiciding melancholia, not blasphemous, not despairing, but a good-natured melancholia, a sadness which is not without sweetness and in which there is a slight smile of irony . . . From the heights of pleasure, we have dropped straight into boredom."[9]

In conscious opposition to the dominant liberal ethos of progress and social evolution, the decadents adopted a cyclical view of history, arguing that European civilization was not at the acme of historical evolution but on the decline, rapidly nearing the end of its natural life. Such notions of historical decline and degeneration, expressed in fragmentary and idiosyncratic ways, did not constitute a genuine philosophy of history. In fact the decadents possessed no distinctive ideology or philosophy of their own. Theirs was essentially a movement of gestures and poses whose goal was not to refute liberal philosophy but rather to shock middle-class opinion by reversing its most cherished beliefs and customs. For the aggressively masculine ideal of the Social Darwinists the decadents substituted a languid, effeminate pose. In place of the moralism of Victorian opinion they affected a cult of sin and perversion. In contrast with the formality of bourgeois manners they assumed an air of frivolity and impudence. In opposition to the established orthodoxies of scientific progress they professed a belief in the exhaustion of modern civilization.

Yet to see decadence as nothing more than frivolous gestures and cheeky parody perpetrated by a handful of literary eccentrics would be to seriously underestimate the movement.[10] Whatever the nature of its tactics, the inner impulse behind decadence was an exceedingly serious one. It was the initial form in which the artistic and intellectual generation of the late nineteenth century registered its alienation from and rejection of the forms and values of liberal society. It represented the first concerted attack against the constraints of Victorian moralism and utilitarianism in the name of consciousness, multiplicity, and indeterminism. The decadents' frankly hedonistic, relativist attitude toward experience was perhaps best expressed in Walter Pater's famous last lines of *The Renaissance*, which constituted the credo of many decadents:

> Not the fruit of experience, but experience itself is the end. A counted number of pulses only is given to us of a variegated, dramatic life. How may we see in them all that is to be seen in them by the finest senses? How shall we pass most swiftly from point to point, and be present always at the focus where the greatest number of vital forces unite in their purest energy? . . . While all melts under our feet, we may well grasp at any exquisite passion, or any contribution to knowledge that seems . . . to set the senses free for a moment, or any stirring of the senses and curious odors, or work of the artist's hands or the face of one's friend. Not to discriminate every moment some passionate attitude in those about us . . . is, on this short day of frost and sun, to sleep before evening.[11]

The new sensibility, first sounded in the works of writers like Walter Pater, was to gain in importance and in time to change from a literary eccentricity into a broadly based cultural enterprise of some seriousness. By the 1880s and 1890s an increasingly large segment of the younger generation was beginning to insist on the primacy of consciousness over external forms and of firsthand personal experience over objectively derived moral and intellectual codes. This impulse was to find an infinite variety of incarnations in late nineteenth-century Europe, depending on national cultures, political traditions, individual personalities. It was, in fact, not a specific movement at all but an underlying mood of questioning, signaling the growing failure of liberal politics and philosophy to provide viable explanatory frameworks for the experiences and expectations of the younger generation.

Not surprisingly, such a profound shift in culture and sensibility generated intense conflicts between the generations, which often confronted each other with hostile incomprehension. As Max Nordau, a well-known spokesman of the liberal establishment, declared in the early 1890s, the new art and literature produced by the more radical segments of the younger generation represented nothing less than the unmistakable signs of hysteria and organic degeneration. Such symptoms, he declared,

> have always existed, but they formerly showed themselves sporadically and had no importance in the life of the whole community. It was only the vast fatigue which was experienced by the generation on which the multitude of discoveries and innovations burst abruptly, imposing upon it organic experiences greatly surpassing its strength, which created favorable conditions under which these maladies could gain enormously and become a danger to civilization. [12]

Supporters of the new artistic tendencies defiantly accepted the label "decadent," but they interpreted it not as pathology but as the hallmark of emancipation, youthfulness, and the testing of accepted truths. As Holbrook Jackson, a sympathetic contemporary observer, recalled, the 1890s had been a time of exuberant experimentation, when young people

> went about frankly and cheerfully endeavoring to solve the question, "How to live" . . . The new man wished to be himself, the new woman threatened to live her own life. The snapping of apron strings caused consternation in many a decent household

as young men and women were gradually inspired to develop their own souls and personalities . . . Life-tasting was the fashion and the rising generation felt as though stepping out of the cages of convention into a freedom full of possibilities.[13]

These views represented the extremes of a highly charged cultural debate rather than serious attempts at understanding or analysis. It was, in fact, virtually impossible for contemporaries to transcend the polemics of the day and generate a more objective, culturally many-sided view of the significance of decadence. For the artistic generation of the 1880s and 1890s, decadence could only assume the guise of a heroic struggle for liberation and the authenticity of art and the self; for outside observers, it could only appear as the nihilistic destruction of all objective standards and moral values. In fact decadence embodied both these tendencies, being at one and the same time constructive and destructive, forward looking and nihilistic. But in order to see these antithetical sides of the phenomenon, the observer had to be both a participant and a critic, both an insider and an outsider.

—

This was the perspective on decadence, or aestheticism as it was often called, that Lukács and his friends acquired in early twentieth-century Hungary, where the impact of the tradition had to be absorbed and eventually transcended within an extraordinarily compressed time span. The initial wave of the aestheticist revolt did not emerge in Hungary until the first decade of the century—almost an entire generation later than in Western Europe. The battles which West European Impressionists and Symbolists had waged against the official salons and academies during the 1880s were to be anachronistically reenacted in Hungary during the early 1900s, by which time these artistic styles were already considered outmoded in the West. Understandably, Hungarian aestheticism had a rather brief flowering, lasting roughly from 1900 to 1910, after which it also was overtaken by newer, more radical artistic and intellectual trends.

One of the earliest manifestations of the new cultural impulse came in 1896, when a group of young painters under the leadership of Simon Hollósy left Budapest to establish their own art school and artists' colony in the village of Nagybánya. The young Impressionists rejected the heroic historical style as well as the anecdotal realism that dominated the official salon (Műcsarnok) and adopted a highly individualistic, natural style that was strongly indebted to the French *plein-air* painters of the 1880s. They asserted the right of each artist to paint nature freely, as he saw it, without any externally imposed literary conventions or political ideologies. "The strength of their individuality and the greatness of nature," wrote Fülep, one of the early defenders of the Impressionists, "is completely sufficient for their art; they have no need of an academy or of foreign examples; they paint out of their own emotions and their innermost souls."[14]

In the realm of music, too, the first decade of the twentieth century brought renewal and innovation. The first break from traditional musical forms came in December 1906, when the unknown young musicians Béla Bartók and Zoltán Kodály published a collection of twenty folk songs entitled *Hungarian Folk Songs for Voice with Piano Accompaniment*. These were much more than literal transcriptions of the peasant folk songs Bartók and Kodály had collected during the previous year. "In our case," wrote Bartók some years later, "it was not simply a question of recovering an individual melody, treating it in the traditional manner, and then building it into our composition . . . This would have resulted in mere copy work and would never have led to a new, unified stylistic solution. Our task was to understand the inner spirit of this hitherto unknown music and to create a new musical style based on this essentially inexpressible spirit."[15]

For Bartók and Kodály the recovery of the primitive musical forms of the Hungarian and Slavic peasantry acted as an invaluable catalyst in the formation of a new, truly modern musical idiom. They liberated the young musicians not only from the stylized gypsy music of contemporary popular entertainment (mistakenly thought to be part of the genuine Hungarian folk tradition), but also from the traditional functional tonality of nineteenth-century music, thus opening the way toward the more idiosyncratic solutions of modern twentieth-century music.[16]

In the same year that Bartók and Kodály brought out their stylized Hungarian folk songs, Endre Ady published his first mature volume of poems, entitled appropriately enough *Új versek* (New verses). Ady's radically innovative symbolist poems, which invented a novel poetic language for expressing the complex inner landscape of the artist's consciousness, ushered in a new age in Hungarian literature. Two years later, in 1908, the periodical *Nyugat* came into existence; it became, as we have seen, the central literary forum for the young, individualistic literary generation which proclaimed Ady as its leader and model.

These different manifestations of artistic and literary innovation in Hungary, like their West European counterparts two decades earlier, lacked any obvious unity of style or artistic goals outside of a common desire to break free from the external constraints of the academic and cultural establishments. "What is occurring here," an editor of *Nyugat* observed perceptively, "is not a revolution . . . but a war of liberation; a war for the freedom of the writer from ignorance and prejudice . . . and from a political regime which attempts to justify its intrusion into literature with the catchword that it is protecting the inner purity of Hungarian art."[17]

The principle of art for art's sake, or the independence of art from all external, nonaesthetic constraints, proved to be even more controversial in the Hungarian context than it had been in Western Europe. Here the official cultural establishment that the young innovators were challenging stood for something more than mere artistic orthodoxy and tradition; it also represented deeply ingrained historical values and national traditions which in the course of time had become fused with the established cultural canons. Thus the bitter and prolonged controversies that raged around the moderns involved questions not only of aesthetic judgment but also of national and moral values. Only a month after the founding of *Nyugat*, for example, a conservative journalist denounced the new literature in terms which were to be reiterated in countless versions during the next four or five years. "It is treason and slander," he wrote, "what they do in *Nyugat* under the pretext of civilizing the barbarian Magyars. They want to ruin our morals, they want to disillusion us of our faith, and they want to crush to pieces our national pride. A storm of outrage should sweep away all those who commit such deep offenses against the nation."[18]

So acute and wide ranging did the public outcry over the new art become between 1906 and 1912 that even important political figures like István Tisza, who became prime minister in 1913, felt compelled to participate in the fray. "The incomprehensible bombast" of the new literature, he wrote in 1912, "is nothing more than the chaotic exterior of spiritual anarchy and an emptiness of mind and heart."[19] *Nyugat* countered with a contemptuous editorial: "Only in our country can it happen that politicians feel justified in interfering in the affairs of literature with such colossal ignorance."[20]

As vehement as official opposition was to the artistic innovators, these did not entirely lack a receptive public. Between the turn of the century and 1910, there had grown up a small but prosperous middle-class public in Budapest whose cultural tastes were no longer satisfied by the art of the official salons and academies. It was they who bought the canvases of the Impressionists, who made up the theater and concert audiences for the new drama and music, who regularly subscribed to *Nyugat* and bought the books of the new writers. By the end of the first decade of the century, the recently beleaguered cultural innovators had found a measure of acceptance—at least among the cultivated urban middle class—and had won for themselves a position if not in place of then certainly alongside the traditional academic writers and artists. Gradually the bitter polemics surrounding the new art quieted down; official accusations of immorality, decadence, and treason became less frequent; and by 1912 the aestheticists could justifiably claim victory. "We have our new literature," proclaimed a 1912 editorial in *Nyugat*, "and a new audience for it."[21]

The triumph of Hungarian aestheticism by the first decade of the twentieth century signaled in effect the end of its viability as a subversive and radical cultural posture for intellectuals like Lukács and his friends. Yet during its relatively brief radical phase, it had played a crucial role in their lives and development. As high school and university students during the early years of the century, they had followed with passionate sympathy the battles of liberation waged by the young innovators. In time, many found themselves actively supporting their various enterprises.

As early as 1902 the seventeen-year-old Lukács was publishing in the daily press little vignettes on the works of modern artists and dramatists, whose products he earnestly defended "against those gentlemen who insist that contemporary art is declining;

where there is such a profusion of interesting, original talent, there can be no question of degeneration. The conflict of tendencies is even fiercer today than among former artists. They agree on only one thing: to express fully, openly, without reservation everything that lies at the bottom of their hearts."[22] Lukács' general interest in the moderns eventually led him to the works of dramatists like Ibsen, Wedekind, and Strindberg, whose plays he helped introduce to Budapest audiences through the experimental theater group the Thália. Lukács' involvement with the Thália between 1904 and 1906 was perhaps the most obvious declaration of loyalty with the moderns, but it was not the only one. Béla Balázs was closely associated with Bartók and Kodály, and he collaborated with Bartók on several early operas and ballets. Lajos Fülep, for his part, became an eloquent and vociferous champion of the Hungarian Impressionists, whose work he explained and analyzed in numerous articles and reviews.

The initial appeal of aestheticism to the radical, socially alienated young intellectuals who were later to form the Sunday Circle is not hard to understand. Aestheticism was associated with radical individualism and with the impulse to liberate not only art but the individual from the constraints of academic conventions, social decorum, and traditional morality. It asserted the truth of the inner self, the ultimate validity of subjective experience in the face of all that was external, conventional, and formalized. Impressionist art, claimed Fülep, "reached down into the depths of the self where one is alone with oneself."[23] It was the great liberator, which forced people to see the world in a new way, with the unjaded eyes of a child who had not yet learned to substitute language and concepts for direct experience. Impressionists taught the modern individual "not to name, but to appropriate an object, so that it may become truly his own."[24]

Effective as the aestheticist impulse was, however, in liberating art and the artist from the tyranny of convention, it proved incapable of generating a positive vision, a genuinely revolutionary artistic style of its own. Aestheticism, and the decadent pose which accompanied it, turned out in retrospect to have been only "an interlude, a mock interlude," which in the words of one of its former supporters "diverted the attention of critics while something more serious was in preparation."[25] This "something more serious" was to become evident in Hungary by 1909, when a group of postimpressionist painters, strongly influenced by Cézanne and Gaugin, seceded from the organization of Impressionists, MIENK (Magyar Impresszionisták és Naturalisták Köre), and exhibited independently for the first time under the title *New Paintings* (Uj képek). The postimpressionists, unlike the Impressionists, were united by common stylistic goals and aesthetic principles. Their canvases displayed a strong sense of form, of plastic contour, and a relative indifference to color or realistic representation. Their motto, appearing on the catalogue of their first exhibit, stated: "We are believers in nature, but no longer do we copy it with the eye of the academies; rather, we dip into it with our intellect."[26]

The need to organize on the basis of positive goals and principles rather than simply through common opposition to official culture was felt by other groups as well. In 1911 the young musicians, with Bartók and Kodály at the center, founded the New Hungarian Music Society (Új magyar zene egyesület), whose main goal, in Bartók's words, "was to organize an independent chorus and orchestra which could perform competently not only the old but also the more recent, and what is more the most innovative, new music."[27]

Lukács and his friends too began to reassess their earlier enthusiasm for aestheticism, and between 1906 and 1910 their cultural and philosophic premises underwent a transformation. By 1910 Lajos Fülep, the former champion of Impressionism, had completely transferred his loyalties to the postimpressionists, who in 1911 adopted the name "The Eight" (A Nyolcak). The Impressionists, he now wrote, had admittedly rediscovered nature, had given individualism a place in art, and had perfected a highly sophisticated artistic technique. But these accomplishments had an effectively negative rather than positive significance. They had helped destroy the hegemony of academic art, but they had not succeeded in creating a genuinely new, original style. Impressionism, from Fülep's new perspective, had simply prepared the way for a future synthetic culture that would provide a real alternative to the defunct academies.[28]

Fülep was not alone in this shattering discovery that aestheticism, with its individualistic, subjectivist, highly fragmented vision, represented not the beginning of a new era but rather the end of the old one. Béla Balázs, who in 1907 spent an extended period in Berlin attending Georg Simmel's seminar on the philosophy of culture, recorded a similar realization in his diary. On this, his first trip abroad, Balázs was still imbued with the traditional expectation of East European intellectuals that the West would offer newer, more advanced cultural patterns than those available back home. Balázs' sense of disenchantment was overwhelming when he found that even Simmel could offer little beyond the aestheticist perspective of the fin de siècle. "This entire cultural milieu in which I find myself," he wrote, "appears somehow outdated . . . I feel it to be claustrophobic . . . I am abroad in Western Europe. All at once I realize it. Where is that famous West European culture which is still fresh and unknown, into which I can enter and from which I can draw sustenance? . . . Everything I meet appears to consist of empty noise and verbosity; I feel decadent weakness here, not the freshness of spiritual energy."[29]

The rejection of aestheticism, with its introverted, individualistic, exquisitely nuanced gestures, embodied something far more complex than still another shift in nineteenth-century literary and artistic conventions. Behind it lay hidden a profound experience of cultural crisis which by 1905 East European intellectuals like Balázs and Lukács shared in full measure with their West European counterparts. The aestheticist experiment, which had appeared to its early followers "an escape from our many imprisonments,"[30] turned out to be an artistic and emotional dead end which had to be abandoned or transcended if continued creativity was to be maintained. The decadents had never really succeeded in creating original artistic forms or new philosophic premises adequate for their novel attitudes, perceptions, and sensitivities. They lacked a positive alternative for the old order and thus remained paradoxically chained to the very society they attacked. As Arthur Symons elegantly summed it up, "Nothing, not even conventional virtue, is as provincial as conventional vice; and the desire to 'bewilder the middle classes' is itself middle class."[31]

A well-known depiction of this crisis came from the Viennese poet Hugo von Hofmannsthal, who through the mouth of the semifictional character Lord Chandos described elements of his own emotional breakdown in the late 1890s. "As once, through a magnifying glass," recounts the protagonist, "I had seen a piece of skin on my little finger look like a field full of holes and furrows, so I now perceive human beings and their actions. I no longer succeed in comprehending them with the simplifying eye of habit. For me, everything disintegrated into parts, these parts again into parts; no longer would anything let itself be encompassed by an idea."[32]

Hofmannsthal's experience was reproduced with individual variations in the lives of a remarkable number of artists and intellectuals of the late nineteenth century. The poetic career of Rimbaud was abandoned in midcourse for a life of adventure in Africa; that of Mallarmé ended in silence and of Arthur Symons in insanity. Some, like Oscar Wilde and Joris Huysmans, sought refuge from psychic disintegration within the fold of the Catholic church; still others, like Maurice Barrès and Gabriele d'Annunzio, found affirmation in a creed of heroic nationalism and "rootedness in the soil."[33]

Their common experience showed them that mere liberation without an overarching framework of values to give meaning and direction to individual experience led inexorably to narcissistic isolation, intellectual paralysis, and sometimes even to psychic collapse. On the most general cultural level, their crisis represented the final disintegration of an older rational-liberal world order which could no longer provide an objective, universally accepted hierarchy of significance for individual experience.

—

Perhaps no one experienced this transition with greater intensity or with more painful self-consciousness than Georg Lukács. For him the failure of aestheticism represented not simply a cultural or philosophic problem but also an emotional and existential crisis of such magnitude that on several occasions only the thought of suicide seemed to offer a way out. Consequently his early essays, letters, and diaries present one of the most exhaustive analyses, as well as one of the most passionate critiques, of the aestheticist phenomenon in modern literature. They shed unique light on that complicated and rarely analyzed process whereby fin de siècle artists and intellectuals severed their last ties with nineteenth-century culture and struck out toward new and revolutionary artistic and philosophic formulations.

Lukács' personal and professional preoccupation with the problem of aestheticism corresponded almost exactly with the years from 1907 to 1911, a period when he was writing and publishing most of the uniquely personal literary essays in his first major book, *Soul and Forms*. This "essay period," as he called it, opened in February 1907, with his winning the coveted Kisfaludy Társaság prize for his first work of literary criticism, "History of the Development of the Modern Drama," and it closed in May 1911, with the suicide of Irma Seidler, to whom *Soul and Forms* was dedicated.[34] As these demarcating events indicate, professional and personal concerns were almost indistinguishable during this period of Lukács' life; neither his life nor his work is comprehensible in isolation. The literary essays echoed the most intimate aspects of his personal life, while his private life became the testing ground for the most abstruse tenets of his cultural philosophy.

The unusual, almost confessional nature of Lukács' literary essays did not escape contemporary observers. As one perceptive *Nyugat* reviewer pointed out:

> The reader who imagines that he will become acquainted in these essays with particular literary figures will be greatly disappointed. Lukács writes for his friends, who happen to be already familiar with these authors. The artist about whom he writes is always much less important to him than his own thoughts and ideas which had become associated in his mind with the memory of the works of these writers . . . The essays reflect his own philosophic, aesthetic, and metaphysical preoccupations.[35]

Leo Popper, Lukács' closest friend of these years, was in an even better position to recognize the intimate nature of these essays. "For you," he wrote Lukács in 1909, "literature is only an opportunity for self-portraiture . . . Of course you are deeply correct in one respect: the essay is a lyrical form, and just as the poet makes nature a symbol of his life, so the essayist makes the poet a symbol of his inner life."[36]

Lukács himself was aware of the fact that *Soul and Forms* was a deeply personal work, one which came closer to providing an intellectual biography of the author than of the literary figures who were the ostensible subject of the essays.[37] The true critic, confessed Lukács in the introductory essay to the volume, makes no pretense to objectivity: "He chooses his own altars and sacrificial animals so that he might conjure up the spirits of only those who can answer his most burning questions."[38] And Lukács left no doubt in his readers' minds that his "burning questions" at the time all touched on some aspects of aestheticism.

By 1909, When Lukács wrote the introductory essay to *Soul and Forms*, the deeply problematic nature of the aestheticist tradition had already found interpreters among contemporary writers and artists. He specifically referred to Hofmannsthal's "Letter of Lord Chandos," whose depiction "of why he could produce nothing, of why every thought he conceived of dissolved into thin air, expresses perhaps more clearly than any tragedy could, the complete fragmentation of contemporary life."[39]

For Lukács the tragedy of the aesthete—and by extension of all modern artists and intellectuals—was summed up in the experience of separation: the separation of the individual from the community, of man from nature, of art from life, of intellect from emotion, of man from woman. He elegantly suggested this theme in the very deliberately chosen title *Soul and Forms*, and he explored the different facets and dimensions of the problem in the individual essays of the volume.

The broad and many-layered cultural crisis that Lukács set out to analyze and document in *Soul and Forms* crystalized around the increasingly problematic identity of the aesthete as an individual who attempted to transcend the flux and contingency of everyday life and to impose form and stability on his being in the same way that the artist imposes forms on the inert matter of nature. But the aesthete used "gestures" in the face of the undifferentiated chaos of events that make up life. "The gesture," wrote Lukács in his essay on Kierkegaard, was a supreme act of will "by which man leaves behind all the relative aspects of reality and reaches the eternal security of forms. The gesture . . . is a single leap through which the absolute can become a reality in life."[40]

The problem was, however, that the supreme heroism involved in the aesthete's gesture toward perfection necessarily involved isolation, self-mutilation, emotional death, for the aesthete's "gesture" was in irreducible conflict with life and nature, a conflict which he ignored only at his peril. This tragic and insoluble dilemma which lay at the core of the aestheticist posture found its quintessential expression, in both Lukács' work and life, in the erotic conflict between man and woman. The characteristic "gesture" through which the aesthete attempted to free himself from the compromising entanglements of life was the rejection of marriage or a permanent relationship with a woman. The hidden and insidious battle of the sexes, claimed Lukács in the essays, was born of the opposite natures of man and woman. Women are creatures of instinct, closer to the primary forces of life than men, and fundamentally opposed to man's striving to create art, culture, eternally valid forms out of the formlessness of nature. But woman is also the nurturer and the creator of bonds, without whose practical sense life would be impossible. "When man first stood face to face with the world," wrote Lukács, discussing the point in the Kierkegaard essay,

> everything around him was his, but the individual objects always eluded him, and his every step seemed to put a distance between himself and objects. And the tragicomic end would have been that he starves to death in the midst of all the plenty of the world, had it not been for woman, who knew from the first moment how to take hold of things, how to use them, and what their significance was. And woman saved man for life . . . but only so she could keep him attached to life, chained to its finitude. Real woman is first and foremost a mother and the deepest antagonist of all yearning for the infinite.[41]

There was, as Lukács realized with increasing clarity during the essay period, no possible resolution to this conflict on the individual level. Just as life remained only flux and chaos without the abstracting, form-giving power of art, so art became a glittering empty shell when severed from the dynamism of life. "The two poles," Lukács wrote, "remain eternal, irreconcilable foes, the man and the woman, art and life, even though they cannot do without each other."[42]

There is little doubt that the intensity of Lukács' perception of the aestheticist dilemma, as well as the symbols through which he expressed it, were closely connected to personal experience. One of the most revealing confessions occurred in an unpublished literary fragment, probably written in the early months of 1909. It was in the form of a letter addressed but apparently never mailed to a woman acquaintance "with whom," he wrote Popper, "I have little inner sympathy, but to whom a hysterical impulse drew me for a brief moment."[43] In the long and passionate monologue Lukács assumed the persona of the quintessential aesthete, or Platonist, as he called himself, who for the first time in his life decided to reach out to a fellow being and to reveal his true self to her. "When I left you," he began, "something wept within me, wept after a great intimacy. I longed, if only for a moment, to take off my impenetrable mask of cleverness, longed for someone to see me, if only for one moment, so that they can say: I see you and love you."[44]

The aesthete or Platonist, it emerged from the letter, was a deeply divided being who habitually faced the world through a mask, who used a façade of intellectual lucidity to hide the sentimentality in his nature. He had turned his life and self into pure intellect, into a deceptively harmonious artifact, only to hide his "deep sense of aimlessness," to "cut the root of his sentimentality." The life of such a man, Lukács elaborated, embodied the problem of "how to live without limits. How to live with the knowledge that one only trespasses on one's own deeds, . . . that the person one embraces remains a stranger forever."[45]

The pure aesthete was the eternal stranger because his emotional life was totally disconnected from his social self. But even more painful than his isolation from people was his metaphysical estrangement from all religious or supernatural realities, a condition he experienced as a perpetual longing for a vague and ill-defined goal. "What does it mean for someone to yearn?" he asked. "Perhaps this: that there is an empty point in his soul which nothing can fill that is his own; perhaps this: that he needs something that detaches itself from his self, that is separate and apart from his life and yet is still his." Ultimately the aesthete was haunted by the religious need for transcendence, by the primitive desire to merge his solitary self in some great communal deed, to lose his constricting individuality in some mystical act of self-abandonment. "There is something somewhere," Lukács concluded, "that perhaps I will melt into; there is a mirror perhaps that will reflect my rays; there is a deed in which I will discover myself. Is there really? I do not know, and I do not know what it could be. I only know that I am journeying toward it and everything is merely a wayfaring station along the way . . . Peraps it is in death—who can tell?—that the soul will become whole; perhaps it is with death that the yearning stops."[46]

This is an astonishing letter which provides an almost painfully graphic depiction of the prolonged depression and intellectual crisis Lukács suffered in the years between 1908 and 1911. The catalyst of the crisis was not the woman to whom the letter was addressed but Irma Seidler, a young painter with whom he had broken only a few months earlier. The facts of their relationship were simple, even banal on the surface. Lukács met Irma Seidler, a cousin of Carl and Michael Polányi, in December 1907 at one of the regular literary soirées held at the home of the Polacsek (Polányi) family. A friendship developed, which by the summer of 1908, following a joint holiday in Italy, had clearly blossomed into something more intense. Given the mores of their social world, a public engagement and eventual marriage would seem to have been in order.[47]

For Lukács, however, the prospect of a permanent attachment harbored subtle but insurmountable difficulties. Seidler spent the summer of 1908 at the Impressionist artists' colony of Nagybánya and attempted to alleviate Lukács' fears and doubts through reassuring letters. "How could you imagine," she wrote him in July, "that the creation of a genuine, nonsuperficial intimacy between two people could take place without pain and suffering? . . . I am not afraid. I look on it as a noble task to be undertaken with honesty and courage."[48] Even Seidler's loving perseverance, however, could not prevail over Lukács' doubts, and in the autumn of 1908 she decided to "ask back the freedom, which perhaps you had never even taken from me . . . For after all," she wrote in farewell, "we could never have been able to leap over that narrow channel that still separates us . . . You, Gyuri, will be able to develop better without me, without a permanent link attaching you to one person . . . Make good use of the inestimable advantage of being able to devote years entirely to your inner growth and development—the chances are given for you to grow into someone at least of the stature of Walter Pater."[49] Shortly after her separation from Lukács, Seidler married a painter colleague and her path diverged from Lukács, though they reestablished a tentative friendship and correspondence during the early months of 1911.

For Lukács the break from Seidler proved traumatic. It began a complex emotional and intellectual transformation that was to be completed more than two and a half years later. His immediate reaction to the separation was thoughts of suicide. In a suicide note of November 1908, which he apparently never sent to Seidler, Lukács began to explore some of the reasons for his inability to commit himself to the marriage both of them wanted. He referred to his exceedingly isolated youth, to his early resignation to a life of solitude, and then to the dazzling and unexpected emotional awakening that the encounter with Seidler had brought. "All former experiences of intimacy," he wrote, "paled in my memory, because I felt that they were lies, that this was the only real one . . . You gave me back my life, and this life, suppressed for so long, wanted to expand to the skies."[50]

The obstacles and inhibitions remaining from the old life, however, proved even more powerful than the promise of happiness in the new one. Lukács seemed convinced that he was incapable of a normal life of emotional fulfillment, that he had no right to undertake such a life. "You wanted to save me," he ended, "but I am not a person who can be saved . . . No person has ever been so close to me as you, and I don't see the possibility of anyone coming so close again . . . I observe with cold objectivity that I have a great deal of talent, but this is not enough for me, to whom you have shown from a distance that there is something else and to whom life has shown that he can never have any part in it. This is why I will die, and this is why I have written so much about myself."[51]

Lukács' hesitations before marriage clearly had psychological roots, which he obliquely hinted at in his letters and essays at the time. He was, he claimed at one point, a man who readily got into conversation with strangers, who formed superficial social and intellectual relationships with ease, but who found the creation of prolonged intimacy almost impossible.[52] He felt unworthy of Seidler, he said in another context, fearing that he could not make her happy, that there was too much sadness and resignation in his nature to be amenable to radical change, to feel at home with conventional happiness.[53]

These were all contributing factors, no doubt, but there existed a more profound motivation behind the seeming paradox of Lukács' actions which emerged only gradually in the course of 1909 and 1910. Lukács sensed, intuitively at first but with growing intellectual clarity as time went on, that his work as a scholar and cultural critic was intimately connected with his personal isolation; that his inadequacy as an emotional being was precisely what provided him with his unique vantage point for understanding the larger philosophic and cultural problems of his time. In his essay on Søren Kierkegaard in *Soul and Forms*, perhaps Lukács' most transparently autobiographical piece in the volume, he referred directly to this deeper professional motivation behind his separation from Seidler. Using Kierkegaard's inexplicable decision to break off his engagement to Regine Olsen as a thin disguise for his own case, he speculated: "Perhaps something in him realized that happiness—even if attainable—would have paralyzed him and rendered him sterile for all time. Perhaps what he was afraid of was that happiness was not unattainable, that Regine's lightness could, after all, have redeemed his great sadness, and that they would both have been happy. But what would have become of him if life had taken away from him his unhappiness?"[54]

The ultimate fear behind Lukács' rejection of Irma was that conventional happiness, the emotional fulfillment of normal, everyday existence, would jeopardize his creativity, would dim the sharpness of his vision for the philosophic task he had staked out as uniquely his own. For the dilemma of the aesthete, reduced to its essential emotional and psychological core, resided in an intense experience of personal and metaphysical isolation; in an absolute estrangement from all forms of sustaining loyalties and communities. Lukács realized that through constitution and fate he embodied this state of mind and attitude toward life in a deeper, more fundamental way than more happily constituted individuals. He possessed, he wrote Popper in the spring of 1909, the sensibility of the aesthete par excellence. "I am no longer afraid," he wrote,

> but I do not believe that I will ever touch the living reality of life . . . I realize this without distress, even though you are here and Baumgarten[55] and someone else I love. And yet, I know that

my love cannot find its way into your real lives, nor yours into mine—because I have no life . . . I think that this is the central problem of the critical sensibility, and I believe that I represent one of the purest examples of the type. There is some sadness mixed with pride in this knowledge—but there is much pride— and today at least much strength as well . . . I believe that my genuine value as a thinker stems from this circumstance; one has to pay a price for it. I pay with "life"—one should not complain against the inevitable; it is vulgar.[56]

Lukács was to devote the next two years to the task of generalizing his personal experience and developing a new, more complex and objective cultural image of the aestheticist personality. Like a modern-day pilgrim, he recorded the stages of his inner struggle in a diary which he kept between the spring of 1910 and the end of 1911. In the diary entries for 1910 it is possible to trace almost step by step the stages by which Lukács transformed the urgent and deeply personal emotions generated by Irma Seidler into a cultural and philosophic problem of universal significance.

By the spring of 1910, when Lukács took up the diary, it is clear that he was past the first shock of separation and that the outline of the resolution he was seeking was well within sight. "Some semblance of hope," he wrote in April 1910, "the 'ice age' has begun. I have died but she lives within me; to the extent that anything can live within me. Quietly. Without reproaches. Without pain."[57] With time the memory of the concrete woman grew increasingly faint, but the pain of her absence paradoxically remained vividly present. "In spite of everything," he mused in May, "only she exists—even if I no longer love her, no longer desire her, no longer want her back. It makes no difference. The memory of one episode with her means more than a lifetime spent with someone else."[58] The lost woman represented warmth, spontaneity, emotion, the unproblematic acceptance of life. She was everything Lukács was not, the embodiment of the possibility of authentic, nonalienated existence. As the symbolic reality separated from the living woman, Lukács had to admit to himself that important as Irma Seidler had been in his life, she was nevertheless only a symbol for larger, more complex issues that transcended her personal attributes. "I am awaiting some miracle," he wrote in June, "which would bring down to earth the unreachable and the unrealizable. And the fact that this mood is, at the moment, generally connected with the figure of Irma is almost an accident. In her time I still had human experiences, and since she was by far and away the most intense among them, in retrospect she will be the symbol of all intimacy."[59]

During the summer, while the image of Seidler gradually metamorphosed into the symbol of community and authentic life, Lukács' own identity and philosophic task came into sharper focus. Slowly the despair of the earlier mood gave way to resignation, then to intellectual clarity, and finally to serenity. "My professional path is becoming clear before me," he wrote on June 26. "I see the direction in which I must travel and how I can travel it—and the fact that outside of me no one has yet seen it."[60] By the end of 1910, slightly more than two years after his separation from Seidler, Lukács had managed to create an almost total identity between his personal and professional life. "These days," he wrote Popper, "my contacts with people have almost completely receded into the background . . . I am at home. In a country where I know the roads, where I travel with confidence."[61]

The seeming resolution of Lukács' personal crisis at the end of 1910 corresponded to the completion of the final stages of work on his book of essays. In early 1910 Lukács wrote Seidler, asking her permission to dedicate *Soul and Forms* to her and briefly summarizing the role she had played in his life during the previous two years:

Even if you should deny my request, it will not alter the fact that this book belongs to you. It was written because you appeared in my life and then departed from it. For me this was the sole reality of that part of life which is customarily called youth . . . Even if the task that is before me, that will occupy my entire life, hardly had intellectual and philosophic roots . . . in our time, the fact that I have reached this point, that I have found my true self and my true vocation I owe to that time and to you. What I want to accomplish can only be carried out by a man who is alone. True solitude, however, can only be bought at the price of, and after, the deepest experience of intimacy. He who does not know what one person can mean to another can only know desolation and loneliness, but never that hard-edged solitude dedicated to

127

knowledge that is without yearning or hope. Only such a man can afford to pass by, calmly and proudly, all the petty and beguiling promises of pseudointimacies and stake his whole life on the uncertain fate of his work . . . This state of mind, this atmosphere, which is the only one I can breathe, which is the only one that can give me the possibility of life, you gave me. Am I not permitted to thank you for it?[62]

The day that Irma Seidler wrote Lukács thanking him for the dedicated copy of *Soul and Forms* he decided to close his diary: "Let this diary end; the time of sentimentality is over . . . I am glad of it . . . Today Irma accepted the dedication of my book: let this be the last thing that I note in here. And let her name be the last I mention, with a simple, sad, and deep blessing for all that she brought and gave. And she is still the only one, and there can be no life without her, but this is how it should be, the only way possible for me."[63]

This, however, was not to be the last entry. In May 1911, after what appears to have been an unhappy marriage and an equally unfortunate love affair (with Balázs), Irma Seidler commited suicide by drowning herself in the Danube. Seidler's sudden and unexpected death closed with tragedy Lukács' essay period. "So arm ist keiner," he wrote immediately after hearing the news, "Gott kann ihn noch ärmer machen. [No one is so poor that God cannot make him even poorer.] I did not know this. Now I know: everything is over. Every tie has been broken because she was the tie to everything, and now all that is left is common strivings, and common goals, and work."[64] Writing to Popper two days later, Lukács made his final farewell to Irma Seidler: "The solitude I wanted has finally descended on me like a judgment of life . . . the only meaning my life ever had was when I could take it to her on an afternoon the way others (better men than me) take roses to someone. But don't worry about me. In a day or two I will even be able to work, and in the future that is all there is, and all there will be."[65]

The inner drama of Lukács' private life in the years between 1908 and 1911 was accompanied by a process of intellectual maturation that was eventually to lead to a coherent refutation of the philosophic assumptions underlying the aestheticist movement. Throughout the essay period Lukács' attitude toward aestheticism was shot through with a complicated kind of ambivalence which rendered him both a participant in and an observer of the tradition he was describing. He was imbued with the aesthete's sense of the irreducible diversity of life, with the feeling, as he later described it, "that every phenomenon is multifaceted . . . and that, at the same time, it is impossible to connect them in any mechanical way . . . to the grand totality."[66] Yet at the same time he longed for the intellectual clarity made possible by abstract theoretical positions. He had a yearning for an integrated philosophy or a dogmatic faith that would create security in the midst of doubts, and order out of the fragmented diversity of life.

The tensions arising out of the contradictory and ultimately irreconcilable nature of these positions created in the essays a misleading appearance of inconsistency and eclecticism, for Lukács' deep ambivalence and dualism during this period stemmed from a consciously maintained posture rather than an unacknowledged conflict. He attempted to create out of the very contradictions that underlay his life a self-conscious literary persona, which he described as that of the typical critic. "In him," he wrote in an essay on Rudolf Kassner,

> the longing for certainty, measure, and dogma was fanatically strong and fanatically disguised, hidden under bitter irony and hardheaded definitions. He is sublime in his uncertainty and hesitations which force him to drop all measuring rods and to see individuals in the sharp light of isolation rather than in the decorative harmony of a grand synthesis . . . Kassner is an advocate of totality, and at the same time—out of scrupulousness—he is an impressionist. This duality is what creates the intensity of his style and its impenetrable ambiguity.[67]

Lukács was shrewd enough to know that the very ambivalence of the "critical" posture would provide him with the deepest, most fertile perspective on the problem of aestheticism, allowing him, in a sense, to combine the subjective insights and experiences of the insider with the objective detachment of the outside observer.

Lukács seemed to sense right from the beginning that the fundamental significance of aestheticism transcended the artistic and literary realms with which it was most commonly associated. Thus the underlying if often unconscious goal of his work between 1908 and 1910 was to find an ever broader and more general philosophic framework within which to understand the aestheticist phenomenon. This impulse toward philosophic generalization was evident even in his analysis of what could be considered the purely stylistic and technical aspects of aestheticism.

As Lukács well knew, the central goal of the art for art's sake movement had been the liberation of art from all external constraints such as morality, utility, or politics. This impulse, understandable and laudable as it was within its initial context, resulted, however, in two unforseen consequences. The first was to render the role and function of art in society radically problematic, for the freeing of art from external pressures had severed what had until then been a self-evident connection between art and life, opening up a whole set of philosophic questions about the relationship of art and reality.

The second was to push the impulse for realism and individualism in art to the farthest possible extreme. As Lukács pointed out in an early essay on Gaugin, the liberation of art from the weight of tradition left only one stylistic direction open for young innovators: an ever more exact and scientifically meticulous reproduction of what they took to be reality. But realism, interpreted in the strictest sense of the word, could only recognize as "real" the momentary sense impressions of the individual artist. The ultimate consequence of this more scrupulous realism on the part of the Impressionists and Symbolists was an extreme kind of subjectivism which attempted to give expression to the fleeting moments, emotional nuances, and states of dream and fantasy of the individual consciousness. Such an art, felt Lukács, lacked "solidity" and "permanence"; it turned everything into moods and impressions which "existed for only a moment: for the moment that the individual 'I'—under the influence of certain experiences, perspectives, illuminations—happened to be looking toward it."[68]

The sincere desire of the Impressionists and Symbolists to communicate the reality of individual consciousness as directly and as truthfully as possible was bound to fail, for subjective vision could never be fully communicated by means of language and paint; and art, no matter how technically perfect, always remained an imperfect copy of inner experience, not the expe-

130

rience itself. Ultimately, Lukács pointed out, Impressionism and Symbolism faced a tragic failure of communication that was identical to the age-old dilemma of the mystic: that the reality at the core of existence is incommunicable. By carrying the tradition of realism to the farthest possible point, the Impressionists and Symbolists had demonstrated the bankruptcy of their tradition. Ironically, despite their iconoclastic challenge to the academies, they turned out to be the last heirs of nineteenth-century realism, not its genuine opponents.

In his stylistic analysis of aestheticism, Lukács stumbled upon a central paradox which permeated all manifestations of the tradition: that its ultimate results often turned into the very opposite of its initial goals. Impressionists and Symbolists strove for greater and greater realism only to become increasingly subjectivist and idiosyncratic; they strove for scientific veracity only to succumb to the ultimate dilemma of mysticism; they strove for intimacy and direct communication only to face increasing isolation within the prison of the self. They had not realized, Lukács concluded, that "the more subjective and fleetingly momentary an experience is, the more problematic is our ability to communicate it. For ultimately, only that which is communal can be genuinely communicated."[69]

With the rejection of individualism as an artistic ideal, Lukács began to grope toward the formulation of a different, more communal aesthetic creed. In his 1907 essay on Paul Gaugin, which despite Popper's advice he chose not to include in *Soul and Forms*, Lukács tentatively explored what seemed to him the communal nature of Gaugin's experience in Tahiti. He came to the conclusion (a conclusion which incidentally was never spelled out in Gaugin's own account of his experiences) that in Tahiti, Gaugin had recovered a sense of community he had failed to find in Europe. "Tahiti healed Gaugin," wrote Lukács. "He had found his place in a society where he was considered neither a luxury item for art lovers nor a dangerous, roving anarchist . . . He had attained his goal; this was what he sought all his life. He is the only modern artist who has arrived home."[70]

The fantasy of "arriving home" could have various embodiments in Lukács' essays. One of the most deeply nostalgic found expression in the essay on Theodor Storm, in which Lukács lovingly recreated the world of early nineteenth-century German patrician society, which still retained some of the attributes of traditional integrated cultures. The Storm essay, in a sense parallel to the one on Gaugin, postulated a mode of existence in which individuals were still firmly enmeshed in a web of social relations; in which desires were defined by custom and ethical norms; in which expectations of life were pegged to the possibilities of life and were, therefore, capable of fulfillment. Within such a society art was not separate from life but a natural emanation of it, and the artist was no genius but a craftsman, calmly and methodically pursuing his work in exactly the same fashion as other craftsmen. In this kind of society work necessarily became a part of the natural rhythm of life, or as Lukács lyrically expressed it, "Life was the melody and everything else the accompaniment to it."[71]

Lukács' gradually emerging aesthetic vision, with its organicist, communitarian implications, ultimately challenged not only aestheticism but romanticism itself, for it was the early nineteenth-century romanticists who had first proclaimed the artist as a unique being, a genius, with a special pseudoreligious mission to fulfill in society. Lukács' broadening criticism of aestheticism inexorably led him back to romanticism, where he felt the ultimate roots of aestheticism could be found. Lukács was by no means the first thinker to remark on the striking similarities between romanticism and aestheticism. As early as 1885 the French essayist and novelist Paul Bourget had pointed to "the unexpected modern rebirth of what was called in 1830 the "mal de siècle.' "[72] But Lukács, unlike others before him, attempted to analyze in some detail the nature of the connection between the two movements.

Aestheticism, he pointed out, was not an exact reenactment of romanticism. Aestheticists were romantics in temperament only, who found themselves living in an age fundamentally uncongenial to their deepest impulses and strivings. They acted out their disenchantment by reversing the romanticist ideals and affirming their direct opposite. In place of the all-embracing intellectual synthesis of the romanticists, the aestheticists advocated radical skepticism; in place of their deism they substituted atheism; in place of their worship of nature they affirmed the worship of artifice. While the romanticists "extended the grasp

of their art over the whole world, . . . [the aestheticists] having
no area left, subordinated everything to art."[73]

Yet, despite the inner connections Lukács saw between aestheticism and romanticism, his attitude toward the romanticists
was more ambiguous, more conciliatory than toward their late
nineteenth-century offspring. He in fact identified to an extent
with the positive strivings of the romanticists, who had also
been "problematic individuals" seeking a way to transcend the
formless, evanescent nature of reality. "To leave behind the
contingent and accidental! This is the goal; this is what Friedrich
Schlegel and Benjamin Constant's Adolph strove for . . . but in
their struggle toward the universal, exemplary life . . . they lost
their way and their selves; they committed suicide or inwardly
sold out."[74]

The romanticists had attempted to reconstitute life through
an all-encompassing synthesis in which "science and art, poetry
and mathematics can be united."[75] But according to Lukács the
very complexity and hubris of romanticist strivings doomed the
movement to failure. Since the romanticists found it impossible
to realize their goals within empirical reality, they enacted them
within the realm of pure imagination and emotion. "Unconscious rejection of life was the price of romantic artistic aspirations," he wrote in his essay on Novalis. "In place of empirical
reality they place another spiritual realm, and because they refuse to give up any possible experience, they have to renounce,
without their wishing to or even knowing it, all possibility of
action."[76]

The ultimate result of romanticist withdrawal and individualism, Lukács pointed out, was the psychological and artistic
paralysis of the aesthete, whose plight he explored in intimate
detail in the essay on Richard Beer-Hofmann. Beer-Hofmann's
characters, he wrote, were no longer bound by the traditional
constraints and limitations of life. They were liberated from the
bonds of family and professional obligations, from the formative
pressures of religious beliefs, national loyalties, intellectual dog-
mas, moral axioms. Such radical liberation, however, resulted
not in freedom but in servitude of the most excruciating kind,
which rendered some of the most basic aspects of life problematic.

For the aesthete, his own identity, his ability to communicate with others, even his sense of reality were in constant danger of disintegration under the unceasing bombardment of ever-new impressions and stimulations. For such a man, wrote Lukács, describing himself as much as the characters of Beer-Hofmann,

> everything is possible and nothing certain; dream and life melt into each other, just as do wish and reality, fear and truth . . . What remains? What is certain in life? Where is a stable point on earth, be it ever so bare and sterile and bereft of all beauty and wealth, where a person can securely anchor his feet? Where is something that does not flow like sand from one's finger, when one tries, if only for a moment, to lift it out of the shapeless mass of life? Where do dream and reality separate from each other, self and the world, deep substance and passing impression?[77]

Lukács' impulse to see aestheticism within the broadest, most general categories possible found its culmination in his essay "Aesthetic Culture" (Esztétikai kultúra), first published in *Renaissance* in May 1910. Here Lukács finally made explicit that for him aestheticism was not just an artistic movement or even a philosophic school but the embodiment of modern, secular society itself. The aesthete, he wrote, symbolized contemporary civilization in the same way that the Sophist symbolized the Athens of Socrates, the Pope and the robber baron the high Middle Ages, the troubadour and the mystic the declining Middle Ages, and the small despot and the militant philosoph the eighteenth century.[78] The modern aesthete was simply the cultural analogue of the specialist who also sacrificed the wholeness of life for proficiency in one small area. The difference between them was that the specialist—be he scientist, engineer, or entrepreneur—focused his interest on a small segment of external reality, while the aesthete concentrated exclusively on elements of the inner life. Both were characterized by an overriding preoccupation with means and a congenital inability to formulate the ultimate ends toward which their activities were directed.

Through imperceptible degrees, Lukács' analysis and critique of aestheticism had metamorphosed into full-blown cultural criticism which was hardly less virulent and uncompromising than that of Nietzsche and other antiliberal thinkers of the late nineteenth century. All the familiar themes and refrains of the radical cultural critic can be plainly recognized in Lukács' later essays. Modern civilization, he maintained, which produced the figures of the aesthete and the technician, lacked all coherence and objective values. In it individualism had triumphed at the expense of the collectivity, and the increasingly frenetic search for novelty and personal fulfillment had banished all possibility for permanence, stability, and objectivity.

The very freedom and individualism which defined the aspirations of contemporary man had become increasingly difficult to attain in a society where everything was permitted, where no intrinsic values existed to differentiate between good and bad, desirable and undesirable, beautiful and ugly. The modern individual aimed at the fullest, most intense exposure to life, but paradoxically lost the ability to experience external reality because he tended to withdraw into privacy and subjectivism. Aesthetic culture attempted to liberate the self from external constraints and yet ended by creating the most "terrible slavery" because it failed to provide order and predictable norms for the individual. "Total passivity," wrote Lukács, "can never become the central principle of life . . . nor anarchy the foundation for order. 'Aesthetic culture,' 'life as art,' represent the permanent glorification of spiritual depravity, of paralysis of will and creativity, of subordination to the fluctuations of the moment, as a central principle of life."[79]

By 1910 Lukács had finally exhausted all the inner possibilities of the aestheticist experience and had found it ultimately untenable, not only for life but also for art. He recorded this observation in his diary shortly after completing "Aesthetic Culture":

> I feel in spite of everything that the shadow of a great crisis is hovering ahead of me. Perhaps it is because I have again been unable to work decently for two days. But this makes no difference. For what kind of life is it which requires the constant narcotic of work in order "to feel well"? . . . I think today: if I reach all my inner and outer goals through work—what then? What have I reached? Is not the meaning of my life—taken in its entirety—directed toward an ever sharper clarification and upward struggle so that one day its ultimate emptiness and futility may stand

revealed in all its nakedness: the tragedy. I feel it coming with a deep certainty as never before.[80]

No conservative or reactionary could have articulated a harsher or more vehement indictment of liberal individualism and rationalism than Lukács did in the later essays of *Soul and Forms* and in "Aesthetic Culture." In fact the more focused his perspective on aestheticism became, the closer he found himself to the position of conservatives who had always condemned aestheticism and romanticism for their unrestrained individualism, their disregard for tradition. And yet no matter how similar their conclusions may have been, Lukács' ideas came out of a totally different matrix of experience from those of mainstream conservatives. He judged aestheticism not from without, on the strength of a preconceived philosophic position, but from within, based on deep personal experience. Only after he had arrived at the extreme peripheries of modern individualism, after he had experienced and understood all its nuances, did he reach the point where, as he confessed in the Beer-Hofmann essay,

> the individual soul becomes tired of the ever new yet constantly repetitive game and longs after tangible, incontestable reality; when the ability of the self to experience all things and accommodate itself to all things, begins to feel like imprisonment . . . when he who is at home everywhere and for that reason is eternally homeless longs at last to settle in one place; when he who understands everything would finally like to find rest in the exclusive limitations of one all-embracing emotion.[81]

Lukács was not alone in these negative conclusions about liberal individualism. It was becoming increasingly clear to many artists and intellectuals of the late 1890s and early 1900s that if the crisis they were experiencing as a generation was to be resolved, they would have to forge or rediscover a new kind of affirmation, a new collective vision. In France the signal for this impulse of affirmation was given by the former aesthete Paul Bourget, who published in 1899 his widely read novel *Le Disciple* (The disciple). In its preface he publicly repudiated decadence and exhorted the younger generation to cultivate such positive virtues as love and will, which had been so singularly lacking in the lives of the decadents. Bourget's call for an end to the uncompromising negativism and individualism of the past was echoed throughout Europe during this period. Young people coming of age began to advocate the need for action, simplicity, physical vigor, and community in place of the passive, overly subtle, and detached attitudes of the decadents.

Particularly notable was the appearance of a new spirit of dogmatism and absolutism in the affirmations of many segments of the younger generation, who rediscovered or reinvented notions of racial community, historic traditions, social hierarchy, and folk customs. They sought refuge in the protective sanctuary of tradition and community and talked, in Maurice Barrès' words, of tasting "deeply the instinctive pleasure of being one with the crowd."[82]

In the circumstances, the pattern of behavior of the young ideologues was understandable. Emerging from the paralyzing nihilism of the decadent experience, they retreated into the apparent simplicity of a national or racial past which had perhaps never existed but which nevertheless served as a symbol of the stability, community, and emotional wholeness they were seeking.[83] The new affirmation was the antithesis of modern skepticism and was in fact, as Barrès made clear, inseparable from it. "I defend my cemetery," he wrote. "I have abandoned all other positions. Religion, scientific certainty, meaning in life, progress. The smoke of all these battles clouds the horizon."[84] The new ideology of conservative nationalism provided for many intellectuals of the fin de siècle a genuine conversion experience through which they freed themselves, in one leap, of all doubts, loneliness, and anxiety by embracing unconditionally a set of absolutes expressed through a community of like-minded individuals.

Not all members of this transitional generation, however, sought to overcome the crisis of liberal individualism through conversion to religious, or political absolutes. Many others—and Lukács and the emerging circle of friends and allies around him were part of this group—believed that the artistic paralysis and personal isolation they suffered as a generation could be resolved not by moving backward to past certitudes, but rather by reaching forward to new artistic forms and new collective truths. They chose neither to retreat from the modern world nor to abandon the search for cultural absolutes.

137

This complex, essentially paradoxical impulse was to form the core of a new cultural posture that Lukács and his friends began to explore and elaborate with increasing self-consciousness in the years after 1910. In their search for totality and a new cultural synthesis, they confessed themselves to be paradoxically related to the romanticists, whose failed task they felt they would finally bring to fruition. "Our days," wrote Fülep with soaring optimism, "are the harbingers of a long-awaited transformation of the world, and in this they show marked similarity to the expectations of romanticists like Schelling, Schlegel, Tieck, and Novalis; but naturally only to their expectations, for their actual accomplishments, for reasons not hard to explain, are puny and insignificant compared to the ones we are aiming for."[85]

Balázs had already expressed such ambitions, though in a rather naive and as yet unformed version, in 1906, when he spoke to Zoltán Kodály of his

> secret dream . . . about the great new Hungarian culture that we have to create . . . It would be a unified "Sturm und Drang" movement, a spiritual rebirth which would cleanse the present of its journalistic art and clownish science and would build in its place a fresh new art, a new science, a great new culture . . . I spoke to [Kodály] of the rehabilitation of art, of the religion of art, which would form the basis of the future culture. Its temple would be the concert hall, the art gallery, and the theater. I spoke to him of the redeeming power of art, that people will improve and society will once again become healthy.[86]

The longing for cultural affirmation which gradually replaced the purely critical, negative gestures of aestheticism found its first rallying point for Lukács and other like-minded intellectuals in Hungary in the defense of postimpressionism. The opportunity for a formal break from Impressionism as well as for a public articulation of the new cultural strivings came in February 1910, on the occasion of a debate sponsored by a radical student organization, the Galilei Circle. The key speaker of the evening was Károly Kernstock, the leader of the postimpressionist painters, and Lukács was the major participant in the debate that followed. Kernstock's talk was brief and unpretentious. He rejected once and for all the optical realism of the Impressionists, maintaining that the artist's attempt to imitate nature was a futile, misguided enterprise which was destined to fail no matter how perfect the technical skill of the artist. For nature, insisted Kernstock, worked with fundamentally different tools from the artist: "We do not have live cells, we do not have mist, we do not have sunshine. All we have are brushes, a flat surface, paint, and a few other similar wretched instruments."[87]

In place of the essentially passive mimesis of Impressionism, Kernstock advocated an activist attitude toward nature, in which the artist would act as a conscious "explorer" (*kutató*) striving to extract meaning and values "out of the huge, eternal gold mine of nature." The "exploring art" (*kutató müvészet*) of the postimpressionists was in direct and conscious opposition to the "accommodating art" (*alkalmazkodó müvészet*) of the Impressionists, who had been satisfied merely to imitate the superficial aspects of nature. The postimpressionists, by contrast, attempted to convey their sense of inner meaning and personal values discovered in nature, and they broke from conventional realism to realize this goal. Rather than depict the surface appearance of the world, they deliberately distorted it, emphasizing elements on their canvases which they considered important and deemphasizing others which they considered less important. Kernstock ended on a utopian note, concluding that the new "exploring art" was part of an enormous cleansing process in contemporary culture which, "similar to a fever, is attempting to get rid of all those externalities which today still assume an important role in painting."[88]

Lukács played a conspicuous part in the general debate that followed Kernstock's speech. In a talk entitled "The Parting of the Roads" (Az utak elváltak), he spelled out the revolutionary philosophic implications contained in Kernstock's unpretentious manifesto. What distinguished the strivings of the postimpressionists, as well as those of a handful of contemporary writers and philosophers, Lukács declared, was "that they wanted to express the essence of things" in their paintings, poems, and philosophic works. In Lukács' skillful hands the seemingly innocuous phrase "the essence of things" became the source of the great divide between Impressionism and postimpressionism, between the culture of the nineteenth century and that of the truly modern epoch, for as Lukács well knew, the very notion of essences or ultimate goals was alien to the vocabulary of nineteenth-century philosophic discourse. This philosophy recognized impartial observation as the only source of legitimate knowledge and relegated all questions of values and ultimate principles to the realm of the unscientific, the unknowable, and the ultimately irrelevant.

By frankly asserting that the central concerns of the new culture were to be metaphysical in nature, Lukács was consciously cutting its ties with nineteenth-century positivism, materialism, and determinism, those firm intellectual anchors of liberal culture. From Lukács' new perspective, it was ultimately positivistic science which was responsible for the fragmented, relativistic world view bequeathed by the nineteenth century to the twentieth. Positivism, he felt, approached nature from a position of passive observation rather than active involvement, and encouraged a view of the world geared to register the reality of atomized individuals and dispersed, disconnected moments. In opposition to such fragmenting, analytic tendencies, Lukács asserted the need for a new kind of affirmation and synthesis. "Today," he declared, "we once again long for order among things . . . We long for permanence, for a common measure of our deeds and unambiguous verification of our words. We long for our daily affairs to acquire meaning and consequence, for them to exclude something. We long for discrimination and differentiation. We long for profundity and seriousness . . . This new feeling has arisen in many spheres of life, and has already found expression in poems and philosophic tracts."[89]

Lukács' talent for concisely summarizing complex philosophic issues in manifestoes like "The Parting of the Roads" made him an effective spokesman for the new postimpressionist art. Yet Lukács was by no means alone in attributing broad cultural and philosophic significance to the emergence of postimpressionism. Lajos Fülep, who did not take part in the Kernstock debate, also maintained that postimpressionism represented something more profound than simply another stylistic shift in the long line of artistic secessions which had characterized the nineteenth century. Fülep, who had become particularly interested in the work of Cézanne, stressed that the French painter's rejection of Impressionism implied the discovery of a brand-new philosophy, a novel kind of objectivity, in the face of the dispersed subjectivism of the Impressionists. "The world outlook of Cézanne," he wrote, "represents the firmest affirmation of the reality of the real world . . . His is a realism—not in the modern sense of the word but in the medieval one—which compares to the outlook of Impressionism the way the philosophy of Thomas Aquinas compares to solipsism . . . The orthodox Cézanne represents a piece of the Middle Ages amidst the age of Impressionism."[90] Like Lukács, Fülep also felt that postimpressionism was the first manifestation of a profoundly new cultural impulse which strove toward creating a new kind of tradition that had nothing to do with the petrified rule of the academies. "Create a tradition for yourself, become your own tradition—this is the call of modern art to itself,"[91] concluded Fülep.

Yet it is important to stress that postimpressionism represented for Fülep, Lukács, and others of their generation only the harbinger of a future integrated culture, not its ultimate embodiment. It helped crystalize among them a mood of apocalyptic expectation and of passionate radicalism which unequivocally rejected all existing social and cultural arrangements. This almost messianic state of mind found expression in a metaphor of Lukács'—though one that was by no means unique to him—which compared contemporary Europe to the decaying Roman Empire, awaiting regeneration from a new religion and a fresh wave of barbarian invasion. Once the enervated culture of nineteenth-century Europe had been torn assunder by the new barbarians, wrote Lukács in "Aesthetic Culture," it would perhaps return to "essentials, even if only after long transitional ages hostile to art and culture."[92]

Lukács was quick to point out, however, that the "new barbarians" would not be the proletariat or the socialists, as many cultural radicals seemed to believe at the time. Socialists, Lukács maintained, far from being genuine antagonists of the bourgeois world, were often only crude caricatures of it. "They are also partly aesthetes," he warned, "They enjoy the same things and in the same way as the bourgeois aesthetes . . . With them too everything remains on the surface as among the bourgeois, and they too remain forever out of touch with the center of life."[93]

If socialism could not offer a utopia for Lukács and his friends, neither could any of the other "isms" which proliferated in such abundance during the prewar years. The distinguishing characteristic of their complicated kind of radicalism lay precisely in its inability to entertain or even conceive of a feasible alternative to the despised present. In his subtle analysis of the pioneer of Hungarian modernist poetry, Endre Ady, Lukács found a happy phrase to describe the essential quality of their common state of mind in the immediate prewar years. They were, he wrote, "revolutionaries without a revolution," for whom "the revolution is only a state of mind, the only positive form in which their endless despair and isolation could even find concrete expression. It is so completely and exclusively only a state of mind, only a yearning, that nothing tangible in the world of reality or even fantasy could possibly fulfill it."[94]

Theirs was a state of expectation and restless searching which not only lacked concrete goals but, perhaps more significantly, resisted all existing goals. As Fülep perceptively summed it up, the postimpressionists were imbued with the sense that "something has to finally happen which will invest contemporary art with a vocation and a significance worthy of comparison with the great ages of the past. The artists of today are 'searching,' but it seems that beyond the reality of the search itself, there is no clear idea of what it is they are searching for; it is as if they were hoping to discover the object of their search in the actual process of searching."[95]

Out of the tensions and paradoxes of this position, delicately poised between radical negation and apocalyptic expectation, emerged the great masterpieces of early twentieth-century modernist culture.[96] And among the most sophisticated interpreters of this fragile cultural moment were the young Hungarian philosophers who began to gather around Georg Lukács after 1910.

5

TOWARD
A NEW
METAPHYSICS

The defense of postimpressionism in 1910 formed the initial rallying point for Lukács and a handful of other like-minded intellectuals in Hungary who were bitterly disillusioned with the aestheticist experiment of the past decade. They saw in postimpressionism a sign of the first break from the negative, analytic temper of the nineteenth century and the first promise of a new organic culture of the future. It was the forerunner, wrote Fülep, of a "new classicism" which would once again express the ethos of an entire age rather than the subjective reality of the individual artist. The twentieth century, he sanguinely prophesied, was destined to give rise to a "unifying, powerful, and monumental art" bearing "the hallmarks of eternity in the same way that the art of Egypt, Greece, and the Renaissance did."[1]

It is important to stress, however, that neither Fülep nor any of his friends seriously believed that this new integrated culture was to be realized directly through a renewal in the arts. Such hopes, they felt, would simply have recreated the discredited illusions of aestheticism and romanticism, which had naively proclaimed the unique independence and mission of the artist in society. Independence, they realized by 1910, was ultimately meaningless without some form of social and metaphysical anchorage, and art could only be the expression, not the cause, of social or religious transformations in society. This was an insight, wrote Lukács in 1910, which "cannot ever again be erased from our consciousness even if our previous state of ignorance were a thousand times richer, finer, more productive. If Herder and Schiller, if Goethe and all the romanticists, had believed in the world-redeeming power of the creative act, their mistake would at most have been a tragic one, had they realized that they were wrong. But today, after everything we know, all attempts to revive an illusion which had once appeared credible would be merely comic."[2]

But acknowledging the impotence of art and the artist to change the world, accepting the verdict that the future resolution was to be the result of fundamental structural changes within society rather than conscious individual effort, did not necessarily imply passivity and despair. As Lukács put it, "the knowledge of determinism drives only the weak toward fatalism."[3] There was room for action, even if the definition and direction of action were to be different from those of the past. In 1913 Lukács stated for the first time, in response to a questionnaire concerning the state of German literature circulated by the periodical *L'Effort libre*, that their collective hopes for the future lay not in the regeneration of art but in the revival of German philosophy and religion.[4] Accordingly, philosophic and aesthetic investigations became increasingly prominent concerns in their writings and discussions during this period, taking precedence over literary and art criticism. Lukács took the lead in this direction when he definitively abandoned literary criticism for pure philosophy with the completion of the last essay in *Soul and Forms*. "I sense that the Philippe essay was the last of the 'Soul and Form' essays," he wrote Popper in the autumn of 1910. "The next stage is to be genuine scholarship. And perhaps, as compensation for the disappearing lyric,—a real metaphysics. That, too, slowly. And I have the patience to wait."[5]

The core of Lukács' philosophic self-definition, like that of his friends, was to be an ever more nuanced critique of nineteenth-century positivism and materialism, an impulse whose roots were already implicit in their repudiation of Impressionism. The declaration of this general philosophic orientation was made in the introductory article of *Szellem*, their first joint venture as a group, which carried a full translation in its opening pages of Emil Boutraux's "Nature and Spirit." "The mathematical-philosophic sciences," wrote Boutraux, in what had by then become one of the classic refutations of the monistic philosophy of the natural sciences, "cannot claim for themselves the exclusive right to repudiate all metaphysics, since they themselves base their fundamental methods and assumptions on irreducibly metaphysical elements: these are the notions of unity, determinism, law, simplicity, and analogy."[6]

Such arguments, however, could form only the starting point of their intellectual and philosophic task as a generation. By 1910 the antipositivist, antimaterialist position already embodied for Lukács and his friends an established intellectual tradition inherited from an older generation of philosophers—Nietzsche, Bergson, Dilthey, Weber—who had first thrown down the gauntlet to positivism in the 1870s, 1880s, and 1890s. Diverse as these thinkers were in methods and interests, they had all insisted on drawing a sharp distinction between the methods of the natural and the social sciences; between the objective world of scientific discourse and the subjective reality of individual consciousness and social existence. They had argued that the methods of the natural sciences, for generations considered the only model for reliable knowledge, were artificial constructs, inappropriately imposed on the dynamic, ultimately subjective reality of individual and collective experience. In Germany this antipositivist impulse found a particularly powerful incarnation in the neo-Kantian movement, which in the words of one commentator fought "to prevent the subordination of consciousness to undifferentiated experience and to protect the integrity of the free individual from all forms of monism and determinism."[7]

During their student years, Lukács and several of his Budapest friends had come under the influence of the Berlin neo-Kantians, particularly Georg Simmel, who liberated them from the shackles of positivism and scientism, still reigning supreme among

Hungarian academic philosophers. Yet important as the neo-Kantian tradition was in their early formation, it turned out to be an ambiguous heritage which they were forced eventually to repudiate and attempt to transcend. Their discontent with neo-Kantianism, which they came to see as the philosophic analogue of Impressionism, emerged gradually over the years, and crystalized around their increasingly problematic relationship with Georg Simmel himself.[8]

Simmel had been not only a mentor but also a personal friend to several members of the future Sunday Circle, who tended to complete their philosophic studies with a semester or two at the University of Berlin, where Simmel lectured. Lukács and Balázs were particularly favored by Simmel, who had them to his house for tea, conversation, or private seminars. In 1906 Balázs participated in one such private seminar on the philosophy of art (*Kunstphilosophie*), and he later dedicated the treatise to emerge from it, "The Aesthetics of Death," to Simmel. By all accounts Simmel thought highly of Balázs, with whom he maintained contact for many years. As late as 1912 he wrote to Lukács: "Though Herr Bauer [Balázs] was in Berlin, I was, unfortunately, able to meet with him only once because of the pressures of work. All the same, it gave me great pleasure to see him. He seems to have achieved an admirable independence and maturity in his development."[9]

Balázs, for his part, already harbored reservations about Simmel at the time of the seminar in 1906. Simmel and the people he met at his home, he recorded in his diary, opened up to him a new and interesting world which nevertheless remained "terribly alien to me. I can appreciate their feeling for symbolism, their sensibility. But I have not yet understood what it is that makes the whole thing so weightless and sterile in my eyes. Simmel is an extraordinarily interesting man with a remarkably developed sensibility . . . He says refined and surprising things. But it is precisely when he is most subtle that he sounds least sincere."[10]

The vague discomfort that Balázs experienced was a premonition of a basic incompatibility between the elder thinker and his young protégés which was to grow into open rejection in the years after 1910. "Simmel," wrote Lukács in a letter of 1910, "who has never been more attentive to me than now (last time

I was forced to spend over two hours at his house), can give me very little; whatever I could learn from him, I have already learned a long time ago."[11] In the following years the "Simmel problem," as one of Lukács' friends called it,[12] turned into an ongoing preoccupation, symbolizing the felt inadequacies of the entire neo-Kantian tradition.

In 1918 both Lukács and Mannheim wrote extensive reviews of Simmel's work, making explicit the nature of their objections to Simmel and neo-Kantianism. Simmel, Lukács wrote, was a consummate critic of contemporary culture, but like the Impressionists, to whom Lukács consistently compared him, he could not go beyond a negative, destructive posture. He was destined to be merely a transitional figure, the forerunner of a new synthetic philosophy "which will immortalize the richness of life in new, firm, and strictly appropriate forms. From this viewpoint Simmel's historical position could be summarized in the following way: he was the Manet of philosophy who has not yet been followed by a Cézanne."[13]

Mannheim's assessment of Simmel, written in the same year, was almost identical. Simmel, claimed Mannheim, remained the "philosopher of Impressionism," whose sensitivity to detail and nuances could not make up for his lack of synthetic ability. "He never fully believed in his subject, he was never fully absorbed by anything because even the most self-evident insight was accompanied by the feeling that all this could be otherwise, only the perspective has to change." Simmel, concluded Mannheim, embodied the inherent weakness of his entire generation: a deep-rooted skepticism which prevented him from formulating any kind of positive vision. "With his writing, he awakens immeasurable longing within us . . . he generates in us a revulsion against all ossified concepts that have existed until now," only to leave the hopes he had awakened unfulfilled and unsatisfied.[14]

Their ambivalent attitudes toward Simmel were refracted, with minor variations, onto the entire antipositivist philosophic generation of the 1880s and 1890s. They felt deeply indebted to the older generation but also slightly betrayed by them, holding that they had left their philosophic tasks incomplete. They had been content, accused Lukács' generation, to destroy the certitudes of nineteenth-century science but had lacked the faith and energy to put new truths in their place. As Lukács wrote about

Dilthey, they had left "everything in shattered pieces," resigning themselves to "an inner compromise with a fragmented universe." Despite Dilthey's pioneering work in challenging the philosophy of the natural sciences, Lukács continued, he shared the limitations which, "with the exception of Hartmann and Nietzsche, existed in all his contemporaries: the fear of metaphysics. The nature of his critique demanded that he push superficialities out of the way and create a new metaphysics . . . But Dilthey always lacked the courage to draw the full consequences from his thinking." Lukács' final epithet for Dilthey contained a judgment on his entire age: "Dilthey the philosopher became an essayist. And if at his grave we mourn the passing of the last great German essayist, we have already mourned during his lifetime the extinction of the philosopher; of an excellent human being who was destroyed by the bad age he was born into and from which he was unable to emancipate himself."[15]

Only two members of the older philosophic generation escaped the condemnation of Lukács and his friends: Nietzsche and Weber. In 1910 Fülep translated Nietzsche's *Birth of Tragedy* into Hungarian and wrote a long introduction to it in which he attempted to clarify his circle's complicated relationship with the great "nay sayer" of the nineteenth century. Unlike most of his contemporaries, wrote Fülep, Nietzsche *did* have the courage to seek a new affirmation, to awaken in mankind a "need for metaphysics." He dared to take a positive stand on man's "suppressed instinct" for religion without leaving behind the earth and man. Nietzsche's metaphysics, wrote Fülep, "belongs to this world. He attempts to prevent the tendency of metaphysical instincts to seek fulfillment beyond history; he attempts to exploit their tremendous energy for the building of the future society in the here and now."[16] Yet even Nietzsche had limitations. His uncompromising individualism, his concern with art as a way of life and as a means of self-creation, betrayed his essential unity with the aestheticist generation of the 1890s. Although Nietzsche talked of transcendence and of an immanent metaphysics, he also lacked the ability to formulate the positive truths of a new culture, for he still approached art and life from the perspective of the individual.

Ultimately Nietzsche provided the greatest challenge for Lukács and his friends precisely because they were able to follow him so much farther than most of the other critical philosophers of the 1890s. And it was in the realm of aesthetics, a central concern for all of them, that their interests converged and eventually clashed. The difference between them, wrote Fülep, was that Nietzsche still viewed art from the perspective of the creative artist, whereas they hoped to approach art from the direction of the work of art itself. This seemingly fine distinction, which Fülep made first, though Lukács was to develop it most fully, had important general philosophic consequences for their entire group. They were convinced that examining art purely from the viewpoint of the artist inevitably led to the negative, merely subjective conclusions of aestheticism rather than to what they were seeking—an objective philosophy of art. "Nietzsche," wrote Fülep, "embedded himself within the most secret corners of the creative artist's body and soul, but what emerged from his fine probing hands . . . is not so much a philosophy of art as the psychology of the artist."[17]

Nietzsche had made the same mistake, argued Fülep, as the aestheticists: he had transposed aesthetic categories onto life itself, unconsciously attempting to make of art a palliative or compensation for the inadequacies of life. Nietzsche had not realized what the following generation was beginning to: that "art can only be valued for itself because it is a separate thing outside of life, and art begins where life ends . . . For us, art is an end, not a means; it represents the goal, the final achievement, the fruit, which life . . . seeks to realize."[18] As Lukács' appreciative review of Fülep's essay made clear, this was still not a fully adequate refutation of Nietzsche—only a new and synthetic philosophy of art could be that—but it was a perceptive summary of their unfolding goals as a generation.[19]

Their relationship with Max Weber—one that was particularly important in Lukács' personal life—was of a different nature. When Lukács moved to Heidelberg in 1912 to undertake the writing of a formal philosophy of art, he became a valued member of the Webers' wide circle of friends and acquaintances, who generally met at the Webers' home on Sunday afternoons. This circle, which Marianne Weber has intimately described in her biography of her husband, was to be for Lukács an invaluable source of intellectual stimulation and social support in the years between 1912 and 1915. In all his later recollections Lukács always referred with warmth and gratitude to Weber, who, though belonging to an older, more austere and rational tradition than Lukács and his friends, never seemed to be the object of the kind of scorn and disappointment that Simmel, Dilthey, and ultimately even Nietzsche became.

The reason for such apparent compatibility lay in the peculiarly tolerant, even indulgent attitude that the Webers extended toward the younger, more metaphysical generation to which Lukács and his friends belonged. As Marianne Weber made clear in her biography, she and he husband were fascinated by the young artists and thinkers, often from Russia and Eastern Europe, who introduced them to a more adventurous, radical, and Bohemian style of life and thought than they were accustomed to. "They wanted," she wrote, referring to herself and her husband, "to learn to understand this strange, unbourgeois world of adventurism and to carry on intellectual dialogue with it."[20] Thus in Lukács' case, relations with the Webers presented a unique reversal of roles. It was not the younger generation who was learning from, and ultimately judging, the older, but the older accommodating itself to the younger. The absence of discernible tensions with the Webers lay ultimately not in a congruence of opinion—Weber remained as skeptical of the possibility of religious and metaphysical regeneration in the modern world as ever—but rather in the civilized urbanity of the Weber circle which made possible intellectual dialogue among a diverse group of thinkers.

—

In her biography of her husband Marianne Weber described Lukács and Ernst Bloch, Lukács' closest friend in Heidelberg, as "messianic young men . . . moved by eschatological hopes of a new emissary of the transcendental God."[21] The description is suggestive but only approximate. It does not even begin to convey the complexity and novelty of the cultural strivings that increasingly preoccupied Lukács and his friends in the years after 1910. As Marianne Weber suggests, their desire to transcend the merely negative, analytic temper of neo-Kantian philosophy, to hasten the emergence of an organic culture in place of the fragmented individualism of the nineteenth century, implied a vaguely religious or utopian alternative. Yet this alternative remained immensely problematic, appearing only as an elusive mirage whose indistinct outlines they sometimes thought to have grasped but never fully possessed. It was in fact the pursuit and definition of the ideal which preoccupied them during these years, mobilizing powerful intellectual and artistic energies which they had not suspected existed in them.

They frequently resorted to religious and philosophic language to express their longing for cultural renewal, but these statements were, characteristically, hedged in with qualifications and ambiguities. Perhaps Lukács' most eloquent expression of their religious longings came in a review of *Ariadne at Naxos*, a tragic drama by his close friend Paul Ernst. Ernst's characters, wrote Lukács, lived in a world

> in which—to use Nietzsche's expression—God is dead, in which man himself has become—in an exalted and moving sense—the measure of all things. But what if there is, after all, a god? If only one god had died and another, a younger, different god, one that stands in a different relationship to us, is in the process of coming into existence? What if the darkness of our aimless time signifies nothing other than the darkness between the dusk of one god and the dawn of another?[22]

There is a tentative, nondogmatic quality about this confession which clearly distinguishes it from traditional religious formulations. In fact Lukács and his friends repeatedly insisted that their use of words like *religious, metaphysical,* and *spiritual* to describe their cultural goals had nothing to do with established religious or cultist spiritual movements. "I am a believer," wrote Balázs in his diary, "and feel myself to be deeply religious, but I do not recognize as my home any of today's existing sects. And I also don't believe that it is possible to invent a religion and that I could make a private religion for myself."[23] Theirs was, cautioned Mannheim, only a "search for metaphysical idealism, which, however, couldn't be further removed from the dogmatic idealism of positive religions."[24]

Metaphysics was the term they used most frequently to characterize their strivings, but their definition of metaphysics, as of religion, was essentially idiosyncratic. They did not mean by metaphysics a spiritual, transcendental, otherworldly reality but rather the striving to overcome multiplicity, to create a unified and homogeneous world in which the division between spirit and matter, subject and object, form and content, art and life, had finally been overcome. "Metaphysics," wrote Anna Lesznai in her diary, "is the art of experiencing things in all their relatedness and yet individually. It is the lifting of the subject-object opposition to such a plane where they cease to be antithetical but become different aspects of one fundamental reality."[25]

The essence of metaphysics, wrote Lukács, was a natural instinct whereby man attempted to transcend his sense of separateness from the universe and thus find a meaning outside himself. It represented, in the final analysis, the demand for the unity of subject and object, and "this ultimately gives rise to an experience . . . which enables one to grasp the inner essence of the world and reach the meaning of the universe."[26]

In the final analysis, however, these attempts to encase their cultural goals in set definitions or formulations could only be provisional and approximate, for there existed no truly appropriate philosophic or religious language to describe them accurately. The nature of these strivings was more adequately reflected in occasional articles and reviews, and casual remarks and debates on such diverse subjects as the nature of postimpressionist art, the meaning of fairy tales and primitivism, the experience of mysticism and erotic passion.

In their minds these were not unrelated questions, as Anna Lesznai made clear in her diary. "What are the phenomena," she asked, "existing in society and the individual psyche, which have retained strong magical tendencies? These are art, certain facets of religion, erotic love, a whole series of spiritual experiences such as presentiment, telepathy, déjà vu, suggestibility."[27] They were fascinated, it is clear, by experiences which transcended the boundaries of modern rationalism and seemed to give a premonition of a radically new form of existence in which direct communion and identity between subject and object would be possible. The unifying emotional force behind their aspirations was the longing for what Lesznai described as the "miracle" that would "break through the walls between the self and the world."[28]

One of the realms where this "miracle" seemed to be occurring was in the scattered manifestations of experimental postimpressionist art, music, and literature which were emerging not only in Western Europe but also in Hungary in the years immediately before the First World War. Lukács, who after 1910 consciously abandoned his role as literary critic, nevertheless remained a sensitive and devoted interpreter of Balázs' poetry, in which he perceived some of the best qualities of the new experimental literature. Balázs, Lukács wrote, was attempting to create a consciously primitive artistic style which had many similarities with the simplicity and austerity of the traditional folk ballad. Such formal simplicity and "primitivism," however, expressed complicated and sophisticated cultural needs. Through it the modern poet attempted to simplify and make homogeneous the multiplicity of the world, to "reduce a spiritual event to one single moment, to the moment when fate becomes fully manifest and fills the soul's stage completely."[29] According to Lukács, Balázs the artist triumphed over the painful dualism between the self and the world by objectifying the inner drama of the self and creating out of it a complete, self-enclosed universe. Modern artists, Lukács concluded, were able to create a new kind of metaphysical unity by expanding the inner self into a cosmos from which the "oppressive limitations of the surrounding world have disappeared."[30]

For Lukács and his friends, however, the new postimpressionist art represented only one—the most recent—expression of man's innate longing for transcendence. They remained very much alive to the possibility of other forms through which the same impulse was expressed. Mysticism was one of these forms, and it became the topic of frequent Sunday afternoon discussions in Budapest after 1915. It seemed to them perhaps the universal expression of man's metaphysical impulse. As Lukács remarked in his appreciative review of Martin Buber's short stories "The Legend of Baalschem" and the "Story of Rabbi Nachmann," there existed an "astonishing congruence between all previous forms of mysticism," whether expressed through Chassidic Judaism, the philosophies of the Vedas, Plotinus, Eckehart, or Böhme.[31]

Lukács himself never explored in a serious way the nature of this congruence, but Mannheim did. His growing interest in the philosophic problems of mysticism coincided with Lukács' discovery in 1911 of Buber's work on Chassidic mysticism. The question all mystics raise, Mannheim wrote Lukács, is that of the existence of an absolute reality beyond the shifting and contingent world of empirical life. For Mannheim the ultimately mystical intuition that there must be such an absolute beyond all empirical or logical evidence became the starting point not only of his own philosophic development but generally of all philosophic inquiry. "All philosophy," he audaciously wrote Lukács, "is ultimately, in its roots, mystical."[32] During the following years Mannheim was to return to this point frequently, feeling that only mysticism had succeeded in raising the fundamental yet "unaskable question" of existence. "Mysticism," he wrote in a review of 1919, "was the conscience of philosophy, reminding it of its ultimate responsibility. This is the reason why the professional philosopher is so nervous when he comes face to face with mysticism: he feels that it reminds him of an old promise he does not wish to fulfill."[33]

Parallel to these philosophic speculations about the nature of mysticism there emerged in the Sunday Circle even more amorphous but equally important discussions about the role of erotic love in human experience. As the fragmentary records of the Sunday discussions reveal, members of the group perceived the erotic and mystical experiences to be analogous in certain ways. Both realities tended to abolish, at least temporarily, the strictly limited boundaries of individuality; to expand consciousness in a sense of communion with something outside the self. Genuine love, declared Lukács in one of the frequent debates on the subject, "redeems the individual, lifting him to his next stage of spiritual development."[34] Only in physical love, wrote Anna Lesznai at around the same time, "does the individual become one with himself, transcending the dualism of body and soul; the self becomes whole and complete and therefore Godlike, and thus, increasingly united with all of life."[35]

Not surprisingly, their remarkable sensitivity to the philosophical and psychological implications of the erotic experience found its most coherent expression in their artistic creations, particularly in the plays and poetry of Béla Balázs. Balázs, as he confessed shortly after completing his dramatic ballad "Bluebeard's Castle," had consciously set out to explore the inner drama of the erotic encounter between man and woman and the sexual struggle which inevitably accompanies such encounters. "Bluebeard's Castle," which Bartók was to set to music, almost perfectly exemplifies this favorite theme of Balázs' generation. It depicted, wrote Balázs, modern man's solitude and his unending and futile struggle to overcome it in the experience of love. In the drama, Judith gains admission into Prince Bluebeard's castle as his new bride. She proceeds, at first cautiously, then with more confidence, to throw open the hidden chambers of the man's consciousness, bringing light and happiness into the gloomy dwelling. Yet as she penetrates deeper and deeper into his soul and memories, she encounters growing resistance and antagonism. She becomes increasingly willful and reckless, insisting on opening the seventh, forbidden door, behind which lies not only the inner secret of the man's self but also the destruction of their love. Total intimacy, implied Balázs in the tragic denouement, can only lead to a struggle for possession and power, and ultimately to renewed solitude.

No matter how painstaking such explorations of the sexual struggle were, they had a serious limitation in common with attempts at systematically exploring the nature of mysticism, for both love and mysticism embody experiences whose core is ultimately inexpressible in language and therefore beyond the range of serious cultural analysis or theorizing. This limitation, however, did not apply to fairy tales, folk legends, and peasant art, which formed perhaps the strongest and most generally shared enthusiasm of the group in the prewar years. Balázs, Lesznai, and even Lukács tried their hand at the writing of fairy tales, and in the case of Lesznai and Balázs, these attempts were remarkably successful, resulting in some classics of Hungarian children's literature. These practical attempts were accompanied by extensive, almost obsessive speculations about the nature and philosophic significance of fairy tales, which they recorded in numerous diaries, conversations, and formal studies.

All fairy tales, they seemed to agree, have in common with mysticism and erotic love the impulse to overcome man's imprisonment within the self, to transcend the imperfections of empirical reality. The fairy tale is simply a primitive expression of this impulse, reaching back to an early phase of human life when man attempted to conquer the world through magic. In a fairy tale there can be no tragedy, no irreducible conflict between the self and empirical reality, because the genre does not recognize the world as foreign from the self, having laws of its

155

own. The fairy tale is a "happy art," wrote Lesznai, in which "everyone has a mission . . . and everyone can return home . . . The world can tolerate miracles because the fundamental assumption of the fairy tale is that all is right with the world. At most, it might be tilted the wrong way, but the pieces can be and must be set back in the right order eventually."[36] In this world the self can undergo transformation from frog to prince and vice versa, being freed from the "prison of a single reality" and the boundaries of an unalterable ego. It is a world in which common, unambiguous values rule and find full expression and realization at the end. Thus the real fairy tale always has a happy ending because "the inner laws of the hero are identical with the laws of his fate and of the tale itself." In other words, the fairy tale is an "antitragedy."[37]

These theories about the nature of fairy tales have great interest in themselves, but they gain added significance from the fact that they embody in a particularly detailed and uninhibited form the personal and collective aspirations of the members of the Sunday Circle. Longings which were perceived as too fantastic and irrational by even these rather unconventional individuals could find oblique expression as speculations about fairy tales. The fairy tale, Lukács admitted in one Sunday discussion, represented nothing less than "a momentary return to paradise."[38]

Such a return could be contemplated theoretically, but given the ethos of the group, could not be undertaken in a direct or obvious fashion. This ethos was defined by a certain intellectual scrupulousness, fastidiousness, even austerity, which existed in paradoxical union with their often-stated metaphysical and religious longings. If we look a little more closely at these longings, it becomes evident that they were primarily of an intellectual and theoretical nature rather than the expression of direct experience. For the Lukács group, antirational phenomena such as mysticism, erotic love, and the world of fairy tales were merely oblique symbols of metaphysical possibilities in some far-off future, rather than genuine options and solutions for the present. They in fact stated quite explicitly that neither art nor mysticism nor love could provide a lasting resolution of the cultural crisis they experienced as a generation. And their empathetic depictions of these phenomena were invariably accompanied by a critique of them as well, which highlighted their inadequacy as final solutions. Lukács, for instance, always insisted that the ability of modern artists like Balázs to create a homogeneous universe from which the painful dualism of the world had been banished was only a pseudosolution, or at best a provisional one. The modern artist had not really succeeded in redeeming a fragmented universe, in genuinely integrating the self with the world, but only in removing himself from it and expanding his inner world into a cosmos. As Lukács put it, enlarging the prison of the self into a world did not alter the fact that it was still a prison.

If art held no permanent solutions for them, neither did mysticism. Mysticism, wrote Mannheim, represented exceptional experiences for a few exceptional individuals. But what was possible for Indian ascetics or Christian saints could not bring salvation to the majority of mankind. "The unelected," he warned, "lose themselves if they try to place themselves outside empirical reality, because they can experience their inner self only through the external manifestations of their life and actions. For this reason the unelected are forced to live within life and become involved in the external cultural reality which surrounds them."[39]

Perhaps most illusory of all was the redemption held out by erotic love, which seemed to offer the possibility of self-transcendence, only to dissolve the illusion the moment love was actually attained. Balázs' "Bluebeard's Castle," as well as his love poetry, was ultimately an exploration of what Lukács tellingly described as the "cosmic hopelessness of love," an expression of the tragic realization that even the greatest love is powerless to break through the walls of individuality. Inevitably, wrote Lukács of Balázs' erotic poetry, "the circle closes again, the walls which had separated individuals once again grow high between them. All is in vain. The man remains eternally unreachable to the woman, and the woman to the man."[40] Erotic love, like other experiences of this kind, could not radically transform life but only point the way to a new metaphysics which would one day succeed in abolishing the barriers between individuals.

These ongoing reservations about the viability of love, mysticism, art, or any other nonrational solutions betray in the group of friends a deep-seated skepticism toward all possible metaphysical resolutions available to them at the time. As Lukács categorically stated in 1910, amidst all their doubts about what was to come in the future, only "one thing is certain: it will not come from pious dreamers or utopian world reformers."[41] Despite their radical hopes and projections for the future, their intellectual temper remained cautious and gradualist in the years between 1910 and 1918. Lukács' letters during this period consistently refer to the long years of study that lay before him as a necessary prelude to the achievement of his final vision. He was, in fact, not even certain, he admitted in one letter, if he himself was destined to see the realization of these distant aspirations. "The goal before me," he wrote in 1912, "appears unquestionably realizable. If I should nevertheless fail to reach it, this failure can say nothing of significance about the ultimate validity of metaphysics; it is merely a judgment about me, and *only* about me, about my lack of talent for philosophy."[42]

Balázs expressed very similar feelings in 1915, when he attempted to console Lukács for the slowness of his progress on his work: "You wrote last time . . . that you are not pleased with your work. Perhaps you are like me, or you are at the beginning of something new whose ripening has to be patiently awaited. We have time, Gyuri. Is it really important that we produce a lot? What *is* important is that we document with sharp, unambiguous clarity the new philosophy—ours—that it may be continued and may never disappear from the world."[43]

Their self-conscious gradualism and instinctive recoil from all sudden and irrational leaps of faith were ultimately based on a deeply felt if not very well examined assumption that events were inevitably moving toward their cherished goals and that, in any case, it was both wrong and futile to artificially hasten the evolution of history. But their characteristic hesitations were also determined by ingrained habits of thought and feeling, which, despite their philosophic strivings, remained unshakably individualistic, analytic, intellectual in temper. They passionately longed for an age that would be communal and religious in nature, yet at the same time they felt themselves to be the products of a rational and individualistic culture whose heritage they were not free to disregard. They felt that the solution for a communal future could come only from the recognition of that which is universal in the self, for, as Mannheim wrote Lukács in 1911, "it is through our own humanity that we have to recognize the links that connect us with others, and it is on the basis of this insight that we must forge the forms which will once more create communion between man and man."[44]

There was at the basis of this posture a scarcely acknowledged contradiction which Balázs, blessed with a less orderly mind than Mannheim's, was willing to admit from the beginning. He was seeking, he wrote in his diary in 1911, an "ultimately valid and unshakable philosophy of religion," but one, he hastened to add, that did not "offend my Enlightenment rationalism."[45] By 1917 he was able to express this same contradiction in a more sophisticated, dialectical form. "I cannot abandon the castle of my intellect," he wrote, "though I know that it will fall, but I have to remain faithful to it. Because what is important is that it be occupied in spite of everything . . . God abandons those who give themselves up to an invisible enemy. He wants to triumph over us and tear from us the weapon of our intellect by force."[46]

Theirs was an attitude of heroic stoicism which insisted on holding on to "the weapons of the intellect" even while straining after a metaphysical solution they knew to be opposed to the intellect. During these years they made the experiment of developing a philosophic posture which was content, according to Lukács, to "measure God but . . . [not to] see or experience him. One has to know and accept this with the defiant humility of the ascetic, and then there is no weakness in it."[47]

—

Perhaps nowhere did these complex attitudes and impulses find more characteristic expression than in Lukács' aesthetic philosophy, which he began in 1912, temporarily laid aside in 1915, only to abandon in incomplete form in 1918. "The Heidelberg Philosophy of Art and Aesthetics," as the fragment is usually called, is an austere, impenetrably esoteric work, ostensibly concerned with highly technical philosophic issues. The treatise, according to Lukács' stated intention, was an attempt to apply phenomenological methods to aesthetics, and through such methods to define aesthetics as an autonomous philosophic category, distinct from both empirical reality and from logic and ethics. Yet to take these goals at face value and to read "The Heidelberg Aesthetics" as a purely analytic and technical work would be to seriously misunderstand and underestimate its scope. It was, in fact, conceived with an openly metaphysical intention, as the forerunner or prologue to a future synthetic philosophy that would transcend the limitations of neo-Kantianism. "Ultimately what is at issue," Lukács admitted in one of his rare direct confessions within the work, "is the triumph over subjectivity."[48]

The individual most directly responsible for inspiring Lukács to undertake this ambitious project was the young German philosopher Ernst Bloch, whom Lukács first met in 1912; they became fast friends almost immediately. "The influence of Bloch was enormous," recalled the dying Lukács in his last account of this period of his life. Bloch convinced him that "philosophy in the grand old manner was still possible. Up until then I was in awe of the neo-Kantianism of my age. Bloch acted as if this entire philosophic tradition did not exist, . . . that it is possible even today to write philosophy the way Aristotle or Hegel wrote philosophy."[49]

Lukács' Budapest friends regarded with some uneasiness Bloch's growing influence over Lukács, though they themselves were not insensitive to the messianic intensity of Bloch's personality. "Bloch," wrote Anna Lesznai in her diary, "is a young man from Berlin who is so Talmudic that he verges on Catholicism."[50] "He is a compulsive philosopher," Balázs observed around the same time.

> There is no minute and thought in his day when he does not speak philosophy. If he puts a cube of sugar in his tea, he asks himself what is the metaphysical significance of the fact that one body dissolves to become the taste of another. He has a hypnotic influence on Gyuri which is unsettling. It is also true, however, that he has set in motion a creative period for Gyuri which surprises all of us, including Gyuri himself . . . He is a spiritual *condottieri* who is redeemed only by the fact that he is at the same time a child and a Don Quixote. Perhaps he is only an empty dreamer, but it is also possible that he will be a great man one day.[51]

Bloch's magnetic personality may have supplied the drive and emotional motivation for Lukács' aesthetic philosophy but hardly the intellectual premises and problems on which it was based.

160

*Budapest around 1890; Deák Square
near Lukács' first school*

József Lukács, Georg
Lukács' father

*Leo Popper, Lukács' closest friend
during his "essay period"*

Irma Seidler, Lukács' early love, to whom
Soul and Forms *is dedicated*

Georg Lukács as a
university student

Georg Lukács and Béla Balázs
on vacation in Italy

Lajos Fülep, a friend of Lukács' who coedited the periodical A Szellem

*Oszkár Jászi and Anna Lesznai in the background, and
in the foreground Jászi's sister, Lili Madzsar,
and the socialist theorist Ervin Szabó*

*Group portrait taken in 1909 at the premiere of Béla Balázs'
play Dr. Szélpál Margit. Front row: Lukács and Balázs.
Back row: Böske Révész, Ilona Waldbauer, Hilda Bauer,
László Révész, Edit Hajós*

Lukács around 1913

"We Want the Republic," 1918, by Mihály Biró (1886–1948):
one of the numerous political posters marking the end
of the Hapsburg monarchy and the founding of
a republic in the October revolution of 1918

"Farewell: Death Song for the Austro-Hungarian Monarchy,"
by Mihály Biró: another political poster from the
October revolution of 1918

*"Proletarians of the World Unite!" by Bertalan Pór (1880–1964):
a good example of the avant-garde poster art that flourished
during the Hungarian Socialist Republic of 1919*

Poster for May 1, 1919, by Mihály Biró

The title page of the German edition of Soul and Forms,
designed by Irma Seidler

Lukács had begun his philosophic inquiry into the nature of art with a problem which reached back to his essay period: the tragic inadequacies of nineteenth-century aestheticism which had failed to create bridges between the self and the world, between art and society. The increasingly sharp distinction between art and life, which grew out of this failure, became the focus of growing interest and study on the part not only of Lukács but also his friends. Anna Lesznai recorded a characteristic discussion on the subject in 1912, in which Ernst Bloch participated as well. "According to Bloch," she wrote,

> art represents a religious failure to complete one's task; a compromise;—for Lukács it is a countercreation; it is Luciferian because it represents a revolt . . . I feel art to be religious, for things are under a spell, compressed into a nutshell, and have to be liberated. Now, the question is whether artistic forms represent an even deeper form of alienation or (as I believe) the first stage of redemption. In that case art is a redemption and not, as Lukács maintains, a conjuring trick which creates a counterworld.[52]

Despite their internal differences, they all agreed on the essential point that art is a reality qualitatively different from empirical life; that it is not simply a more nearly perfect, more concentrated, more powerful form of communication between the artist and the world but a new, unprecedented act of creation. This perception of art was not unique to Lukács and his friends during these years. Essentially similar ideas were being advocated in numerous manifestoes of modernist, nonrepresentational art, such as Wassily Kandinsky's *Concerning the Spiritual in Art* (1911) and the *Blaue Reiter Almanach* (1912), which proliferated in the decade before the war. Most of these declarations stressed that art should not be viewed as a copy or duplicate of some prior reality existing "outside" in nature or "above" in some ideal realm. Art, as they conceived of it, was an autonomous creation which owed its existence to immanent laws of its own that had nothing to do with external nature. The radical, iconoclastic implications of this assertion, when implemented literally, became evident on the canvases of expressionist and Cubist painters, who increasingly cut their ties with all realistic or mimetic representations of nature.

The philosophic implications of this striking phenomenon in

the arts were, however, rarely examined in any systematic way. One of the most interesting attempts at such examination came from Wilhelm Worringer, a student of Georg Simmel's, who wrote a remarkably influential dissertation on the subject in 1908. In *Abstraction and Empathy*, which became well known throughout Europe in the years before the war, Worringer argued that the dramatic shift from realistic to nonrepresentational art, occurring in Europe at the turn of the century signaled nothing less than a major cosmological shift in European culture and a fundamental transformation of Western man's symbolic universe.

Artistic realism, which had characterized Western culture since at least the Renaissance, had been, argued Worringer, the expression of a unique attitude of trust and security in the external world. It had been founded on the individual's belief that the external universe was fundamentally benevolent, understandable, and controllable. The expression of this "sense of assurance . . . this unproblematic being at home in the world," wrote Worringer, was "a happy, world-revealing naturalism in art." Such periods of cosmic security, however, were anomalous and fragile episodes, interrupting ages of anxiety and insecurity in which mankind experienced the physical universe as shifting, unpredictable, potentially hostile. Such attitudes, maintained Worringer, gave rise to abstraction in art, whose goal was not to imitate or copy nature but, on the contrary, to cut loose from it and create a new reality that actually stood opposed to it. The urge for abstraction, he wrote, represented for most ages the only "possibility of repose within the confusion and obscurity of the world picture. It is the consummate expression . . . of emancipation from all the contingency and temporality of the world picture."[53] Ironically, claimed Worringer, the very rationality and technical sophistication of contemporary civilization resulted in modern man's renewed sense of cosmic insignificance and fear in face of nature. Like primitive man, the modernists too used abstraction to create an oasis of order and stability in a universe which had become alien and incomprehensible to the human intellect.

As anthropology, or even as art history, Worringer's thesis may have been fanciful, but as an expression of the broader, nonaesthetic impulses of prewar modernism, it was highly illuminating. Lukács knew Worringer's work and carried on a limited but cordial correspondence with him, sending him a copy of *Soul and Forms* when it came out in German. Though Lukács by no means regarded Worringer as a predecessor, his aesthetic philosophy was in many ways parallel to Worringer's work. Lukács too established as his starting point the rarely analyzed perception that modernist art, with its claims to radical autonomy and independence from nature, was the expression not simply of a stylistic shift from nineteenth-century realism but of a deep crisis in Western philosophy as well.

Even at the time of undertaking the aesthetic philosophy, Lukács was convinced of the originality of his approach. He sensed, as he wrote Leo Popper, that his "way of posing the problem is so original that no one has even come close to seeing it this way before."[54] Though Lukács was to revise radically his overall opinion of "The Heidelberg Aesthetics" in later life, he never changed his mind on this essential point. He liked to recount in autobiographical sketches throughout his life that his unique approach to the question of aesthetics had been the one factor responsible for the strong initial impression he had made on Max Weber in Heidelberg. As he put it shortly before his death, "I said to Max Weber at one point: Kant maintained that the essence of aesthetics is the aesthetic judgment. I maintain, there exists no a priori aesthetic judgment; the only thing that exists a priori is *Sein* [being]; *es gibt Kunstwerke, Wie sind sie möglich?* [There exist works of art. How are they possible?] This is how I put the question to Weber, and this made a very great impression on him."[55]

Lukács' memories are confirmed by outside observers, such as Paul Hönigsheim, who recounted in his reminiscences of the Weber circle that Weber had indeed been struck by Lukács' original approach to the question of art. "Whenever I have spoken with Lukács," Weber is supposed to have remarked, "I have had to think about it for days."[56] What appealed to Weber, as he himself explained in a letter to Lukács, was the younger thinker's insistence on the autonomy of the work of art and the need to examine its structure independent of all external considerations. "My impression is a very strong one," he wrote Lukács, "and I am quite sure that the posing of the problem is the definitively correct one. It is a boon that the 'work' as such is now finally given a voice after attempts to write aesthetics from the standpoint of the receiver and more recently from that of the creator. I am curious to see how it will be when your concept of forms emerges."[57]

In beginning with the question "Art exists, how is it possible?" Lukács was broaching a problem even more fundamental than that of the nature of the artistic phenomenon. He was raising the larger philosophic issue of why this particular perception of art emerged at that particular time and not before. He realized that his initial question was itself the product of an unprecedented cultural situation which needed to be explained and made self-conscious. In a series of fascinating letters written to Leo Popper between 1909 and 1910, he grappled with this question, wondering why it was that the aesthetic realm had never appeared problematic to previous generations of thinkers; why art had, until his time, been considered simply a more nearly perfect, more concentrated means of communicating some preexisting truth rather than what it actually was: a radical and thus far unexplained act of creation.

Lukács' conclusions, which remained tentative and intuitive, never finding their way into the formal aesthetic treatise, are nevertheless crucial for understanding the implicit goals and aspirations of the final work. Previous philosophers, he confided to Popper in a letter of June 1910, had overlooked the true nature of aesthetic activity because they had consistently subordinated it to a priori assumptions about the nature of reality. They had projected a preexisting metaphysical order onto the world, not realizing that the order they saw in the universe was the result, not the source, of man's aesthetic activity. The problem of all rational philosophers until that time, he elaborated in a later letter, was that they were naive and unself-conscious. They had simply failed to realize that the reality they attempted to order was already unified and homogeneous and meaningful. For such philosophers, "if we think it through logically, art is superfluous. For the world that they describe, the world which according to them is actual reality, is already *art*. Thus for them, art is simply a preposterous tautology, a weak copy of existing reality . . . They can, tragically, never reach their goal, because they are already at their goal; they run in circles, trying to overtake their own tails."[58]

Lukács' probing analysis into the broader philosophic implications of modernist aesthetics had a purpose that went far beyond disinterested scholarly curiosity. His aesthetic philosophy was in fact only a first step toward more distant and audacious goals. As he confessed to Popper, his ultimate intention was to refute and undermine all previous rational philosophies which, by denying the absolute autonomy of the work of art, had created a false, untenable image of the universe. His aesthetic philosophy, by positing the immanence of the aesthetic realm, would be at the same time an implicit "refutation of all rational philosophies, which had projected [artistic] forms onto nature, saying: forms = the world = the *Ding an sich* [thing in itself]."[59] Lukács' ambitions did not stop here, however. Though he rarely allowed himself the self-indulgence to articulate this idea, it is clear that he expected his radical philosophic criticism to lead to positive results as well. "Do you remember," he wrote Popper in December 1910, "I once mentioned to you that what I hope to accomplish is an inverted Platonism. Only now do I realize that you thought of this idea first. It is you who brought down absolutes from the sky to the earth and placed them within the soul of man, within the brush of the painter and chisel of the sculptor. Our task now is to rebuild the palace of absolute ideas here on earth, for the old one has collapsed, having been built only on words."[60]

What is perhaps most remarkable about these broad metaphysical aspirations underlying Lukács' work is the immense reticence he felt about expressing them directly. He seemed to consider them intimate elements of his private life, to be shared with close friends like Leo Popper or trusted groups of friends like Weber's circle in Heidelberg and the Sunday Circle in Budapest, but not to be indiscriminately promulgated in print.

Certainly, nowhere in "The Heidelberg Aesthetics" did Lukács refer directly to these goals. One finds in the formal aesthetic philosophy two distinct but interrelated themes which Lukács developed, repeated, and intertwined like musical motifs in a symphonic composition. The first of these was the elaboration of the idea that the work of art is a utopian reality, distinct and separate from the empirical world. The second was the attempt to analyze the structure of this utopian reality, with a view to unmasking it, and showing it to be only an illusion of perfection, or as he often called it in private conversations, a "Luciferian antiworld" which only anticipated "the harmony before true redemption."[61]

Of these two themes, Lukács was far more successful with the first, which he explored with a lyrical intensity reminiscent of his earlier essays in *Soul and Forms*. The perception of art as utopia, as a perfected microcosm distinct from empirical reality, was itself the sign of man's terrible alienation in the world, he wrote late in 1911, shortly after Popper's death. It was predicated on the opening of a chasm between "life and work, the world and forms, between the creator, the work, the forms, and the audience." Such a view of art could emerge only after the individual had become aware of the "horrible inadequacy of life, when he came to see that in empirical life all things are driven by blind force and governed by falsified fictions."[62]

In contrast to the formless, fragmented; alienated world, the work of art was to Lukács the embodiment of harmony, homogeneity, completeness, community. Art creates "a perfect world, which, in the immediacy of its physical reality, silences all pain and suffering . . . which exists in the here and now with undeniable concreteness and yet seems to have descended from regions far removed from the evanescence of the present." The aesthetic realm abolishes the painful separation between object and subject, the gulf between reality and values, the chasm between being and possibility, because everything that is possible in it, according to its constitutive principles, becomes reality in it. Here and only here, Lukács concluded, "the categories of 'possible,' 'real,' and 'necessary' become absolutely identical and lose their distinctness." Art, in fact, is the only activity in life in which man gains the illusion of fully communicating the deepest realities of his subjective self: "Whatever the artists want to tell us in their works . . . comes to us in unbroken and authentic form, and when it reaches us, the world that surrounds us is freed of its frequently oppressive incoherence, of its tormenting silence: it becomes simple, clear, communicative, and self-evident."[63]

Despite the emotional intensity of such passages, Lukács' basic intention in "The Heidelberg Aesthetics" was not to glorify the work of art as the only utopia possible in an imperfect world. On the contrary, he meant to undermine this perception, to show it as the illusion that it was. As he pointed out, the ful-fillment offered by art could never be anything other than "is-lands within the sea of fragmentation and struggle after unity . . . For this reason we have to abandon the world of art, and looking at it from the distance, as an alien reality, we have to learn to . . . understand the true structure of the work of art and the exact relationship of its constituent parts."[64]

Lukács' shift in perspective from an internal to an external view revealed novel, hitherto unexplored aspects of the aesthetic phenomenon. When viewed from the outside, it became evi-dent, Lukács argued, that the redemption offered in art was only an illusion, a mirage which deceived both the creator and the viewer. The tragic inadequacy of the aesthetic experience was perhaps most acute in the case of the artistic creator, who, once he had completed his work, lost all living connection with it. The completed work of art became an autonomous, alien object which confronted the artist in all its perfection without redeeming him or leaving him better off than ordinary men. Having completed their work, Lukács wrote, artists remain more "mute and voiceless" than ordinary men. "And though their works are the embodiment of the highest perfection human beings can reach, they themselves remain the most unhappy, the least redeemed individuals among their fellow human beings."[65]

If the work of art cannot redeem the artist, even less so can it redeem the spectator. The work of art, it is true, appears to have transcended the limitations of rational, linear discourse and gives the impression of being able to communicate subjective truths and inner experiences. "It seems," Lukács mused, "that art is the one sphere where the directness of communication does not take place at the expense of oversimplification, and thus as if it were able to abolish all individual anxiety and worry over being imprisoned in the subjective self." However, Lukács then raised the question whether the aesthetic experience does in fact communicate new truths to the receiver, whether there is any guarantee at all that in the work of art the receiver has experienced the same reality that the artist did and meant to communicate. The answer, of course, is that there is no guar-antee at all; that in fact the enduring quality of all great art proves indubitably that the work of art can suggest only very general schema which the individual fills with his own subjective ex-

167

periences. The work of art can mobilize experiences and emotions within the range of the individual's own reality but can never convey totally new experiences. Thus art can enrich the world of the individual but can "never break through the hermetic isolation of this world by bringing to it truly new, qualitatively different perceptions."[66]

These intricate formulations about the nature of the aesthetic phenomenon had, as Lukács well knew, overwhelmingly negative and critical implications. By showing that art was an autonomous realm distinct from ordinary existence, Lukács was actually challenging all doctrines of naturalism and realism which had considered art merely a reflection of nature. Then, by proceeding to expose the illusory nature of the aesthetic utopia, Lukács was also discrediting the more recent theories of aestheticism and art for art's sake which had attempted to hold up art as an alternative to empirical reality.

Yet Lukács' success in demolishing or undermining all existing philosophies of art proved to be a Pyrrhic victory, for these critical methods did not, and could not, lead to the positive results Lukács had originally envisioned in his written conversations with Leo Popper in 1909 and 1910. As the fragmentary state of "The Heidelberg Aesthetics" indicates, once Lukács had succeeded in showing that art was neither a copy of nature nor a utopian substitute for the inadequacies of life, he could proceed no further. The ultimate question as to how art was possible, how aesthetic activity created order and values out of the undifferentiated chaos of empircial life, kept eluding Lukács, no matter how hard he strained for a solution. It is striking that whenever Lukács attempted to address these issues, he was inevitably reduced to irrational, semimystical explanations. The work of art, he was forced to admit, was a "miracle," a "paradox," a "mystery," an "improbability or even impossibility become reality." Aesthetic creation, he concluded, "is always a leap, always something which, from the standpoint of unaided personality, is inexplicable. Yet its potentiality exists within the personality and only needs the spark of grace which, with the explosion of the leap, brings into existence the work of art."[67]

Lukács' inability to substitute for the discredited theories of the past a positive aesthetic philosophy of his own cannot ultimately be explained through an internal analysis of "The Heidelberg Aesthetics." The failure lay, as Lukács was to realize in retrospect, within the fundamental premises of the work itself, which were paradoxical and ultimately nonviable. He had set out, he wrote shortly before his death more than fifty years later, to write an ontology of aesthetics and had ended up writing a metaphysical critique of aesthetics.[68]

What the older Lukács failed to add, however, is that these two tasks—the one constructive and the other destructive—had not appeared contradictory to the philosopher of the prewar years. On the contrary, the young Lukács had been convinced that only by criticizing and eventually undermining all established philosophies of art could he arrive at positive solutions of his own. As he wrote to an acquaintance in the summer of 1911: "What I aim for is to point out as clearly and forcefully as possible the inhumanity of pure artistic forms, their rigid and absolute separateness from ordinary life. [Such separation] is the essential and necessary precondition for any viable philosophy of art; and it is something which has never been accomplished with sufficient rigor. Whether at the end of this task there emerges some kind of vital truth, some kind of true and eternal life for me personally—that I cannot tell at the beginning of my task."[69]

The note of uncertainty as to the eventual outcome of his work was mostly rhetorical—the assumed modesty of a young scholar who knows himself to be in the forefront of a new field of inquiry. During this phase of his life Lukács had little doubt that a novel, hitherto undiscovered theory of art would eventually emerge from his purely critical, destructive work in aesthetics. "Positive answers are still far off," he admitted to Popper in 1910. "They are not really important at this point. But I think I am finally able to tell you what the goal of my book will be: to describe the crisis of our present notions, from which, it is to be hoped, the solutions will automatically emerge."[70]

As these early letters indicate, the young Lukács' entire aesthetic philosophy was based on the paradoxical but deeply held belief that only by sharpening the critical tendencies of his age could he hope to establish the basis for a future philosophic integration. This faith was not unique to Lukács, of course, but was part of a more general cultural attitude he shared with the friends and acquaintances who gathered around him during these years. As a generation, they were convinced that their philosophic mission was an essentially negative and critical one, for only by destroying the last vestiges of a discredited past could they hope to pave the way to a new future. As Lukács put it in 1911, only after they had solved all the remaining philosophic questions inherited from the past could they begin to "lay the foundations for a great new synthetic philosophy that could create a culture and become a worthy successor to the great past."[71]

It was Karl Mannheim who perhaps expressed most eloquently the paradoxical nature of their collective task as a generation. What united them, he wrote in his essay *Soul and Culture* (Lélek és kultúra) in 1918, was not necessarily common opinions or interests as scholars but rather a shared relationship of distance and estrangement from the objective culture surrounding them. This tragic historic situation necessarily defined the nature of their tasks and attitudes as intellectuals, for the perspective of outsiders allowed them to perceive the formal, structural elements of culture in a way not possible for earlier, more fortunately located generations. Given their unique angle of vision, it was natural for them to undertake such critical researches as "logic, aesthetics, the philosophy of history," which for the first time allowed them to present culture in a "unified cross-section." But this purely critical activity, Mannheim stressed, was only the prelude, the necessary preparation for a new religious age of the future:

> That the structure of the objective culture around us has become transparent . . . is connected to our historical situation. And I think it is the appearance of new subjective realities which has alienated us from the old structure, making them transparent in our eyes. We as individuals cannot yet speak of the form that these new objective realities will take; such developments can only be the result of the collective life of entire epochs . . . It may never be granted us to see the new contents embodied in the clarity of new cultural forms, yet we believe that we have, nevertheless, prepared the way for the new culture by making the old one comprehensible.[72]

Lukács and his friends created a coherent cultural identity out of the very imperfections and incompleteness of their life task. Their negative, critical work was given ultimate meaning by the positive promise of the future. And, as Lukács put it, the tragic isolation of his generation was lifted beyond tragedy by its faith in its mission. People like themselves, Lukács concluded, "do not create positive culture and do not want to create positive culture; the sanctity of their lives comes from the loss of all illusions. They do not create a positive culture, but they act as if they lived in one; they act in such a way as to deserve to live in one. The atmosphere of their entire life could perhaps best be defined by one of Kant's deepest categories, the category of *als ob* [as if]. This heroism, which expects nothing, is what justifies and sanctifies their lives."[73]

This curiously complicated posture of theirs, poised between radical negation and apocalyptic expectation, proved to be a fragile one which, in the long run, could not realize those all-encompassing metaphysical goals that it aimed for. In retrospect it is clear that the enterprise was doomed to fall short of its radical aspirations, in part because it was still based on axioms unconsciously inherited from the traditions of rational philosophy it was trying to displace. Ultimately the group's basis for optimism rested on the deeply humanistic assumptions that the historical process had an immanent telos which would gradually unfold from the vestiges of the past, and that criticism and reason were potentially positive as well as negative tools that could help bring about the positive solutions of the future.

Though their posture was based on assumptions that were philosophically problematic, or at any rate unself-conscious, it proved to be nevertheless an immensely fertile one in the realm of artistic and cultural innovation. The very passion of their optimism generated an explosion of creative energies which successfully undermined the last vestiges of liberal high culture. In this development, Lukács and his friends were typical of the various avant-garde groups in Western Europe during the pre-war years, for the paradoxical dualism which the Hungarian circle chiseled to such infinite refinement during these years underlay, in less exaggerated and less self-conscious forms, most of the achievements of the early modernists. As their statements and manifestoes from the early years of the century make clear, they all shared a general perception that their iconoclastic art was both the manifestation of a broadly based cultural crisis and the potential solution of that crisis.

Perhaps even more intensely than the romanticists, the modernist innovators felt themselves to be involved in an enterprise that went beyond merely artistic and technical experimentation. Their intention was not only to break from the forms and techniques of nineteenth-century realism but also to give voice to a radically new kind of artistic intention which, in Kandinsky's words, was devoted "not to the reproduction of natural phenomena, but rather, to the expression of the artist's soul." Nor was there any doubt in their minds that there existed a direct link between this new artistic impulse and the larger cultural and ideological crisis of their time. "When religion, science, and morality are shaken," wrote Kandinsky, "the last two by the strong hand of Nietzsche, and when the outer supports threaten to fall, man turns his gaze from externals in on himself."[74] Hofmannsthal expressed the same idea when he wrote that the new art "was born from a terrible doubting of the world . . . and with its existence, it now covered over forever the dreadful chasm of yawning nothingness."[75]

At the heart of the modernist affirmation was a powerful if vaguely defined messianism which assumed that the new art was destined to point the way out of "the spiritual darkness, insecurity, ignorance, and fear"[76] in which modern man found himself. It contained what Stephen Spender has called a "pattern of hope" based on the belief that "art might re-connect the life, which has been driven inwards into the isolated being of the artist, with the external world by accomplishing a revolution in the lives of people converted to share the vision of modern creation."[77]

Diffuse and intellectually unresolved as these notions remained, they were strong enough to form the basis of a seemingly new artistic philosophy which consciously repudiated all previous theories of art, but especially that of art for art's sake. Art, the early modernists declared, was not a rarefied, isolated realm of beauty, created as an escape from the real world, but rather a dynamic process indissolubly linked to the living forces of society. The French cubist poet Guillaume Apollinaire expressed these new activist, socially engaged views of art quite bluntly. "The new poets," he wrote in 1918, "are creators, inventors, and prophets; the attention they demand for their work is for the greatest good of the collectivity to which they belong . . . The new spirit is above all the enemy of aestheticism, formulas, and all snobbism. It does not reject any particular school because it does not aim to be an artistic school but one of those broad movements of culture which transcend all schools since Symbolism and naturalism."[78]

Despite the energy and conviction of such pronouncements, they had at their core a serious flaw which Lukács was gradually uncovering in his aesthetic philosophy of these years. The modernists repudiated the claims of aestheticism only in words, not in fact, and despite a shift in emphasis, the modernists' theory of art did not differ in essentials from that of their predecessors. Their claim that the work of art was an autonomous reality independent of external nature turned out to be only a more extreme, more consistent expression of the aestheticists' earlier demands for independence from external social, moral, and political pressures on their art. Their desire to create a new artistic idiom that, in Kandinsky's words, was to help raise "the spiritual pyramid which will some day reach to heaven,"[79] resulted not in a new, objective culture but in a more thoroughgoing individualism than even the Impressionists and Symbolists could have conceived of.

These fatal weaknesses inherent in the early modernist enterprise were, however, not apparent in the first years of its development. They would probably have manifested themselves gradually over time, but the outbreak of the war crystalized them in a particularly brutal and unambiguous fashion. Visions of a universal rebirth of culture faded abruptly as the first total war in European history unfolded a vastly different alternative.

6

WAR AND THE
FRAGMENTATION
OF THE SUNDAY CIRCLE

The outbreak of the First World War came
as a violent, and on the whole unexpected,
intrusion into the lives of Lukács and his
friends. "We are at war! What is more, in
a world war!" wrote the shocked Balázs
in July 1914. With characteristic self-
consciousness, he immediately wondered
why he had not seen the catastrophe coming and what impression his singular
shortsightedness would make on some future historian. "How will it seem," he
mused, "when many years from now,
someone reading this diary will suddenly
come across in it: 'We are at war!' How is
it possible that there has never been any
mention of politics in these pages, of the
society and people living around me? Was
it simply frivolity or fate?"[1]

Despite his chronic self-absorption, Balázs had an unerring instinct for the important problems, if not answers, raised by
the events unfolding around him. He was
already intuitively touching upon the root

of the dilemma that was to preoccupy him and his friends throughout the war years. The dilemma was twofold: first, it had to do with the group's hitherto unresolved relationship to the world of politics, which, by 1918, in the context of total war and accelerating social and political disintegration in Hungary, could no longer be ignored or postponed; and second, it concerned the broader and more fundamental issue of the viability of their prewar cultural posture, with its peculiar mixture of messianism and radical individualism, in the changed political and cultural ethos of postwar Europe. There were to be no immediate or unambiguous answers to these complex questions, but the inexorable pressure of inner and outer events was to shatter the former consensus among the group of friends, exposing the inner tensions and contradictions of their collective aspirations.

The question of political engagement was to play a particularly important role in Lukács' life. In late December 1918 he joined the Communist party of Hungary, setting out on what he later aptly called his "path toward Marxism."[2] Lukács' sudden turn toward revolutionary Marxist politics in late 1918, a decision he shared with over half the members of the Sunday Circle, was in many respects a complicated, overdetermined event, which cannot adequately be described within any single explanatory framework or paradigm. As Lukács himself, along with scholars like Michael Löwy, rightly stressed, this decision to become a communist "grew logically out of . . . [Lukács'] previous development"[3] and was intimately related to the "romantic anticapitalism"[4] implicit in his prewar position. And yet the politicization of cultural radicals like Lukács in late 1918 would have been inconceivable without the powerful pressure of such external political events as the Russian Revolution of 1917, the collapse of the Hapsburg monarchy in October 1918, and the emergence of Béla Kun's short-lived Bolshevik regime in Hungary in 1919.

Ultimately, however, the logic of personal development and the vicissitudes of the political world could only act as catalysts, crystalizing the inherent paradoxes of a philosophic and cultural posture which was unstable and precarious to begin with. As Lukács was later to realize, the ambitious enterprise he had undertaken in his "Heidelberg Philosophy of Art and Aesthet-

175

ics" was ultimately unrealizable in the form he had conceived it. "Here," he recalled in his last autobiographical account, "I had maneuvered a theory into a dead end. There was no direct way out. Therefore, if all things had gone according to plan, I could have become an interesting, rather eccentric university professor in Heidelberg."[5]

Gradually Lukács and his friends were forced to acknowledge the fact that their cultural messianism, which had been anchored in the assumption that communal values are compatible with individual freedom, that metaphysical transcendence could be achieved without abdicating reason, could not be continued indefinitely in the face of evidence to the contrary, and that a choice between the antithetical poles of their vision was inevitable. The necessity of this choice was eloquently expressed in a contemporary novel, by a main character closely modeled on Lukács:

> Individual existence has the tendency to pass without meaning, falling back into nature like the leaves of a tree. In previous ages, the defense against this fate lay in the development of individuality . . . in the realization of a creative act or a work of art. In our time however . . . such a separate deed means that the individual places himself beyond history and the will to redemption which today has no other embodiment and stage than politics. Today, everyone who wants to give objective sense to his existence has to surrender his separate existence; the separate mission of the individual has ceased to make sense because we are in complete darkness . . . and whoever does not want to wade through the darkness remains in the dark no matter where he may stray.[6]

Lukács' formulation, with its overtly anti-individualistic conclusions, formed, however, only one possible response to the historical crisis of 1914–19. Others, like Mannheim and Lesznai, confronting identical circumstances, came to the opposite conclusion, feeling that the communal and metaphysical elements of their prewar strivings had been the anomaly, and that individuality was the inescapable goal as well as burden of human existence. "I see now," wrote the chastened Lesznai in the 1920s,

> that the kind of love I strove for . . . is a mystic wonder and therefore can never become a permanent and objectified fact of

life; it comes as a grace of God, but it cannot be willed. One cannot base one's life on it. My mistake was perhaps that I wanted to force this divine grace, which is the foretaste of a future impossibility, into an actual, institutionalized social order. The bankruptcy of my forty-six-year existence lies in the realization that this one thing which I wanted with my whole being cannot completely be realized either through art, or through love, or through motherhood. One remains ultimately alone, and if one longs after spiritual communion, one can play with one's God, but only play with the idea.[7]

Both Lukács' and Lesznai's confessions, with their undercurrent of self-sacrifice or resignation, signaled the bankruptcy of those collective hopes and aspirations which had united them as a generation before the war. These hopes, which received the coup de grace during the political crisis of late 1918 in Hungary, had in fact already been radically undermined and eroded by the realities of four years of war, which Lukács and his friends experienced with unusual and tragic intensity.

—

Like other European intellectuals in the summer of 1914, the Hungarian cultural radicals found themselves caught off guard by the outbreak of hostilities and were left lacking any sort of collective attitude toward the events unfolding around them. Yet by the autumn of 1915, when they formally organized the Sunday Circle, they had become united in an unambiguous hatred for and condemnation of the war. The writings of Balázs and Lukács during the autumn of 1914 and early 1915 are especially revealing of the process whereby even opposite initial reactions to the war coalesced into almost identical conclusions by late 1915.

Balázs shocked his friends and family by volunteering for active military duty in August 1914. His reasons for this step, which he compulsively discussed, analyzed, and reanalyzed, were more complicated than they appeared on the surface. He wanted, he wrote in his diary, to atone for his "monomaniacal individualism." He hoped to "pay back a debt and create links with [his] society by risking [his] life and taking part in its struggles."[8] But the war represented for Balázs something even more complicated than a way of identifying with the national community. It also seemed to offer entry into the primitive world of male camaraderie and high adventure. "The men," he wrote in his published war memoir, "who for hundreds of years have been separated from one another by female arms, have somehow once again found one another. It is a moving, remorseful, mutual rediscovery. A return home among the men."[9] Ultimately Balázs began to see in the war a highly irrational symbol of fate or destiny that was to be mysteriously revealed to him in the extremity of battle. In a strikingly Kafkaesque image he compared his anticipation of battle to the feelings of "a petty bureaucrat whose entire existence depends on a bureau chief he has never set eyes on. Then one day, he is summoned into the inner office, and he puts on his black coat to personally receive his orders."[10]

Balázs was acute enough to realize from the start that his complicated emotions about the war had little to do with political or national enthusiasm. Even while impatiently awaiting his marching orders, he remained markedly unaffected by the reports of the newspapers and almost completely skeptical about the publicly proclaimed goals of the war. "I read in the papers," he wrote, "that the German government has called the Russians liars, the Russians the Germans, the Germans the French, etc. etc. The probability is that they all lie and cheat, and even if they don't it is not for moral considerations that they refrain. The diplomats lie, cheat, forge, steal, and in the end, the soldiers murder."[11]

There was a curious and not unfamiliar contradiction in Balázs' position, which was characterized by a deep longing to belong to a group and an equally deep skepticism about all existing communities and causes. His uncensored emotions drew him toward the communal experience of war while his judgment and intellect condemned everything about the war. He was uncomfortably aware of this paradox, and he actually attempted to resolve it dialectically. The final stage of his development, he explained in his diary, was to be "a mystical anarchism, but I have to earn the right to this. Only after I have done the most that a man can do for the collectivity, only after I have offered up my life in its war, only then will I have the right to say: and now, adieu!"[12]

Balázs need not have wasted his dialectical skills in reconciling the conflicts of his position; his experience on the front proved to be a disappointment in any case. The heroic community he had hoped to discover in battle turned out to be only a fantasy. Even in the midst of the most dramatic situations, he remembered afterwards, he remained in the grip of his old self-consciousness, more "preoccupied with what was happening within myself than with the outside world." By March 1915, after recovering from a serious illness contracted on the front, he had to admit to himself, "How little effect the sight of misery, suffering, death had on me. It is true that I was miraculously spared the worst sights, and though I was everywhere, there is perhaps no soldier who saw so little of the horrors of war than I. But what I saw appears cloudy and insubstantial in my mind."[13]

What remained real, and if anything became intensified, was his original mistrust of institutions, his abiding dislike for all political and ideological systems. The war confirmed in his mind the hollowness of the professed values of European liberal society, which, as he wrote Lukács in December 1914, "suppresses a hundred million small individual conflicts only to horde them up in one huge collective slaughter involving hundreds of millions."[14]

Lukács came to similar conclusions about the same time, without Balázs' tragicomic military detour. When war was declared, Lukács was living in Heidelberg, working on his aesthetic philosophy, which he had every reason to believe would gain him an academic post in Germany. Perhaps his strongest initial reaction to August 1914 was shock at the unqualified enthusiasm German friends like Max and Marianne Weber, Georg Simmel, and Thomas Mann showed toward the war. In an unfinished article entitled "The German Intellectuals and the War," Lukács lashed out against his friends, characterizing their state of mind as "general, spontaneous euphoria, lacking all clear and positive content."[15] The article was, however, more than an act of reproach leveled at friends whom Lukács considered morally deluded. It was also a bitter if curiously indirect indictment of the war itself, containing in compressed form the essential points of his antiwar posture.

The war, Lukács began, had given rise to a new kind of heroism which had less to do with individual courage and chivalry, as was the case in former wars, than with discipline, obedience to orders, and ultimately the total abdication of personality. The modern soldier, created by universal conscription and the psychological pressures of the mass army, was interchangeable with his fellows and anonymous even to the point of lacking personal hatred for the enemy. Lukács saw proof of this in the fact that soldiers in the war frequently fraternized with the enemy, whom they considered not hostile aliens but fellow sufferers.

Whatever historical accuracy his analysis may have had, its polemical intention was unmistakable and consistent with his earlier views on modern society. Lukács was no pacifist then or later, and he could lay aside his instinctive dislike of violence if that violence was directed toward goals he approved of. What he abhorred in the war of 1914 was not its senseless slaughter but rather its anonymity and impersonality. It lacked, Lukács implied, genuine goals or comprehensible principles which could have provided meaning for the sacrifices of individuals. It reduced soldiers to tools of murder who carried out their tasks simply as a matter of duty, without even hating the enemy. For Lukács the ultimate lesson of the war was a familiar one, though presented in infinitely more tragic terms than in the world of peacetime: the individual in modern society had become utterly powerless, reduced to helpless passivity by a world he had created but over which he had lost control.

Balázs, who knew of Lukács' sentiments, closely identified with them, and in fact, drew conclusions from them that Lukács only implied at this point. "Your writing about the impact of the war on you," he wrote Lukács in December 1914,

> affected me strongly. Almost the same thing happened to me, though perhaps with a different emphasis. As you will see from my war memoirs, to be published by *Nuygat*, it started with socialism [sic!]. But it seems it will end with complete (though amorphous) anarchism. For I have come to realize that every human collectivity which has a common, possibly centralized administration, is, of necessity, immoral. It lacks a focus and combustion point for moral responsibility. Only the individual can possess moral responsibility . . . Today, every existing collectivity can only be the source of open and unabashed egotism.[16]

By 1915 these extreme conclusions were, significantly, not unique to Lukács and Balázs. To varying degrees they were shared by their entire circle of Budapest friends, many of whom had just recently returned to Hungary from research trips or prolonged sojourns abroad and seemed as impervious to nationalistic rhetoric as Lukács and Balázs. As a group they felt an overpowering sense of hopelessness and helplessness in the face of a world that seemed to have gone mad around them. Their reaction was an even more uncompromising withdrawal from external political realities than before the war. They were, wrote Lukács in an oblique reference to the Sunday Circle, like a small band of exiles "retreating from the war psychosis of their environment in the same way that the characters of the *Decameron* retreated from the plague."[17]

In many respects the war simply reinforced and intensified their earlier rejection of liberal culture, providing concrete political evidence for their uncompromising critique of the modern world. Contemporary Europe, they concluded, as it manifested itself in the first world war, had become an ossified civilization that bore no living connection or relationship to the inner realities of individuals. The gulf between the subjective and the objective, between the world of values and empirical reality, between authentic and inauthentic existence, had widened to such an extent that no reconciliation seemed possible. As György Káldor, one of the youngest members of the Sunday Circle, put it in 1919, "The outbreak and continuation of this war have become living proof of the truth a chosen few have possessed and proclaimed for a long time . . . that we are witnessing the last convulsions of a dying civilization, that the eternal forms which characterized the spiritual life of previous ages . . . have become empty of meaning."[18]

Such catastrophic views of contemporary culture were by this time not entirely without a responsive echo from the larger cultural world. From the middle years of the war on, the Sunday Circle began to exercise a limited but unmistakable impact on young Hungarian intellectuals radically disaffected from the old order and hungering for a philosophy more spiritually compelling than any liberalism could offer. Lukács in particular was becoming the focal point of a youthful following, which Balázs observed with considerable irony. "It is amazing," he wrote in 1917, "how immensely Gyuri's reputation has increased here over the years. He is starting to have a growing circle of admirers, though most of them hardly know why they praise him."[19] These flickering signs of public recognition did not go unnoted by Fülep, either, who expressed downright uneasiness at the prospect of their success. "Until now we have been twelve fishermen," he confided to Balázs in 1918, "and now we might turn into an apostolic church."[20]

Despite such fears, they decided in early 1917 to organize a series of lectures through which they hoped to summarize their collective goals and clarify their philosophic outlook for the younger generation. The lecture series, which they called the Free School for Humanistic Studies (Szellemi Tudományok Szabad Iskolája), proved even more successful than they had anticipated, attracting approximately seventy regular students. "I have never seen such a good, attentive, inspired, and grateful audience in Budapest," Balázs congratulated himself in 1917. "We have done well with this."[21]

The series of lectures continued for two semesters, the first opening in the spring of 1917 and the second in the early winter of 1918. Not limited to any particular subject matter or even discipline, they covered issues as varied as aesthetics, discussed by Lukács, Balázs, and Hauser; phenomenology, by Sándor Varjas; Marxism, by Ervin Szabó; and Hungarian folk music and modern music, by Kodály and Bartók.[22] Despite the enormous diversity of topics, these lectures were conceived and presented with a unified object in mind. "Nothing is farther from our intentions," declared Mannheim in the keynote address to the second semester of lectures, "than to bring to the school a haphazardly selected group of individuals to lecture on various and sundry themes that happen to interest them." What unified the lectures, he claimed, was not so much their content as the common perspective from which the lecturers approached their subject and the common assumptions of radical opposition to existing culture that pervaded their methods. They all belonged, he said,

> to a novel type of European intellectual just in the process of evolving. This new spiritual type substitutes the problem of transcendence for outworn materialism, the universal validity of principles for relativistic impressionism, the pathos of normative ethics for an anarchic world view . . . We know that the representatives of the new culture are already numerous in Europe, possibly even in Hungary. Our lectures aim merely to help them get acquainted

with one another and to draw strength from the consciousness of a new generational unity.[23]

The Free School for Humanistic Studies was the culminating expression of a sense of generational solidarity which had been gathering force among the group of friends since at least 1910. It gave voice not only to their extreme alienation from contemporary cultural forms but also to their passionate belief that their analysis of these cultural forms was in some way destined to contribute to the birth of a new, nonalienated world. Nevertheless, these common assumptions, based on prewar theoretical premises, were also in the process of being radically undermined by new perceptions and intuitions emerging from their apocalyptic visions of the war and destruction around them. If modern civilization had truly become an alien reality existing beyond human values—as they were beginning to feel—then their hopes for a cultural revival to emerge gradually from within this civilization might turn out to be utterly quixotic and unattainable.

The extremity of despair manifest in their common reactions to the war fostered a state of mind that was potentially just as receptive to a religious leap of faith as to long-range cultural goals and projects. Fascination with overtly religious and mystical solutions did, in fact, grow appreciably among members of the Sunday Circle by the end of the war years. According to Anna Lesznai, their discussions frequently focused on religious thinkers like Kierkegaard or Meister Eckhardt and other medieval mystics, and words like *redemption, salvation,* and *transcendence* became key concepts in their ongoing debates. Yet these new overtly religious concerns never entirely preempted or challenged the cultural and philosophic strivings of the prewar years. They simply existed as a radical undercurrent of thought and feeling which developed parallel to their older concerns, intertwining with them in a way that transformed the emotional texture of their views without actually changing their philosophic underpinnings.

Perhaps the only thinker in the group who seemed to be self-conscious about the potential contradiction between their religious and cultural interests was Georg Lukács, who for deeply personal reasons was already sensitized to the implications of a

religious breakthrough for his work. In his case the conflict between religious longings and gradualist cultural commitments
was quite an explicit one which he later acknowledged as the
leading motif of the war years. During these years, he wrote
shortly before his death, "opposing ideological tendencies and
world outlooks waged battle within me. Thus, parallel with the
development of those idiosyncratic philosophic currents which
were to lead me to Marxism, there also continued my former
idealistic assumptions, which not only remained dominant but
reached their maximum unfolding [during these years]."[24]

The inner battle between these opposing currents began in 1915,
when Lukács suddenly laid aside his aesthetic philosophy in
order to commence work on what he hoped would be a book
on Dostoevsky. Max Weber, personally involved in Lukács' academic career, strongly disapproved of this step, fearing that
his protégé's sudden detour showed a lack of serious commitment to sustained scholarship. For this reason, he later wrote
Lukács, "I hated and still hate this work of yours [the Dostoevsky
book] . . . If you truly find it an insufferable burden and frustration to complete a systematic work before beginning another,
then with a heavy heart, I advise you to give up all thought of
habilitation."[25] Weber had no way of knowing that Lukács had
not definitively abandoned his aesthetic philosophy or his ambitions for a German academic career. But the outbreak of the
war had unleashed such profound emotional and intellectual
turmoil in him that he had no choice but to confront these reactions in the context of an entirely new kind of work that was
not bound by the formal, scholarly framework of aesthetic philosophy.

In the introduction to the Dostoevsky book, which he later
published as *The Theory of the Novel*, Lukács returned to the
themes of his essay period, using aesthetic and historical categories as avenues for self-confession. As in the early essays,
here too the fundamental contrast was between the closed, organic ages of the past, this time embodied in the Homeric epics
of classical Greece, and the fragmented world of modern Europe,
exemplified in the art form of the novel. If anything, the contrast
between these two aesthetic forms, which were really anti-

thetical ways of relating to the world, gained sharpened expression in the later book. With a lyrical pathos unmatched in the essays of *Soul and Forms*, Lukács painted a Homeric world of innocence and harmony where the individual was still at one with the world and with himself. In the Homeric epic, Lukács wrote, "the soul does not yet know inner conflicts which seduce it down into the depths or drive it up into the pathless mountains . . . [Here] being and fate, adventure and fulfillment, life and essence, are still identical concepts."[26]

The world of the novel, by contrast, was one of separation, of eternal homelessness, where individuals lived tragically estranged not only from each other but also from the objective world of nature and the metaphysical realm of God. In passages that provide a transparent mirror of his state of mind during the early years of the war, Lukács described his anguish in the face of a world he perceived as literally godforsaken. In such a world the weight of institutions assumed demonic power over individuals, and traditional ethical and intellectual concepts no longer provided guidance or assurance. The novel, he wrote, "is the epic of a world that had been abandoned by God; the psychological reality of the novel's hero exists in the realm of the demonic; the objectivity of the novel comes from the mature insight that intellect is never able to completely penetrate the world and that the world without intellect falls back into the chaos of meaninglessness." The novel, Lukács repeated several times, can only be described in Fichtean terms, "as the characteristic form of an age of absolute evil, and while the world remains under the power of this star, the novel will remain its ruling aesthetic form."[27]

The stark dichotomies of this essay, with its intense nostalgia for an idealized past and its equally intense hatred for an imperfect present, recall the traditional themes of cultural criticism. Yet, as Lukács later correctly warned, *The Theory of the Novel* was not a continuation of the past but rather "an explosive work" leading toward revolutionary conclusions.[28] It represented, in fact, Lukács' first formal attempt to transcend the dichotomies of the past and to repudiate the premises of cultural criticism.

These revolutionary tendencies found expression in two new themes which surfaced for the first time in *The Theory of the Novel.*

The first was the emergence of the demonic motif in his analysis of modern society, which now for the first time was described not simply as an ossified, lifeless civilization but as a demonic one, radically cut off from the realm of the divine. The other was a hitherto unsounded note of resignation in the face of this world of absolute evil. The novel, Lukács pointed out repeatedly in the course of the book, was the specific art form of "developed manhood," of "ripe adulthood," of "disenchanted maturity." It was characterized, he insisted, by a pervasive melancholy stemming from the insight that mankind was powerless to transcend its metaphysical estrangement through creative effort or will. The individual, Lukács concluded for the first time, could never be the source of new values, of metaphysical truths. The individual subject could "annihilate the objective world, but it remains forever incapable of creating out of itself the totality of life."[29]

The philosophic implications of these new themes were momentous, though they were not spelled out explicitly in *The Theory of the Novel*. Only in his recollections did Lukács explain that in this work he was no longer "analyzing the present through Hegelian, but through Fichtean categories."[30] What this meant was that Lukács was gradually abandoning the idealistic premises of his prewar philosophy, which were based on two implicit assumptions: that a solution for the crisis of the modern world was to emerge from within this world itself, and that individual philosophic and artistic activity, no matter how negative or subjectivist, could nevertheless lead toward the new culture of the future. The old hope, which now for the first time Lukács labeled "utopian," was replaced by a sense of intellectual and philosophic deadlock which could not be resolved in terms of his old categories.

Yet the vague outlines of a revolutionary solution were suggested toward the end of the essay. If the demonic reality of modern civilization could not be transcended from within, it might nevertheless be overcome from without, through religious and nonrational means. Lukács associated this new religious solution with the figure of Dostoevsky, whose work, he thought, transcended the form of the novel and prefigured the redeemed culture of the future. Only in the fictional world of Dostoevsky, he wrote toward the end of *The Theory of the Novel*, "can one already recognize the outlines of this new world, presented not as a desperate opposition to the present but as a visionary reality."[31] *The Theory of the Novel* was in fact to be an introduction to a large-scale study of Dostoevsky in which Lukács intended to explore systematically the possibilities of religious transcendence in the modern world.

That he never actually completed the Dostoevsky book was linked to a complicated set of reasons, not least of which were the distractions and interruptions imposed on him by the war. As he explained to Max Weber in 1915, he had decided to publish the work in incomplete form as *The Theory of the Novel* simply because he could not foresee the possibility of systematic work for some time to come. "If I were not forced to perform military duty," he wrote Weber, "or if the end of the war were in sight, I would draw the logical conclusions and would wait to publish this work in its entirety in connection with Dostoevsky. Since, however, I have to contend with the fact that for a long time to come I will not be able to work seriously . . . and then (perhaps years from now), I have no way of knowing if I will immediately return to this work and not to the aesthetic, I cannot think of it [delaying publication]."[32]

The letter is revealing, but it gives only part of the reason for Lukács' difficulty in completing the Dostoevsky book. The very style of the letter, with its convoluted phrases and indecision about the the future, betrays the enormous inner conflict Lukács felt about the project. It represented the irrational undercurrent of his psyche, competing with the philosophically more optimistic and academically more respectable aesthetic philosophy of the prewar years, which he was not yet willing or able to abandon. Only during the tumultuous final months of 1918 did he make a final decision between the two competing currents, deciding in effect to translate the Dostoevsky book into action and thus finally bridge the gulf between life and art which had tormented him since early youth.

Though Lukács was never to write the Dostoevsky book, it is nonetheless possible to reconstruct from notes, letters, diaries, and earlier articles the personal and philosophic components of the projected book. The fascination with Dostoevsky did not, in fact, begin with the war years but reached back to 1911, when Lukács had suffered a dual personal tragedy with the suicide of

Irma Seidler in May, and in October the death of Leo Popper. The loss of the two dearest friends of his early manhood unleashed in Lukács a profound emotional crisis which several times brought him to the brink of suicide. It also crystallized in unexpected ways those radical religious-mystical questions that were to assume such importance in his life after 1914.

Lukács' immediate reaction to Irma Seidler's suicide was a devastating sense of guilt and personal responsibility. "If anyone could have saved her," he wrote Popper immediately after the event, "it was I . . . and I did not and could not: I was her 'good friend,' I know—but this is not what was needed. Something else. More. And the necessary deeds for this were not in me. And with this, judgment is passed."[33] The difficulty was that judgment could not be passed, not at least in conventional ethical terms. In a transparently autobiographical dialogue, "The Poor in Spirit" (later published as "Von der Armut am Geiste"), which takes place between Lukács' alter ego and the dead woman's sister, he confronted the full ethical dilemma of the situation. "According to every law of human society," the man explains to his listener, "I am innocent—what is more, I have scrupulously fulfilled all my responsibilities toward her." Lukács' conclusion was not that his sense of guilt was, therefore, exaggerated, but rather that the ordinary laws of morality used to evaluate human actions and motives were unsatisfactory. The postulates of social obligation, of ethical commandments, he claimed, were inadequate categories of life, detached from subjective truths, like the aesthetic and cultural forms he had criticized in his essays in *Soul and Forms*. Kantian ethics, he concluded, like nineteenth-century culture, had become autonomous forms resembling bridges that separate rather than unite individuals. "We come and go on them," he wrote, "and we only encounter ourselves, never the other."[34]

In place of the formal postulates of duty, Lukács for the first time suggested a new, more adequate category of life: that of personal goodness as exemplified by Dostoevsky's fictional characters. "Goodness," the man explains to his listener, "makes possible a kind of all-embracing recognition of the other in which subject and object have become as one. The truly good person does not explain the inner world of the other but reads within it as if it were his own. For this reason, goodness is a miracle, an act of grace, an experience of redemption. And, if you like, it is also authentic life, genuine life."[35]

This quality of radical goodness, deeply connected as it was to Lukács' agonizing sense of inadequacy in his relationship with Irma Seidler, nevertheless had general philosophic implications which transcended the personal circumstances from which it emerged, for radical goodness in Lukács' mind represented not simply an extension of, or a more perfect form of, ethical conduct but rather its direct antithesis. In what amounted to a repudiation of ethics and all forms of rational morality, Lukács pointed out that "true goodness is not mild, calculating, or resigned. Goodness is wild, cruel, blind, and adventurous. In the soul of him who is good, all psychological content has disappeared, all causality and calculation are absent. His soul is like a clean white sheet on which fate writes its own absurd commands. And he fulfills this command blindly, recklessly, cruelly. And when the impossibility turns into deed; blindness into light; cruelty into goodness—this is the miracle, the state of grace."[36]

Lukács' conception of radical goodness, with its undercurrent of irrationalism and paradox, contained in embryonic form those religious themes and political opinions which were to become so important to him during the war years. In an uncanny way he sensed even at the time that he was destined to return to these ideas at some future date. In August, when he mailed the completed dialogue to Popper, he asked his friend whether it should be published and forecast its significance in his future development. "As for my opinion," he confessed, "I have no idea whether the piece is worth anything as it stands. Perhaps it's just as well that it is so subjective and not 'scholarly.' I wrote it out of inner necessity, and only in five or six years will these thoughts ripen into scholarship. They are deep and certain even now—but they do not yet exist in the sphere of philosophic objectivity, only in the realm of the essay."[37]

This was to be one of the last communications Lukács would have with Popper, who was mortally ill at the time and died only two months later. Popper's death plunged Lukács back into the depression he had just barely conquered after Seidler's death. This time he recorded his thoughts and emotions not in published form but in an intensely private diary which he kept until the end of the year.

189

If Seidler's death had raised painful ethical issues in his mind, Popper's triggered agonizing doubts about the mission of the aesthetic philosophy which he was about to commence, and which he had discussed with soaring ambition during the previous months with his friend. With the sudden loss of Popper's affirming presence and affectionate support, Lukács' confidence in his own work crumbled. "My intellect works in weightless, empty space," he records in October.

> There exists no pressure or resistance anywhere, no trace of life anywhere. Not even in my work: I can do nothing. Is this an ordeal or a temptation? . . . It seems that I am brought to punishment for my arrogance, for my confidence in my work, and for my sense of efficacy through it . . . The intellect works in dark, weightless space: there is nothing, no sign, no road . . . Humility! Humility! And yet, I remain hard in spite of everything: I have still not broken down completely. I have still not been annihilated. Something in me still holds on to my work—I have still not been humbled enough.[38]

As the crisis progressed, the thought of suicide became increasingly compelling. "I have reached," he recorded in November, "all that is possible for man to reach by mere intellect. It now turns out that it is nothing. Would it not be more decent and more logical—both intellectually and philosophically—to put an end to everything rather than be gradually forced into compromises?"[39]

As in the crisis over Irma Seidler's death, here too Lukács was keenly aware of the broad philosophic dimensions of his problem. For it was not simply his own status as a philosopher that tormented him but also the general question whether philosophy as practiced at the time had any relevance to the ultimate questions of life and human existence. His intellectual efforts and achievements, he felt in the crisis of the moment, amounted to nothing more than "an experiment to create a reality surrogate out of intellectual clarity . . . This illusion, however, is over."[40]

The alternative to philosophy, to mere intellect, once again appeared to Lukács in the form of a religious breakthrough, which was at the same time a reversal of conventional ethical categories. "Now I see clearer than ever," he wrote in October, "that the saint has to be a sinner first; only through sinning, only by committing an act of sin, can he completely conquer life; and at the same time, he can only find his way to God by having been in a state of sin beforehand."[41]

At the time Lukács drew paradoxical conclusions from these radical insights. On the level of his most intimate emotional life, he had gained a searing vision of the ultimate inefficacy of ethical categories or philosophic inquiry. In the realm of public conduct, however, he was not ready to act on these intuitions and openly abandon conventional ethics or professional philosophy. By the end of 1911 he seems to have repressed his inner conflicts and was ready to resume his work and normal life. "It seems," he wrote in mid-December, "that the crisis is over. I have once more escaped into epistemological studies and into frivolity. I am afraid it is going to succeed . . . I feel my intellect to be decadence; through suicide I could have reached the essence and logical conclusion of my being. This way, all is heartsick compromise and gradual demoralization."[42]

Lukács, however, consciously left open the possibility of a religious breakthrough at some distant point in his life, when he would have reached, as he put it, the ultimate peaks of despair, from which only descent into the abyss or ascent into the transcendental is possible. "I have never foreseen anything in the future with such absolute certainty," he wrote in October, "as the breakthrough of my intellect, its breakthrough into the religious; and yet, I see it only as a necessity, as a logical postulate—I am far from being ready yet, far from being desperate enough yet."[43]

The descent into complete despair seems to have come in August 1914, when the world confirmed on a macroscopic level what Lukács had experienced on the level of personal tragedy: that ethical and rational standards had become inadequate categories, mere ossified forms in a world of "perfected evil." A civilization, Lukács felt for the first time, where inherited culture could no longer provide any form of mediation between individual and external reality had ripened for some kind of transcendental, religious solution. From the sketches Lukács made for the Dostoevsky book, it is clear that he intended to resurrect the religious themes of 1911, encompassing them within a more objective, more universal framework.

What remains from the projected book are only cryptic notes, brief historical quotations, elliptical references, often expressed in incomplete phrases. Yet the broad problems Lukács intended to deal with are not hard to decipher. Here for the first time Lukács expressed the opposition between the world of culture and institutions and the religious possibilities of a Dostoevskian world as the conflict between two different ethical universes which he simply referred to as the "first and second ethic." The first ethic evidently referred to external, merely formalistic standards; the second to the possibilities of genuine communion, of individuals interacting without the distorting medium of language, culture, ethics. Lukács conjured up the vision of a mystical, frictionless community where people would live their lives "without distance," without "attachments to social position, class, family origins, etc." Such ties as they had would be "new concrete relations reaching directly from soul to soul." These kinds of interactions, Lukács pointed out, had been experienced up till then only by mystics in their relationship with God. The great accomplishment of Dostoevsky was to show that they could also exist between individuals, that it was possible to break through the solipsistic isolation of the past. From the new perspective it was possible to realize that "we are all responsible for each other's sins and for everything in the world—and not only because of the general sinfulness of the world; every individual is personally responsible for everyone collectively and individually on this earth. And this insight is the height of life."[44]

Perhaps the greatest novelty of the Dostoevsky notes, however, lies in the practical direction in which these insights began to point. Lukács was becoming increasingly convinced that the religious-mystical state of mind he associated with Dostoevsky could have political manifestations that were intimately related to the psychology of terrorism. In a significant exchange of letters with his friend Paul Ernst in the spring of 1915, Lukács stated explicitly that the question of terrorism was directly linked in his mind with the philosophic problems of the Dostoevsky book. In March he requested Ernst to forward the autobiography of Ropsin (Boris Savinkov), a noted Russian anarchist who had been head of a terrorist organization in Russia between 1904 and 1906. He wanted to become better acquainted with the book, he explained, not for its literary merits but rather "in order to understand the psychology of Russian terrorism about which I intend to write extensively in connection with Dostoevsky."[45] In the example of Ropsin, he elaborated a month later, "we have a new type of man whose nature is important to understand."[46] For Lukács, the terrorist had evidently become the political incarnation of the Dostoevsky hero, who not only pointed to but actually helped bring about a new religious age by substituting for the formal ethical commandments of society the higher impulse of self-sacrifice. "I see in Ropsin," Lukács wrote Ernst,

> not the sign of pathology but a new manifestation of an old conflict in which the individual is forced to choose between two different ethical systems: the first being responsibility toward institutions, the second responsibility toward his soul. The conflict always finds peculiar dialectical expression in situations where the politician, the revolutionary, directs his soul not inward but outward toward humanity. In these cases—in order to save his soul, he is forced to sacrifice it. On the basis of a mystical ethic, he has to become a cruel *Realpolitiker*, and break the absolute commandment, "Thou shalt not kill." In its ultimate roots, this is an ancient dilemma which perhaps Hebbel's Judith expressed in its clearest form: "And if God had placed between me and my foreordained deed the act of sin,—who am I to withdraw myself from under it?"[47]

Lukács' transcendental religious longings, which emerged only as flashes of intuition during the personal crisis of 1911, clearly acquired increasingly concrete and self-conscious expression as a result of the external crisis of world war. And as Lukács proceeded deliberately to explore their implication, first as theory in the Dostoevsky book and gradually as potential politics in the correspondence with Paul Ernst in 1915, a new kind of dualism surfaced in his thinking. If before the war the fundamental polarities of his thought had revolved around the contrast between organic and inorganic cultures, after the war they began to converge on the contrast between mystical-religious and individualistic-ethical values. The new set of dichotomies, which were to dominate Lukács' thinking increasingly by the last years of the war, explicitly juxtaposed the values of individualism and community, freedom and salvation, personal autonomy and self-abandonment in a way that the old categories had not. The need for radical distinctions and for fateful personal choices was already foreshadowed in these new religious categories which

Lukács and his friends were beginning to use with increasing frequency by the end of the war.

Yet it is doubtful whether even Lukács knew in 1915 the direction in which these new ideas and assumptions were leading him. In late 1918 he was to resurrect almost word for word his 1915 letter to Paul Ernst, which explained terror as the ultimate act of religious self-sacrifice, as his personal justification for joining the Communist party of Hungary. The politicization of Lukács' religious vision was an immensely complex and in many ways unique phenomenon whose inner progress is impossible to trace with any detail or certainty. Yet it is quite certain that it could not have occurred without those radical political changes in the outside world which brought Bolshevism to power in Russia and caused the collapse of the Hapsburg monarchy in Hungary. These momentous historical and ideological events radically redefined the options for most Hungarian intellectuals during the last years of the war, channeling individual energies into directions almost none of them could have foreseen.

—

In 1914 or 1915 Lukács and his friends would have been incredulous had they been told that revolutionary Marxism was to play a central role in their lives within four years. They were, of course, aware of and even sensitive to the Marxist oeuvre before the war, but like so many prewar cultural radicals, they remained deeply ambivalent about its implications. Orthodox Marxism was too closely associated in their minds with nineteenth-century scientism, materialism, and determinism, and seemed particularly ill suited for their complex cultural concerns and analyses. The Marxist sociology of art, wrote Lukács in 1910, "was made hopeless by the fact that it attempts to make connections that are too direct and simple-minded. The attempt to derive literary content from economic relations cannot bring results."[48] Their disdain for what they considered the crude reductionism of Marxist methods continued well into the war years. Béla Fogarasi, for instance, who was to be one of the most passionate converts to communism among Lukács' friends, could still write in 1916: "Epistemological investigation can easily demonstrate that Marxist determinism—with its claim that the economic modes of production are as independent of human will as the cultural and intellectual formations they give rise to—is itself only an intellectual formation, and what is more, a well-known form of dogmatic metaphysics."[49]

Perhaps more serious than their reservations about Marxism as a philosophy were their doubts about the socialist movement as a political force. To them the prewar social-democratic parties, with their parliamentary representation and increasingly bureaucratic organization, had ceased to offer a revolutionary option or a genuine alternative to liberal society. As Lukács tellingly put it in 1910, "Socialism lacks the kind of religious energy that could fulfill one's entire life and that primitive Christianity possessed."[50] Even working-class culture, in which some prewar radicals saw an alternative to bourgeois life, appeared to them simply a retarded version of middle-class culture. There existed, Lukács pointed out in a book review of 1915, no "positive motifs which distinguish the cultural structure of workers from those of the bourgeoisie." If working-class life appeared to be more communal, less fragmented than middle-class life, it was only a sign of "its temporary spiritual underdevelopment," which was bound to disappear with growing affluence.[51]

These deeply ambivalent, if not overtly hostile, attitudes toward socialism began, however, to shift subtly from the middle years of the war on. The cause was directly related to the fragmentation of the European socialist movement after 1914, and to the emergence within it of an intransigent revolutionary left wing which was committed to ending the war without delay. In later life Lukács always stressed that for him it was the example of Rosa Luxemburg, Karl Liebknecht, and after 1917, the Bolsheviks, that represented the first ray of light showing a way out of the total darkness of the war years. Significantly enough, neither Lukács nor his friends had actually read the works of Luxemburg, Liebknecht, or Lenin in any detail before 1918. Nor did they seem aware of or interested in the very real practical and doctrinal differences that separated these revolutionary socialists. What they derived from them was not specific ideological truths but rather points of identification, moral examples of courage and resistance against the war. Theirs was a convergence of political outlook and sensibility growing out of common attitudes toward the war and a common revolutionary frame of mind toward existing society.

The parallelism is perhaps most strikingly demonstrated in Rosa Luxemburg's initial reactions to the war, which bear unmistakable resemblances to those of Lukács and Balázs. In her 1915 pamphlet *The Crisis of German Social Democracy* she painted an apocalyptic vision of Europe which Lukács himself could have written at that period. "Shamed, dishonored, wading in blood, dripping with filth," she wrote, "thus capitalist society stands. Not as we usually see it, playing the role of peace and righteousness, of order, of philosophy, of ethics—[but] as a roaring beast, as an orgy of anarchy, as a pestilential breath, devastating culture."[52]

There was about the radical socialist leaders who came into prominence during the war years none of the timidity and philistinism which had so alienated Lukács and his friends from the prewar socialists. Through such leaders the socialist movement gained a new stature, a new moral authority in their eyes that it had clearly lacked in the years before 1914. Yet it is also undeniable that the moral example of revolutionary socialists like Luxemburg, Liebknecht, and Lenin could have had few direct political or even ideological consequences by itself. As Lukács later admitted, his sympathy for wartime socialists was before 1918 only an abstract, theoretical position, without "even the remotest possibility of following in their footsteps."[53]

The catalyst that was to change this general moral sympathy for socialism into the potential for concrete political commitment and action came specifically from Hungarian conditions at the end of 1918 and early 1919. There is considerable irony in this development, since Lukács always considered Hungary to be the place where he felt most alienated and therefore least likely to be confronted with external social or political choices. This certainly was his reasoning in the autumn of 1917, when he decided to return to Hungary for a longer stay in order to finally complete his aesthetic philosophy. "What is certain," he wrote Paul Ernst in September 1917, "is that I am going to Budapest; it represents the only possibility for me right now to live only for my work, disconnected from external life."[54]

Lukács' calculation was proven wrong within less than a year. In Hungary the end of the war brought such extreme social, political, and economic dislocation that not even Lukács could afford to live aloof from and unaffected by external events. "The framework of normal existence disintegrated," Lukács recalled of these months, "and with this the chief direction of my philosophic problems was swept into new channels without my even realizing the significance of this turn of events at the time."[55]

The signal for general political dissolution in the Hapsburg monarchy came, ironically, from the young emperor, Charles IV, who in October 1918 issued a decree authorizing the different nationalities to form national councils with the view of transforming the monarchy into a federal state. The proclamation would have constituted a serious concession to progressive demands before the war, but now was too late. It became the source not of consolidation but of the dissolution of the monarchy. During the month of October the Poles, the Czechs, the Romanians, the Croats, and the Slovenes did form national councils, not with the intention of laying the foundations for a federal state, though, but rather for the purpose of creating independent nation-states of their own.

In Hungary too the emperor's decree mobilized progressive forces, and the National Council was formed in mid-October under the leadership of the liberal aristocrat Count Michael Károlyi. Károlyi's National Council represented a genuinely novel phenomenon in Hungarian political life. It was a representative left-wing coalition which for the first time included socialists and radical liberals like Oszkár Jászi, and was openly committed to far-ranging democratic and economic reorganization, including universal manhood suffrage and land reform. Hopes ran high in the autumn of 1918 among left-wing intellectuals, who tended to see in Károlyi's platform the fruition of decades of labor and agitation.

For the general public too Károlyi and the National Council stood for positive values: they represented peace, fresh leadership, a new beginning after the sufferings of war. During the last week of October, Budapest was agitated by large-scale demonstrations, work stoppages, and mass rallies all aimed at demanding the abdication of the conservative government and the nomination of Károlyi as prime minister. Lukács and his friends, who were socially connected as well as politically sympathetic with Jászi and the radicals, could not help being affected by the bracing, hopeful atmosphere that settled over left-wing circles in Budapest in late October. They certainly felt strongly enough about Károlyi's cause to participate as a group in one of the largest demonstrations on his behalf on October 28. Balázs, Lukács, Mannheim, Lesznai, and a handful of other Sunday acquaintances were present in the crowd that assembled outside the Károlyi party headquarters to show their support for the National Council. When the excited crowd decided to head toward the royal palace in Buda to demand the immediate nomination of Károlyi as prime minister, the group of friends followed suit. "On the banks of the Danube," Balázs recalled the incident a few weeks later,

> we encountered a terrible row of fire and the crowd started to head back. We pressed forward. Mali [Anna Lesznai], who thought her husband was out at the front, rushed ahead like a terrible Valkyrie, pulling people with her. Mannheim, pale and clutching on to me, proceeded with determination. (The others got lost somewhere) . . . When we got to the Ritz, we suddenly faced a row of mounted police. The crowd headed back, and we three found ourselves alone on the square in front of the statue of Deák; behind us they were shooting, and ahead of us, a few people lay on the pavement.[56]

This initiation by fire was to be only the beginning of an experience of accelerating political and social dissolution for members of the Sunday Circle. The demonstration was, in fact, the direct antecedent of the revolutionary coup that brought Károlyi and the National Council into power two days later. On the night of October 30–31, armed soldiers and organized workers occupied key military and administrative installations in the city and took over power in the name of the National Council. The next morning the socialist press triumphantly proclaimed the revolution and prepared its readers for armed resistance. "The revolution has broken out," read the headline of *Népszava* (The people's voice). "Workers! Comrades! It is now your turn! The counterrevolution will probably try to regain power . . . Stop work! . . . Out to the streets!"[57]

The call to arms proved unnecessary, for there was to be no official resistance. The next morning Archduke Joseph, the representative of the monarch in Budapest, called Károlyi, Jászi, and other leaders of the National Council to his palace and named Károlyi prime minister, authorizing him to form a government. The news of his nomination, recalled Károlyi, "produced general euphoria in the city, for this meant peace. People danced in the streets, strangers embraced and shed tears of joy. Everywhere people were distributing white tuberoses, which men and women pinned on their lapels. In their enthusiasm people forgot that they had lost the war. They felt themselves victorious because the revolution had triumphed."[58]

Lukács and his friends too felt elated at the triumph of Károlyi's revolution, which seemed to hold out the promise of a new social and political order in Hungary. Some were actually drawn into the day-to-day administrative life of the new regime; Balázs, for example, assumed a temporary post in one of the improvised municipal offices. He was astonished at this peculiar development, which had suddenly transformed him into a "practical man of action." "It was," he recalled in late November, "a fantastic nightmare. I, the outsider-poet, the public school teacher and librarian, found myself dealing with war ministers, municipal commanders, chiefs of police, managers of train stations, and provincial judges, without having any official position, simply because decisions had to be made quickly and people turned to me and everyone was free to assume whatever task he chose." After a few weeks of feverish activity, once power had begun to be consolidated into "ordinary organized offices with paying and titled positions," Balázs decided to quit, already feeling out of place in the emerging political establishment. He was, he wrote, eager to return full time to his unfinished novel and other more customary activities.[59]

Balázs' desire to resume the tasks and routine of normal life, however, proved to be infeasible. The October revolution was the commencement not of consolidation but of a wide-scale political and economic collapse which Károlyi's government found increasingly difficult to contain. During the month of November, the pent-up social resentments of the war years exploded in a series of jacqueries throughout the countryside. Peasants broke into the estates of local landowners, confiscated stores and restaurants, even occasionally attacked local judges, priests, and administrators associated with the hated old order. In the cities the situation was not much better, as the dislocated economy floundered, and the urban population, especially in Budapest, faced drastic shortages of fuel, food, clothing, and housing.

But perhaps the most devastating setbacks for the new government occurred in the realm of foreign affairs. Both political insiders and public opinion had assumed that Károlyi, who had been pro-Entente throughout the war, would be in a particularly favorable position to negotiate a lenient peace treaty after the war. This illusion was shattered in the first week of November, when military commanders of the Entente made plain that Károlyi was to be treated as the heir of the discredited old regime, and would be expected to pay in full the price of military defeat. "Optimistic public opinion," recalled Károlyi, "which up till then attempted to delude itself, was now forced to confront the full weight of reality."[60] The reality was that in the course of 1918 and 1919, Hungary was to lose three-fifths of her territory and over half her population, as Czech, Romanian, and South Slav troops pressed forward to claim territories formerly under Hungarian rule.

Not surprisingly, Károlyi's left-wing coalition, precarious from the beginning, could not withstand such disastrous internal and external setbacks. It began to disintegrate, rapidly losing both inner cohesion and moral authority among the population. By the new year only the organized forces of the Social Democratic party seemed to retain a semblance of discipline and coherence within the demoralized coalition. In fact the fate of Károlyi's moderate government was clearly in the hands of the socialists. In early January, Károlyi appeared unannounced before the party convention to plead for their continued support of the existing government. "If you withdraw support from me," he recalled his own words, "I will be forced to resign. If, however, you want to assume power alone, I will go along with that."[61]

By early 1919, however, Károlyi's plea for parliamentary legalism and moderation was growing ineffectual if not quixotic. As the diplomatic situation worsened and the political power structure disintegrated into near anarchy, the attractions of extremist solutions increased correspondingly. Political groups on the radical right and left, which had been organizing since November, began to gain in strength and credibility, and in fact reinforced each other. "The stronger the forces of the counter-revolution appeared," recalled Károlyi, "the more fuel it supplied to communist propaganda, and the more powerful the communist agitation became, the more excuses it gave to the organization of the reactionaries."[62]

The appeal of the communists, whose core consisted of Bolshevik-trained prisoners of war recently returned to Budapest from Russia, was both simple and compelling. Headed by the former journalist Béla Kun, they seemed to offer decisive leadership, simple analysis, and above all hope for the future. They formally established the Communist party of Hungary on November 24 and by early December had a highly effective daily paper in operation, which proclaimed the failure of social democracy and the need for immediate revolution. "Capitalism," claimed the opening editorial of *Vörös Ujság* (The red paper) on December 7, "has ripened for destruction . . . not only morally, but also economically . . . But who will lead the proletariat in this struggle? The old social democratic parties throughout the world have become allies of the criminal bourgeoisie . . . This is why we, communists, stand at the head of the Hungarian proletariat, to prepare it for the inevitable, and what is more already present revolution."[63]

The opposing claims of social democracy and revolutionary socialism or communism had become, of course, a topic of burning controversy not only in Hungary but throughout the entire European socialist movement by late 1918. The major tactical disagreement between the two camps was over the question of gradualism and parliamentary politics on the one hand and immediate revolutionary takeover on the other. The theoretical issue of contention was whether terror, the suspension of individual rights and democratic means, could ever constitute a legitimate basis for a socialist takeover in Europe. Only the summer before, Karl Kautsky, the head of the German Social Democratic party, had categorically rejected terror in his well-known pamphlet *Dictatorship of the Proletariat*. In the autumn of 1918 Lenin had responded in *The Proletarian Revolution and the Renegade Kautsky*, pointing out that "the proletariat cannot triumph without breaking the resistance of the bourgeoisie, without forcibly suppressing its enemies . . . Where there is forcible suppression, there is, of course, no 'freedom,' no democracy."[64]

The peculiarity of the Hungarian political situation in late 1918 was that this same debate, which constituted an essentially internal theoretical and tactical conflict within socialism, took on general significance and expanded beyond the socialist camp to encompass whole layers of politically aware, progressive intellectuals. The real power of the Hungarian communists in late 1918 came from the fact that despite their small numbers, they had the ability to define the limits within which both socialist and nonsocialist intellectuals were forced to confront the political choices of their time. For the communists' claim that the major ideological question of the day revolved around the conflict between social democracy and communism happened to be true in an immediate and practical sense in Hungary. Pragmatically, most left-wing intellectuals in late 1918 were confronted with the same unavoidable dilemma: were they to continue Károlyi's legacy and remain loyal to an increasingly ineffectual parliamentary democracy, or were they to join the communists and turn eastward toward a Bolshevik alliance?

Perhaps nothing illustrates the generality of this dilemma more clearly than the left-wing press of Budapest in late 1918. The December issue of the radical liberal *Szabadgondolat* (Freedom of thought), for example, was entirely devoted to the problem of Bolshevism in Hungary. The editors of the journal canvassed a broad spectrum of left-wing opinion in Budapest, ranging from radical liberals like Oszkár Jászi to apolitical scientists like Michael Polányi, asking them to express their opinion on the desirability of a possible communist takeover in Hungary. Lukács himself was one of the intellectuals who contributed to the debate, and it was in the pages of *Szabadgondolat* that he first publicly formulated his attitude toward Bolshevism.

What is immediately striking about the responses published in *Szabadgondolat* was not so much the conclusions reached, which were almost evenly divided for and against Bolshevism, as the immense diversity of perspectives from which these decisions were arrived at. As even a brief sampling of the responses makes clear, individuals tended to bring to the question categories of thought which had less to do with Marxism than with their former philosophic and ideological preoccupations. Jászi, for instance, remaining true to his deep-rooted liberal, humanistic commitments, rejected Bolshevism out of hand, arguing that "no individual or class in society is justified in imposing a dictatorship on others."[65] Michael Polányi, already preoccupied with the general question of intellectuals in politics, rejected Bolshevism for more fundamental reasons. "Let us assume," he warned in words very similar to Julien Benda's argument a decade later,[66] "the ancient traditions of the skeptics . . . It is not the task of creative intellectuals to spread their ideas among the masses. The words would have frozen in Christ's mouth had he been able to forsee his future Church. Nietzsche would have laid down his pen if he could have imagined the Nietzscheans and Marx if he had seen his contemporary followers."[67] Others, like Miklós Sika, imposed Freudian concepts on Bolshevism, welcoming it, ironically, as the final liberation from the rule of the primal father. "They have actually killed the fathers of today's generation," he wrote. "With today's generation it is no longer possible to reestablish the old state, forced discipline, forced solidarity." The essence of Bolshevism, he concluded, was "the alliance of the brothers, the dethroning of the fathers."[68]

In the intensely polarized and politicized atmosphere of Hungary in late 1918 it had clearly become difficult or impossible for progressive intellectuals not to take a stand on the question of the relative merits of social democracy and communism. The problem had been defined by the pragmatic and inexorable political realities of the time and not by individual theoretical or ideological proclivities. Under the circumstances, it is hardly surprising that the general debate was theoretically heterogeneous and only rarely defined by specifically Marxist or even socialist concerns. The general and understandable tendency was to continue thinking in terms of the old philosophic categories and to transpose these onto the new ideological and political issues of the time.

———

Not surprisingly, Lukács' article in *Szabadgondolat*, entitled "Bolshevism As an Ethical Dilemma," betrayed unmistakable traces of earlier non-Marxist concerns, harking back to those transcendental, religious longings that had been preoccupying him since 1915. Lukács began the article with the familiar distinction between "first and second ethics," between unredeemed empirical reality and a transcendental realm of harmony which he had been exploring in his notes for the Dostoevsky book. In the article, however, these familiar polarities were for the first time associated with aspects of Marx's philosophy. The

Marxist oeuvre, Lukács began, had two separate components or dimensions, between which a sharp distinction had to be made: his sociology, which contained descriptions and analyses of empirical reality, and his philosophy of history, which postulated a transcendental utopia where all class antagonism and conflict ceased.

The pragmatic choice between social democracy and communism, between individual ethics and revolutionary terror, had to be made, Lukács argued, with consideration to this basic dualism in Marx's work. The central question was what relationship the actual socialist struggle bore toward the empirical and transcendental realms implicit in Marxism. If the socialist movement was seen to exist within bourgeois reality, then the ethical laws of this realm still applied to its actions and tactics. If, however, the class struggle embodied within it the transcendental utopia that was the ultimate goal of socialist politics, then it was not to be constrained by the legal and ethical norms of existing society.

Lukács' position on this key issue seemed unambiguous at this point. "The class struggle of the proletariat," he insisted, "which is destined to bring about the new world order, as class struggle does not yet contain this world order." This being the case, parliamentary legality, traditional ethical norms, could not be suspended for the sake of the socialist struggle, and Bolshevik terror, even if committed in the name of the future utopia, would nevertheless constitute nothing more than "the former oppressed becoming the new oppressors." For the dilemma of the Bolsheviks, he wrote in a surprisingly passionate ending, "sounds like this: is it possible to do good through evil, to bring about freedom through oppression; can a new world order come about if the instruments of its realization differ only in superficials from the justly hated methods of the old order?" With the problem posed in this way, the answer had to be a resounding rejection of Bolshevik terror in the name of social democratic gradualism. "Bolshevism," Lukács concluded, "is based on the metaphysical premise that out of evil, good can come, that it is possible to lie our way to the truth. The writer of these lines is incapable of sharing this faith, and for this reason sees an insoluble ethical dilemma in the roots of the Bolshevik position."[69]

In many respects the tone of finality and resolution at the end of the article was deeply misleading. Despite appearances, "Bolshevism As an Ethical Dilemma" was not an argument against Bolshevism but rather an externalized dialogue between the antithetical impulses battling for supremacy within Lukács' own psyche. On the one side was individual ethical responsibility, associated with his incomplete aesthetic philosophy, and on the other the promise of a transcendental metaphysics, originally associated with Dostoevsky, and only recently invested in Bolshevism. The very passion with which he rejected the Bolshevik option betrays the deep attraction that its metaphysical elements held for him. He had, after all, been preoccupied with just such paradoxical solutions that he associated with Bolshevism as far back as 1911, when he had described the act of radical goodness as "the impossibility turned into deed; blindness into light; cruelty into goodness."[70] And he had again discussed such a nonrational ideal in his correspondence with Paul Ernst in 1915, when he referred to the terrorist as a man who on the basis of "a mystical ethic has become a cruel *Realpolitiker* and breaks the absolute commandment, 'Thou shalt not kill.' "[71]

The conclusions Lukács reached in "Bolshevism As an Ethical Dilemma" could have no ultimate validity or finality, for they expressed only one side of his nature, one pole of his divided self. And as his later actions indicate, it turned out to be the weaker, less dominant side. A few weeks after writing his repudiation of Bolshevism, Lukács suddenly reversed his position and officially joined the Communist party of Hungary. His reasons for this decision were outlined in an important article entitled "Tactics and Ethics" (Taktika és etika), which he must have written in late 1918 or early 1919 but only published in the spring of 1919, under the Béla Kun regime. The central question posed in the article was identical to the one in the earlier piece: was it justifiable to realize socialism through terror, through the violation of individual rights, or were such tactics fundamentally antithetical to the inner goals of socialism? The answer this time was that terror *did* form a legitimate component of socialist tactics and that Bolshevism was indeed a true embodiment of socialism. The reasoning underpinning this conclusion, however, was tortuous and contradictory, betraying the identical conflict and dualism that Lukács had given voice to in "Bolshevism As an Ethical Dilemma."

There existed, in fact, two separate levels of argumentation which remained distinct and unreconciled in "Tactics and Ethics." On the first level, Lukács simply abolished the familiar dualism of his earlier position and asserted that there could never be a conflict between socialist tactics and traditional ethics since socialism as a movement did not exist "within the framework of existing social reality" but rather as a "given beyond such boundaries." The transposition of the socialist struggle from the realm of "sociology" to that of the "transcendental" made the crucial difference in determining political tactics, for if the class struggle existed within the realm of empirical reality, "the established legal order was a necessary and normative given defining the tactical possibilities of action." If, however, it already existed within the realm of the transcendental, then legality and individual ethics could be regarded as simply "part of the power structure of empirical reality," to be swept away with the other aspects of the past. Lukács performed here a logical sleight of hand, and on the level of theory at any rate created an irrefutable solution. The class struggle of the proletariat, which already embodied the future socialist utopia, was liberated from the rules of external reality and by this fact abolished the conflict between "is" and "ought," subject and object, tactics and ethics. "The Marxist theory of class conflict," Lukács argued, "(and in this aspect, it follows completely the Hegelian formulation) makes immanent the transcendental goal; the class struggle of the proletariat constitutes at one and the same time both the goal and the realization of the goal."[72]

This philosophic solution, which already embodied in embryonic form Lukács' later formulations in *History and Class Consciousness,* did not yet command complete conviction in Lukács' inner consciousness, for parallel to his new argument there continued a second train of thought that still drew heavily on the concepts, preoccupations, even language of the Dostoevsky notations. Bolshevism, Lukács pointed out in the second, lengthier part of the article, though historically necessary, was, in the subjective realm, fraught with tragic conflicts and sacrifices. The acceptance of Bolshevism, he insisted, could not abolish on the level of individual conscience the force and validity of ethical commandments. "Everyone," he warned in words that echoed a passage of his Dostoevsky notes, "who at the present moment opts for Bolshevism is ethically responsible for the life of every individual who is destroyed in the struggle for socialism." Theirs, concluded Lukács, was one of those tragic historical situations "in which it is impossible to act in such a way as not to commit sin; but it also teaches us at the same time that even the choice between two evils has a measure. This measure is the greatness of the sacrifice. The individual, when forced to choose between two evils, chooses correctly when he sacrifices his lower to his higher self."[73]

Lukács left no doubt in "Tactics and Ethics" that this tragic choice between two evils really involved a new embodiment of the psychological reality of the Dostoevsky hero who, through an act of radical goodness, sacrifices his personal life for the higher good of others. As in his 1915 letter to Paul Ernst, Lukács once again invoked the example of Ropsin, though not as an intellectual curiosity this time but as an alter ego whose life and sacrifices paralleled his own. It was the Russian terrorist, he wrote at the end of his article,

> who saw not the justification (for that is impossible) but the ultimate ethical validation of his terroristic deed, in the fact that he sacrificed for his fellow human beings not only his life but his purity, his morality, his soul. In other words: murderous actions can be tragically ethical only of those who know . . . that to kill is forbidden under all circumstances. Or to express this ultimate human tragedy in the unutterably beautiful words of Hebbel's Judith: "And if God had placed between me and my foreordained deed the act of sin—who am I to withdraw myself from under it?"[74]

These pivotal articles of 1918, with their inner contradictions, philosophic inconsistencies, and persistent echoes of the past, clearly did not yet constitute a coherent Marxist position in Lukács' life. As he liked to stress in later recollections, his entry into the Communist party in late 1918 was just the beginning of a long process of inner transformation that only gradually gave way to his mature Marxist philosophy in the 1930s and 1940s. Even more than portents of future development, Lukács' articles on Bolshevism represented final assessments of the past, whose implicit assumptions were exposed as contradictory and ultimately incompatible with action. Lukács' insistence that the political decision between social democracy and communism ultimately involved tragic and inevitable choices between individualistic and communal values implied at the same time a judgment on his prewar cultural strivings which had attempted to reconcile precisely such antithetical values. The pervasive implication of these articles was that rational judgment was incompatible with metaphysics, that salvation was possible only at the price of abdicating the autonomy of the self. Lukács was in effect proclaiming the bankruptcy of his aesthetic philosophy, which had been based on the assumption that radical analysis was compatible with metaphysics, the two forming necessary elements of the same historical solution. From his new perspective, shaped by the disillusions of war and the challenges of political crisis, Lukács no longer believed that a fragmented world could be redeemed by culture, that discrete individual efforts could ultimately culminate in a grand communal synthesis.

This sense of broken illusions was shared by his Sunday friends as well, who seemed to have arrived at a similar position of cultural and philosophic deadlock by 1918. As discussions in the Sunday Circle gradually shifted in late 1918 "from philosophy to the realm of theoretical politics or revolutionary theory,"[75] the ethical dilemmas that Lukács had outlined in his articles on Bolshevism became the focus of prolonged and passionate discussion. "Metaphysics and ethics are in conflict in empirical reality," acknowledged Anna Lesznai, "though they are one and the same in the realm of redemption . . . We constantly have to choose between ethical and metaphysical values, and we sin sometimes against ethics, sometimes against metaphysics."[76]

The consensus in the Sunday meetings about the necessity for radical choices did not, however, imply general agreement with Lukács' pro-Bolshevik conclusions. Anna Lesznai and about half the Sunday Circle argued strenuously against Lukács' position in "Tactics and Ethics," feeling that traditional ethical standards could not, under any circumstances, be subordinated to a higher collective goal. The values of individual autonomy and ethical responsibility, Lesznai maintained, had logical priority over collective solutions. "The individual," she pointed out in her diary, "could not sacrifice himself completely for the future generation: otherwise the history of mankind would provide the paradoxical picture of a never-ending deadend."[77] Her conviction that genuine transcendence could be achieved only by deepening inner life rather than subordinating it to an external ideology gained force with time and found expression through the familiar symbols of fairy tales. "In the fairy tale too," she observed in 1929, "the redeemed world exists below the earth, at the bottom of the well, within the depths of the self . . . The hero who tries to gain redemption by climbing up a beanstalk or by flying away on a broomstick usually finds only a magpie or an ugly princess at the end of the quest. Most such fairy tales (at least in Europe) are satirical in nature and end with a debacle, symbolizing the truth that one cannot climb up into redemption, one can only reach it by submerging oneself within the self."[78]

Whether they opted for or against Bolshevism, the conflict between individual consciousness and communal values formed the central, ultimately insoluble dilemma of their lives during these crucial transitional months. The issues they were grappling with, wrote Balázs in 1919, involved "not *individual* problems, but rather the problem of *individualism*." In his own life, the commitment to communism meant the acceptance of "solidarity out of a sense of honesty and a struggle for universal principle, where I accept the principle but not the struggle for the principle. I accept the principle, but the struggle for the principle leads me away from all principles and from myself, from my true work. I am forced to choose between the 'ethically just' and the 'authentic' life. (Gyuri's tragedy.)"[79] Their deepest conflict, Balázs wrote two years later, came from the fact that they were suspended between two worlds, living in "two presents. We cannot transform our inner experiences into ethical deeds, because they have no external forms yet . . . Our ethical present represents a bygone spiritual age. Our most compelling ethical commandments are the consequences of antiquated, already ossified inner experiences. We are already walking in the shadow of fresh green foliage, but the ground under our feet is still covered with a litter of dry, long-dead leaves."[80]

The final political implications of these tragic alternatives, which ultimately crystallized around the choice between "ethical" and "authentic" life, could not be fully assimilated during the turbulent months of late 1918 and early 1919. Whether they tended to emphasize the priority of ethics or of metaphysics, most members of the Sunday Circle found themselves drawn into active involvement within the cultural life of Béla Kun's Bolshevik regime. Under Lukács' leadership as deputy commissar of public education, the solitary artists and philosophers who had formed the Sunday Circle organized unemployed actors to tell fairy tales to proletarian children in the suburbs of Budapest; participated in committees to nationalize private art collections; and generally assumed an important role in the regime's somewhat traditional cultural policies, which centered on efforts to bring the achievements of Hungarian high culture within the reach of workers.[81]

By the summer of 1919, however, it was evident that these decidedly quixotic cultural gestures, along with the entire Kun regime, were doomed to failure, as Hungarian right-wing forces under Admiral Miklós Horthy were reorganizing and reestablishing control over the country. By the end of the year almost all the former members of the Sunday Circle had been forced to flee Hungary, for no individual compromised by radical or even moderately left-wing associations was safe. Within the atmosphere of growing political violence and extremism which had been gathering force in Hungary since late 1918, there was no longer any room for fine ideological distinctions and philosophic nuances.

Perhaps nothing illustrates more strikingly the dangerous revolutionary mystique that the Sunday Circle had acquired in the annals of the new regime than a peculiar incident in the autumn of 1919. In November Balázs' apartment was apparently searched and his diaries confiscated by the police. The event was considered important enough for reporting on the front pages of the right-wing daily *A Nap* (The sun), which gave the following account of the seizure: "The Budapest police have taken into custody the diaries of the writer Béla Balázs . . . since they consider it their responsibility to examine all documents which might shed light on the secret springs and as yet unclarified sources and leaders of communism. As the favorite of Dr. György Lukács, Balázs played such a significant role in the Commissariat of Public Education that every line he wrote, despite its lack of literary merit, has a special interest for the police." Balázs' diaries turned out to be somewhat disappointing, however. Instead of revolutionary theories and diabolical Marxist plots, they contained for the most part "wittily malicious gossip about literary foes" and indelicate, compromising details about ladies (which the police chivalrously vowed not to divulge).[82] Lack of direct evidence, however, was no deterrent; the police continued to view the Sunday Circle as a "special and particularly dangerous secret political organization."[83]

Most of the former Sunday participants fled to nearby Vienna, hoping—incorrectly as it turned out—that Horthy's regime would prove to be ephemeral and that they could shortly return to Budapest to resume their former lives. For a while, the Sunday Circle was actually reconstituted in Vienna under the drastically changed circumstances of emigration, professional insecurity, and political disorientation. Lukács was actively engaged in the underground communist movement by this time, and Balázs provided the following portrait of his friend in December 1919:

> He presents the most heart-rending sight imaginable, deathly pale, hollow cheeked, impatient, and sad. He is watched and followed, he goes around with a gun in his pocket . . . There is a warrant out for his arrest in Budapest which would condemn him to death nine times over.
>
> And here [in Vienna] he is active in hopeless conspiratorial party work, tracking down people who have absconded with party funds. And in the meantime his philosophic genius remains repressed, like a stream forced underground which loosens and destroys the ground above . . . He was born to be a scholar, a solitary savant, a seer of eternal things . . . he who does not speak his own language if more than five people in the world understand him. His is a terrible homelessless; he has become truly homeless because he has lost his spiritual home.[84]

Despite his growing political commitments, Lukács continued to attend the meetings of his Sunday friends, which were now actually held on Mondays. "The ties among us refuse to break," recorded Balázs in 1920. "And only now do I feel what a shame it is that our Sundays did not have a faithful chronicler. It would at least have formed an accurate document of what those brutes have destroyed in Hungary."[85] The Viennese meetings occasionally even succeeded in recapturing some of the vitality of earlier debates. "We have had some wonderful Sundays lately," reported Balázs in the spring of 1921. "On these Sundays the only subject of discussion centers on the problem of communism—that is to say, on the fate and significance of our ethical individualism and artistic-philosophic 'Platonism' in the new world which we want . . . but whose outlines none of us can yet conceive in our minds."[86]

—

From the content of the Viennese debates and discussions it is evident that the former Sunday members were beginning to feel dated by the 1920s, no longer in the forefront of artistic and philosophic innovation, a place they had taken for granted in the years before and during the war. Their many-sided and irreducible individualism seemed out of step with the new age of sectarian politics and professional specialization; their uncompromising cultural elitism out of step with the realities of democracy and mass society; their philosophic idealism and hopes for cultural renewal out of step with the nihilism and cynicism of postwar youth. As a group, Lukács concluded in 1920, they represented "a wonderfully elegant idealism, which is destined to die and to be replaced by something entirely different."[87]

There was no agreement among them as to what this "something entirely different" was to be, though by 1920 Lukács was clearly looking to revolutionary Marxism as the new incarnation of those unfulfilled philosophic and cultural hopes they had cherished as a generation before the war. It was certainly easiest to describe their sense of dislocation in explicitly political terms, as Balázs did in connection with Mannheim and Hauser. In 1921 the communist sympathizer Balázs remarked on the ideological homelessness of friends like Mannheim and Hauser, who had not joined the communist movement in 1918 and had failed to find any alternate source of allegiance. "They are," he wrote in his diary, "orphaned and rootless outside the Sundays, and they can find no appropriate spiritual or professional niche anywhere . . . For today, all intellectual activity that is not somehow rooted in the [communist] movement gains the quality of an idiosyncratic hobby that is no better than stamp collecting. And they are aware of this. They feel that they have missed the train in a provincial way station. They have been pushed to the periphery."[88]

What is noteworthy in this description is the fact that it did not apply exclusively to the noncommunist members of the Sunday Circle. Balázs, sensitive as always to the nuances of the cultural scene around him, was giving expression to a current of anxiety that stemmed as much from his own situation in the postwar world as from that of his non-Marxist friends. As he himself had begun to speculate, "there is something dated in my style"; "I have somehow been left behind" in the realm of literary and artistic innovation.[89] Balázs' anxious self-searchings were prompted in large part by the challenge of a group of young Hungarian avant-garde artists and writers who had coalesced as a group sometime around 1915 and were known for their militant pacifism, their radical socialist sympathies, and their expressionist, surrealist, and futurist orientation in art. The leader of the group, Lajos Kassák, was a self-taught man of working-class origins who maintained close ties with the Italian futurist Marinetti, as well as with leading members of the Dada and later the Bauhaus movements in Germany.

Balázs had become aware of the young avant-gardists as early as 1915, when they brought out the first issue of their experimental pacifist literary journal *A Tett* (Action), closely modeled both in format and ideology on the German *Action*. His immediate reaction to the journal was friendly and receptive, and he sent off an encouraging note to Kassák asking the young editor to place him on the subscription list. Balázs, in fact, had begun to entertain hopes that he was witnessing in the Kassák group the emergence of a youthful following that would continue the cultural legacy he and his Sunday friends had been struggling to establish for the past decade.

Such hopes were not entirely unfounded, since the young artists evidently shared many of the political, cultural, and aesthetic reflexes characteristic of the older group of cultural radicals. The activists, as they liked to call themselves, were also fundamentally opposed to the war, seeing in it the culmination of a corrupt and ossified civilization. They repudiated nineteenth-century realism and Impressionism with possibly even greater fervor than the Sunday Circle, and they too predicted a cultural renewal that, according to Kassák, was to mark the "beginning of a new epoch in the development of mankind."[90] The future culture, proclaimed the activists, again in striking agreement with the Sunday Circle, was to be communal and synthetic in nature, based on a "new, unified way of life."[91] Nor is it a coincidence that both the older group and the young activists admired Bartók as one of the important pioneers of the new art that was to lay the foundations of a future culture. "Bartók," declared an editorial in *Ma* (Today), the successor to *A Tett*, "is the first artist who, liberated from sentimental romanticism and melancholy Impressionism, manages, in this most impressionistic age, to be monumental."[92]

Yet despite such undeniable congruences between the two groups, the activists made clear from the beginning that they wanted to have nothing to do with the slightly older scholars and artists of the Sunday Circle. Just as Lukács and Balázs had rebuffed in their time the well-meaning advances of liberal scholars like Bernát Alexander, so now they in turn were being rejected in no uncertain terms by the young avant-gardists. "The recent lead editorial in *A Tett* was directed at me," Balázs recorded ruefully in 1915. "They instructed me that I have nothing to do with them. They are futurists, activists, world reformers, and deny the inner life of the soul. They don't know what they are talking about, but from all this confused chatter one thing is clear: they don't feel any affinity or solidarity with me, and they want no part of me. Otherwise, one or two of them are talented, though they are green and without taste."[93]

The activists' reservations about Balázs in particular and the Sunday Circle in general were subtle and, initially at any rate, rooted in temperamental incompatibility rather than any major philosophic or aesthetic disagreement. What they objected to in Balázs' poetry and prose was its passivity, its paralysis in the face of the world of action. Balázs was, wrote one reviewer of his published war memoirs of 1915, remote from external realities, overcome by an excess of individualism that made it impossible for him to act without acute self-consciousness. With such a man even "the great gesture becomes a pose," for "the world of realities does not readily tolerate the dreamer of the shadow of eternity."[94]

At the very time that Lukács was proclaiming in lengthy reviews Balázs' unique place in modernist, experimental literature, the young avant-gardists were mercilessly pointing out how irrelevant the older man's scruples, conflicts, pains, and hesitations had become for them. Balázs' abiding themes of the irreducible conflict between subjectivity and objective culture, of the dilemma of the self, helplessly struggling in a world unmediated by values, was, they declared, "no longer a problem for us."[95] According to their numerous militant manifestoes, the avant-gardists resolved this key conflict not by the discovery of a new, more meaningful social order but rather by a more un-compromising, more aggressively hostile rejection of the old one. The new artists, declared Kassák in a striking metaphor borrowed from the French cubist poet Apollinaire, stood for absolute liberation from all institutions, morality, family ties; in fact, from all previous conditions of mankind which, "carrying its father's corpse on its back and its helpless child in its lap . . . could never arrive at the most worthwhile goal, at the source of uncompromising, dynamic life."[96]

Clearly, what had started off as a mere difference of temperament and emphasis between the two groups gradually blossomed into a major philosophic disagreement involving a fundamental reinterpretation of the relationship between the self and the world, between individuality and culture. In striking contrast to the older cultural radicals, the younger avant-gardists had succeeded in abolishing the duality between subject and object, between inner experience and outer reality, without seeming to resort to those tragic and ultimately impoverishing ideological choices which members of the Sunday Circle felt it necessary to make in late 1918 and early 1919. The activists, who had been self-proclaimed socialists since the outbreak of the Bolshevik Revolution in 1917, emphatically denied the existence of an insoluble conflict between their communist sympathies and their radical, iconoclastic individualism. For them socialism did not constitute a necessary historical truth embodied within an organized party or even within a particular class but rather a dynamic, ever-changing ideal which could in no way conflict with the fullest expression of artistic and personal freedom. So certain did they feel of their views that they did not hesitate to challenge Béla Kun himself on this issue. Despite Kun's repeated invitations, the activists conspicuously refused to join the Communist party in December 1918, declaring that they could more effectively serve the socialist cause as spokesmen of "the individual revolution of mankind"[97] than as docile followers within an existing socialist organization. When Kun and other socialist leaders disagreed, Kassák publicly put him in his place in an open letter which declared: "I honor you as one of the greatest political leaders, but allow me to express doubts about your understanding of art . . . Your superficial criticisms harm not individuals but the fulfillment of the revolution."[98]

The issue of contention that separated Kassák from the leaders of Hungarian communism in 1919 was, ironically enough, similar to the one that had alienated him from Balázs and the Sunday Circle somewhat earlier. Kassák and his followers, unlike the older cultural radicals, were, according to their own admission, "ideological anarchists,"[99] whose self-declared role in society, even in a socialist one, was that of perpetual critics and revolutionaries. For them the revolution could never be embodied in any particular social order or ideology because it was an independent force always to be found in the future, never contained in the present.

The implicit differences of attitude between the older cultural radicals and the young activists erupted in the early 1920s into a heated aesthetic controversy which, in many respects, crystalized the underlying philosophic viewpoints of both groups. The protagonists in the controversy were Kassák and Balázs, who were both living in Vienna at the time, and the subject at issue was the meaning and implication of the most recent avant-garde art, especially expressionism.[100] Kassák reiterated that the essential creed of avant-gardism was radical liberation not only from external and internal constraints but from all conceivable aesthetic rules. True modern art, he declared, was "comparable to nothing, measurable with nothing: for all artistic creation is a new synthetic objectification of the world process . . . And the essence of the world is movement, eternal revolution against its very self . . . All artistic creation is an endless revolutionary assault against the reader, the viewer, the listener, against the state, society, against the defenders of the status quo."[101]

Balázs, forced on the defensive in spite of himself, responded that an art which repudiated all aesthetic standards, all conceivable social norms and stable cultural values, necessarily opened the floodgates to chaos and nihilism. The newest avant-garde, of which Dada was the most consistent representative, Balázs argued, was not so much a

new artistic current as a movement against art and all of culture . . . It is a new barbarian invasion. The expression of cultural decay, a revolutionary symptom . . . it acknowledges no fixed point, no eternal values to which it might subordinate itself. As with the insane, its existence has become autonomous (because outside of itself nothing exists). This is why they militantly oppose all faith, all science, all art . . . The complete relativity of the physical world is only proof that the absolute and eternal realities exist within the soul.[102]

Though Balázs had been pushed into the unenviable posture of criticizing youth, innovation, and novelty, his was not a conservative standpoint intransigently defending the status quo against the youthful newcomers. On the contrary, he himself remained a radical critic of existing culture, and he understood only too well the source and nature of the young avant-gardists' radical malaise. Theirs was essentially a family quarrel, which hinged not so much on disagreement about the need for cultural innovation as on the definition of the nature and foundation of this activity. The root of their conflict was ultimately philosophic and metaphysical in nature: it concerned the existence of objective values and truths that could become independent of the self and form the basis of artistic creation. Balázs, Lukács, and most of their contemporaries in the Sunday Circle still maintained the belief in, or at any rate the nostalgia for, some form of universal philosophic truth to be embodied in a revitalized, nonfragmented social order. The young activists, by contrast, while paying lip service to the notion of synthesis and totality, had pushed it so completely into a distant, ever-receding future that it ceased to have any concrete implications for their life and art. As Balázs realized with unerring intuition, the activists' declarations of hostility to existing society were nothing more than declarations, for they remained deeply enmeshed within the very society they criticized, lacking the essential conceptual tools for transcending its limitations. Their art, wrote Balázs, was ultimately only a form of "hysterical anarchism which remains more individualistic than the most eccentric manifestations of bourgeois literature." The activists had indeed overcome the tensions of dualism and alienation that the older artistic generation had struggled with, but only at the expense of reformulating and essentially abandoning the notion of absolute values, aesthetic form, and cultural totality. "Instead of merging the individual self into the multiplicity of the whole," concluded

Balázs, "they had ended up shattering the individual self into the multiplicity of fragments."[103]

The debate between Balázs and Kassák had to remain inconclusive, for in a sense both men, both generations, had truth on their side. Kassák was positing an irrefutable position when he pointed out to Balázs that "an age has closed, a new age has begun, and the sons of this new age have acquired a different aesthetic sensibility and valuation. I ask you: why do you refuse to acknowledge in this age drowning in fire and blood that we are experiencing the agonies of historic death and rebirth?"[104] For their part, Balázs and his friends, having been raised and formed within the peaceful and seemingly stable universe of prewar liberal culture, could not understand the full depth and violence of the newer generation's experience of discontinuity. The older radicals did not feel the need for or the possibility of entirely rejecting the last vestiges of rational humanism which had formed the bedrock of the old philosophic order.

It is ironic, but not illogical, that their continuing loyalty to the values and philosophic premises of the past should eventually find expression in political commitments and ideologies that set some of the group diametrically at odds with others. Those who, like Lukács, chose "authentic" over "ethical" life in 1918 slowly evolved a more viable, less paradoxical form of Marxism than the one he had articulated in "Tactics and Ethics." As was usual in Lukács' case, the process of reorientation proved to be an immensely creative period; it resulted in perhaps his best-known work in the noncommunist world, *History and Class Consciousness*, first published in 1923.

Those who, like Mannheim and Lesznai, chose to emphasize the priority of ethics over metaphysics ended up in the opposing political camp, reaffirming a new form of liberal commitment which prided itself precisely on its clarity of vision and lack of illusions about the future. Mannheim, in a letter addressed to Oszkár Jászi in 1936, expressed concisely the nature of this stoical, disenchanted liberalism that had come to replace the utopian hopes of the prewar years. "As far as I can see," he admitted to Jászi,

> we are both at our roots finally "liberals," but you attempt to fly in the face of our age with noble defiance, whereas I, as a soci-

ologist, would like to divine the secret springs of the age (even
if these springs are diabolical); for I believe this is the only way
that we can prevent the social structure of the new age from
gaining ascendancy over us and to try to make sure that we gain
ascendancy over it. To transpose with the aid of technology liberal
values into modern society—perhaps a paradoxical enterprise—
but the only viable route if one does not wish to react simply
with defiance. Though I can understand this gesture too, and
perhaps it is merely a question of time before I follow suit.[105]

From this new perspective, the Hungarian revolution of 1919,
which had tried to create a new world out of the ashes of the
old one, came to appear a premature and ultimately futile exercise. Anna Lesznai, in a 1954 sketch for her autobiographical
novel about the Hungarian fin de siècle, pronounced final judgment on the Hungarian Bolshevik experiment of 1919. "Our
attempts to change the world," declares one of the heroes of the
projected novel, "cannot come to fruition if events do not unfold
naturally in and of themselves. The gentle humanists raped history when they attempted to alter radically the course of events.
Such actions can only bring trouble . . . You see, every world
whose birth had to be aided by human hands has turned out to
be worse than the previous one. To awaken people's consciousness before their time is like trying to open the bud of a flower
with one's fingers."[106]

The political fragmentation among members of the former
Sunday Circle, which was becoming increasingly evident by the
late 1920s, did not result in a complete severing of social or
intellectual contacts among the group of friends. Significantly
enough, many continued to debate and argue with one another
throughout the 1920s, trying to understand the divergent currents which were carrying them in such different directions. In
1928, for instance, Anna Lesznai recorded a revealing conversation with Lukács in which she asked him to define

> what has remained intact in his current communist world outlook
> from the spiritual values of the past. Let us say from the soul:—
> as far as I can see, he kept everything which is able to comprehend
> more or less completely the historical process, but named it in-
> dividual consciousness. Is the maximum to be hoped for, I ask,
> simply understanding? It turns out that this understanding is not
> passive, but an active engagement in the historical process which

makes possible the appropriation of fate, the humanizing of the world order.[107]

Lesznai was not alone in her curiosity about the elements of continuity in Lukács' thought. A year earlier Mannheim had apparently posed a similar question to Lukács, wondering to what extent he had been able to incorporate in his Marxist philosophy those "organic and dynamic values which 'romantic cultural criticism' embodies and demands." Lukács' answer, that Marxism had nothing to do either with the organic values of romanticism or with the rationalism of capitalism, nevertheless revealed certain deeper philosophic continuities with the past. "The organic and dynamic can also be rational," he is reported to have answered, "*even* if it transcends human rationality today. Individual reason itself can be transcendental—for it is a spoke extending outward to a higher network of reason beyond individual knowledge."[108]

Such debates and contacts understandably became rarer and less intense with the passing of years. Yet the fact that they remained possible for as long as they did reveals the survival of a common ground for discourse that transcended even those political, ideological, and linguistic barriers which came to separate the group increasingly by the early 1930s. This common background of philosophic values and cultural reflexes was evident in their instinctive aesthetic preferences, which remained remarkably similar. None of the former Sunday members ever fully reconciled themselves to the irrationalist, existentialist perspective of the new avant-garde, which had first appeared on their horizon in the guise of the Kassák group. Even Lesznai, who was frankly interested in the experiments of postwar expressionists, futurists, and Cubists, found it impossible to follow in their footsteps. "I do not understand, I do not experience from within, the modern perspective," she complained in the late 1920s. "Since I have tried to make it my own, my paintings have gotten worse. I feel that I should understand it in order to be able to consciously reject it. But what should form my own perspective? I no longer know—in words or in my life."[109] Unable to identify with the ethos of the avant-garde and equally unable to formulate an authentic perspective of their own, many former Sunday members ended up reaffirming nineteenth-century realism or classicism, which could at least provide a morally congenial and intellectually comprehensible vision. This transformation of aesthetic judgment was to be most dramatic and self-conscious in Lukács' case. He gave the following account of it in a letter of 1940. During the twelve years followng his entry into the Communist party, he wrote to Balázs, he had been forced to undertake "a thoroughgoing revision of all my views, of all my assumptions about reality . . . Only after this process of inner transformation had been completed did I notice that the entire system of my aesthetic categories had also changed. Balzac had come to replace Flaubert in my estimation; Tolstoy, Dostoevsky; Fielding, Sterne; etc."[110]

These strikingly conservative aesthetic conclusions formed the logical though not inevitable culmination of a tortuous line of development which was, nevertheless, deeply rooted in the cultural soil of the prewar years. Lukács and his friends had been part of an essentially transitional generation, uneasily bestriding two epochs, fully at home in neither but intuitively understanding both. Their radical cultural critique had expressed in the most uncompromising terms possible their tragic perception that the forms and values of liberal culture could no longer encompass the living experiences of individuals entering the twentieth century. And yet their passionate faith in the possibility of an integrated culture of the future, their abiding nostalgia for totality and communally defined values, unmistakably revealed their continuing links to the philosophic traditions of nineteenth-century idealism and rationalism.

Unlike their younger artistic contemporaries, the activists, Lukács' generation did not succeed in completely exploding the heritage of the past or in fully liberating the self from the painful dualism between subject and object which defined their malaise in the modern world. Nevertheless, their ambiguous position, with all its psychological discomforts and intellectual paradoxes, had proven to be a uniquely creative one, mobilizing energies and crystalizing insights that would not have been possible in less exposed, less marginalized positions. And it could perhaps also be argued that precisely because they so stubbornly held on to the values and standards of the past, they were able to mount a more sustained and consistent critique of modern industrial civilization than the younger avant-garde, who possessed no vantage point beyond their personal rage, no historic memories beyond the fragmented present.

In retrospect, it seems clear that Lukács and his friends had been more dependent on the despised liberal order they hoped to transcend than they could possibly have realized in the years before the war. The old culture had ultimately provided not only the ideals in terms of which they opposed it but also the social tolerance and political stability that had made such an opposition possible in the first place. Of all of them, it was perhaps Lajos Fülep who in later life was most willing to admit their collective indebtedness to the culture of the past. Unlike most members of the Sunday Circle, Fülep did not emigrate in 1919, choosing instead to retreat into internal exile as a Protestant pastor in an out-of-the-way little village in southern Hungary. Speaking in the name of his entire generation, he wrote in 1932 to an old friend peripherally associated with the Sundays: "You, along with a few others, represent for me that world in which, and for which alone, it is worthwhile to live. They have destroyed this world and now we sit like Robinson Crusoes scattered on different desert islands, and occasionally we wave to each other with the flag that we still hold on to."[111] Ten years later, writing to the same friend amidst rumors of deportations and concentration camps, Fülep returned to the same theme and in a sense completed the thought of the earlier letter. "We are the few—and the fewer the more dependent on one another—remaining members of a common world . . . This world is worth holding on to because it represented the values of spirit and intellect in a larger world that was not one whit less abominable than today's. Today's is only the inevitable result of that earlier one."[112]

BIBLIOGRAPHICAL NOTE
NOTES · INDEX

BIBLIOGRAPHICAL NOTE

The single most important source for Lukács' early life is his pre-1917 letters, unpublished manuscripts, and diaries, which are found at the Magyar Akadémia Filozofiai Intézet, Lukács Archivum és Könyvtár, Budapest. (Most of the early letters are in Hungarian, but from 1910, German and occasionally French begin to predominate.) A selection of Lukács' early letters has been published by Éva Fekete and Éva Karádi, eds., *Lukács György levelezése (1902–1917)* (Budapest: Magvetö, 1981). A complete collection of Lukács' early articles and reviews, including the essays he published in *A lélek és a formák* (Soul and forms), can be found in Árpád Timár, ed., *Lukács György, Ifjúkori művek (1902–1918)* (Budapest: Magvetö, 1977). Lukács' major pre-Marxist philosophic work, his incomplete aesthetic, has been published by György Márkus and Frank Benseler, eds., as *Heidelberger Philosophie der Kunst 1912–1914*, and *Heidelberger Asthetik 1916–1918* (Neuwied: Hermann Luchterland Verlag, 1974). The aesthetic fragment has also been translated into Hungarian and published as Lukács György, *A heidelbergi művészetfilozófia és esztétika* (Budapest: Magvetö, 1975). His last pre-Marxist writing, *Die Theorie des Romans*, is available in English as *The Theory of the Novel* (Cambridge, Mass.: MIT Press, 1971).

Throughout his long life, Lukács had the habit of summarizing the course of his tortuous personal and philosophic development in prefaces, interviews, and autobiographical accounts, which provide important guideposts for the historian. See in particular Lukács' 1969 introduction to his *Utam Marxhoz: Válogatott filozófiai tanulmányok* (Budapest: Magvetö, 1971); his 1969 introduction to his *Magyar irodalom—Magyar kultúra: Válogatott tanulmányok* (Budapest: Gondolat, 1970); and perhaps most important, his last autobiographical sketch, "Gelebtes Denken," which has been published by István Eörsi, *Gelebtes Denken: Eine Autobiographie im Dialogue* (Frankfort on the Main: Suhrkamp, 1981).

The most important recent secondary sources which deal with Lukács' pre-Marxist and early Marxist career are David Ketteler, "Culture and Revolution: Lukács in the Hungarian Revolutions of 1918/19," *Telos*, no. 10 (1971); 35–92; Michael Löwy, *Pour une sociologie des intellectuels révolutionnaires: L'évolution politique de Lukács 1909–1929* (Paris: Presses Universitaires de France, 1976); Paul Breines and Andrew Arato, *The Young Lukács and the Origins of Western Marxism* (New York: Seabury Press, 1979); Lee Congdon, *The Young Lukács* (Chapel Hill: University of North Carolina Press, 1983); Ágnes Heller, ed., *Lukács Reappraised* (New York: Columbia University Press, 1983); and J. M. Bernstein, *The Philosophy of the Novel: Lukács, Marxism and the Dialectic of Form* (Minneapolis: University of Minneapolis Press, 1984).

The lives of the other members of the Sunday Circle are, understandably, less well documented, though several of them have left extensive diaries which give invaluable insight into their prewar and wartime concerns. Perhaps the most important is Béla Balázs' diary, which begins in 1905 and continues until the midtwenties, found in the Magyar Tudományos Akadémia Könyvtára, Kézirattár, Budapest. Of Balázs' published works before and during the war, his autobiographical novel *Lehetetlen emberek* (Budapest: Szépirodalmi Könyvkiadó, 1965), and his war memoirs, *Lélek a háborúban* (Gyoma: Kner Izidor, 1916), are perhaps the most directly useful. His later autobiography, *Álmodó ifjúság* (Budapest: Magvetö és Szépirodalmi Könyvkiadó, 1976), is especially revealing about his early youth and social milieu. A good biography of Balázs is Magda K. Nagy, *Balázs Béla világa* (Budapest: Kossuth Könyvkiadó, 1973). In English, see Lee Congdon, "The Making of a Hungarian Revolutionary: The Unpublished Diary of Béla Balázs," *Journal of Contemporary History*, 8, no. 3 (1973), 57–74.

Anna Lesznai's diaries, personal accounts, and sketches for novels are in the Petöfi Irodalmi Múzeum, Budapest. Her autobiographical novel *Kezdetben volt a kert*, 2 vols. (Budapest: Szépirodalmi Könyvkiadó, 1966), is an invaluable source for both Lesznai's early life and the Hungarian fin de siècle. A recent biography of Lesznai is Erzsébet Vezér, *Lesznai Anna élete* (Budapest: Kossuth Könyvkiadó, 1979).

Lajos Fülep's correspondence is found in the Magyar Tudományos Akadémia Könyvtára, Kézirattár, Budapest. His early articles, reviews, and studies have been published in Árpád Timár, ed., *Fülep Lajos, A müvészet forradalmától a nagy forradalomig*, 2 vols. (Budapest: Magvetö, 1974). For the other members of the Sunday Circle, an excellent collection of reminiscences and articles is Éva Karádi and Erzsébet Vezér, eds., *A Vasárnapi Kör: Dokumentumok* (Budapest: Gondolat, 1980). For the collective philosophic goals of the Sunday members, the most important source is their short-lived journal, *A Szellem*, March and December 1911. See also Dénes Lajos, ed., *Emlékkönyv Alexander Bernát hatvanadik születése napjára (Dolgozatok a modern filozófia köréből)* (Budapest, 1910); Béla Fogarasi, *Zalai Béla: In Memoriam* (Budapest, 1916); and Karl Mannheim, *Lélek és kultúra* (Budapest: Franklin Társulat, 1918). Scattered articles, book reviews, and essays by members of the Sunday Circle can also be found in prewar literary and philosophic journals like *Nyugat, Huszadik Század, Renaissance,* and *Athenaeum.* For secondary works about members of the Sunday Circle, see Árpád Timár, "Hauser Arnold pályakezdése," *Ars Hungarica,* no. 1 (1974), 192–204; Lee Congdon, "Mannheim as Philosopher," *Journal of European Studies,* 7, no. 25 (1977), 1–18; and Zoltán Novák, *A Vasárnapi Társaság* (Budapest: Kossuth Könyvkiadó, 1979).

There does not yet exist a full-length biography of Oszkár Jászi and the radicals in Hungarian; the best source for their ideas remains their journal *Huszadik Század,* 1900–1918. Some of the more important articles of the radical sociologists have been published in Attila Pók, ed. *A Huszadik Század körének történetfelfogása* (Budapest: Gondolat, 1982), and György Litván and László Szücs, eds. *A szociológia első magyar műhelye: A Huszadik Század köre,* 2 vols. (Budapest: Gondolat, 1973). Jászi's early correspondence is in the Országos Széchényi Könyvtár: Levéltára, Budapest. His papers dating from his emigration are located in the Butler Library, Columbia University, New York City. For official reactions to the radicals, the most useful source is the government-sponsored political journal *Magyar Figyelő,* 1911–1914.

Hungarian cultural life in late 1918 and early 1919 is best reflected in contemporary periodicals like *Szabadgondolat,* whose issues of December 1918 and February and March 1919 were almost exclusively concerned with the debate about Bolshevism. For an analysis of this debate, see György Litván, "Apáink válaszútja: Tallózás a *Szabadgondolat* 1918–1919-es számaiban," *Új Irás,* 19, no. 3 (1972), 109–117. The official journal of the Hungarian Communist party, *Vörös Ujság,* and the Social Democratic *Népszava* and *Az Ember* give slightly conflicting versions of the aims and cultural policies of the Béla Kun regime. Contemporary novels dealing with the events and personalities of late 1918 and early 1919 are Ervin Sinkó, *Optimisták: Történelmi regény 1918/19-ből,* 2 vols. (Budapest: Forum Könyvkiadó, n.d.); Lajos Kassák, *Egy ember élete* (Budapest: Magvetö, 1966); and József Lengyel, *Visegrádi utca* (Budapest: Szépirodalmi Könyvkiadó, 1962). Michael Károlyi gives an excellent firsthand account of 1918–19 in *Hit illúziók nélkül* (Budapest: Magvetö, 1977). (In English, *Memoirs of Michael Károlyi: Faith Without Illusion*, London: J. Cape, 1956.) See also Iván Völgyes, ed., *Hungary in Revolution 1918–19: Nine Essays* (Lincoln: University of Nebraska Press, 1971).

The nature of the Hungarian avant-garde that crystalized around Kassák during the war years is best reflected in their own wartime journals, *A Tett* (1915–1916), and *Ma* (1916–1919). Kassák's correspondence is found in the Kassák Múzeum, Budapest. For secondary sources on the Hungarian activists, see Júlia Szabó, *A magyar aktivizmus története* (Budapest: Akadémiai Kiadó, 1971); Krisztina Passuth, *Magyar művészek az európai avantgarde-ban 1919–1925* (Budapest: Corvina, 1974); and György Rónai, *Kassák Lajos: Alkotásai és vallomásai tükrében* (Budapest: Szépirodalmi Könyvkiadó, 1971). For the debate between Kassák and Balázs, see the newspaper *Bécsi Magyar Újság* for 1920.

For a general intellectual and cultural history of the Hungarian turn of the century, a dated but still useful book is Zoltán Horváth, *Magyar századforduló* (Budapest: Gondolat, 1961). It has been published in German as *Die Jahrhundertwende in Ungarn. Geschichte der 2. Reformgeneration (1896–1914)* (Neuwied: Luchterland, 1966). More recent studies dealing with the same period are Endre Kiss and Kristóf Nyíri, eds., *A magyar filozófiai gondolkodás a századelőn* (Budapest: Kossuth Könyvkiadó, 1977), and Kristóf Nyíri, *A Monarchia szellemi életéről: Filozófiatörténeti tanulmányok* (Budapest: Gondolat, 1980). The best historical treatment of prewar Hungary and the crisis of Dualism can be found in Péter Hanák, ed., *Magyarország története 1890–1918*, 2 vols. (Budapest: Akadémiai Kiadó, 1978).

NOTES

Introduction

1. See Robert Wohl, *The Generation of 1914* (Cambridge, Mass.: Harvard University Press, 1979).

2. See Lee Congdon, "Mannheim as Philosopher," *Journal of European Studies*, 7, no. 25 (1977), 1–18.

3. Leszek Kolakowski, *Main Currents of Marxism* (Oxford: Oxford University Press, 1981), III, 253.

4. Paul Breines and Andrew Arato, *The Young Lukács and the Origins of Western Marxism* (New York: Seabury Press, 1979).

5. D. H. Lawrence, "Georgian Poetry," *Rhythm* (March 1913), quoted in Malcolm Bradbury, "London, 1890–1920," in Malcolm Bradbury and James McFarlane, eds., *Modernism, 1890–1930* (New York: Penguin Books, 1976), p. 187.

6. Renato Poggioli, *The Theory of the Avant-Garde* (Cambridge, Mass.: Harvard University Press, 1968), p. 4.

7. Richard Ellmann, "Two Faces of Edward," in *Edwardians and Late Victorians* (New York: Columbia University Press, 1960), p. 196.

8. Stephen Spender, *The Struggle of the Modern* (Berkeley: University of California Press, 1963), p. 209.

9. Ibid., p. 106.

10. Malcolm Bradbury, "The Cities of Modernism," in Bradbury and McFarlane, *Modernism*, p. 100.

11. Béla Bartók, "Magyar népzene és új magyar zene" (Hungarian folk music and modern Hungarian music), in *Önéletrajz: Írások a zenéről* (Autobiography: articles on music) (Budapest, 1946), p. 22.

12. Carl Schorske, *Fin de Siècle Vienna: Politics and Culture* (New York: Alfred A. Knopf, 1980), p. 120.

13. Karl Mannheim, quoted in Anna Lesznai, Diaries, 1920–1930, Petöfi Irodalmi Múzeum, Budapest.

14. For an interpreation of Lukács' "classicism," see Ferenc Fehér, "Lukács in Weimar," in Ágnes Heller, ed., *Lukács Reappraised* (New York: Columbia University Press, 1983).

15. Quoted in Bradbury, "London, 1890–1920," p. 188.

1. The Sunday Circle

1. Karl Mannheim, "Heidelbergi levelek" (Letters from Heidelberg), *Tűz* (Bratislava), 15 November–1 December 1921, pp. 46–50. All translations are my own unless otherwise noted.

2. Peter Gay coined the phrase to describe the ethos of Weimar Germany in *Weimar Culture: The Outsider as Insider* (New York: Harper and Row, 1968).

3. Karl Mannheim, *Lélek és kultúra* (Soul and culture) (Budapest: Franklin Társulat, 1918), p. 1.

4. See Robert Wohl, *The Generation of 1914* (Cambridge, Mass.: Harvard University Press, 1979).

5. Mannheim, *Lélek és kultúra*, p. 1.

6. Georg Lukács (b. György Lukács), 1885–1971.

7. Karl Mannheim (b. Károly Mannheim), 1893–1947.

8. Arnold Hauser, 1892–1978.

9. Charles de Tolnay (b. Károly Tolnay), 1899–.

10. Antal Frigyes, 1887–1954.

11. Béla Balázs (b. Herbert Bauer), 1884–1949.

12. Lajos Fülep, 1885–1970.

13. Béla Balázs, Diaries, 23 December 1915, Akadémiai Levéltár, Budapest.

14. Béla Balázs kept an extensive diary, now in the Akadémiai Levéltár in Budapest, which is probably the most useful source for accounts of the Sunday Circle. Anna Lesznai also kept a diary, which can be found in the Petöfi Irodalmi Múzeum in Budapest. For glimpses of the Sunday Circle in fictional accounts, there is Béla Balázs' novel *Lehetetlen emberek* (Impossible people), also translated into German as *Unmögliche Leute;* Anna Lesznai's two-volume novel *Kezdetben volt a kert* (In the beginning was the garden), translated into German as *Spätherbst in Eden;* Emma Ritoók's *A szellem kalandorjai* (Adventurers of the spirit); and Károly Tolnay's *Ferenczy Noémi* (Naomi Ferenczy). An excellent collec-

tion of interviews of, and written reminiscences by, former Sunday members is Éva Karádi and Erzsébet Vezér, eds., *A Vasárnapi kör: Dokumentumok* (The Sunday Circle: documents) (Budapest: Gondolat, 1980). I was able to gain a great deal of valuable insight into the Sunday Circle from repeated conversations in New York with Tibor Gergely (1900–1978), who was one of the youngest members of the group and was later married to Anna Lesznai.

15. Emma Ritoók, Diaries, courtesy of Erzsébet Vezér.

16. Imre Kner to Lajos Fülep, 18 February 1934, Akadémiai Levéltár, Budapest.

17. Karl Mannheim to Béla Balázs, 15 February 1930, Akadémiai Levéltár.

18. Charles de Tolnay, "Reminiscences," in Karádi and Vezér, *A Vasárnapi kör*, p. 49.

19. Georg Lukács, "Gelebtes Denken," Lukács Archive, Budapest. A version of this autobiography was published by István Eörsi, ed., *Gelebtes Denken: Eine Autobiographie im Dialogue* (Frankfort on the Main: Suhrkamp, 1981).

20. Edit Hajós to Georg Lukács, 8 October 1916, Lukács Archive.

21. Balázs, Diaries, 1917.

22. Edit Rényi (b. 1896), today called Edith Ludowyk Gyömröi, is a practicing psychoanalyst in London.

23. Edit (Gyömröi) Rényi, "Reminiscences," in Karádi and Vezér, *A Vasárnapi kör*, p. 65.

24. Béla Balázs to Mihály Babits, 26 September 1910, Országos Széchényi Könyvtár, Kézirattár, Budapest.

25. Lajos Fülep, "Introduction," *A Szellem* (March 1911); reprinted in Lajos Fülep, *A Művészet forradalmától a nagy forradalomig: Cikkek, tanulmányok* (From the revolution in art to the great revolution: articles, sketches), 2 vols. (Budapest: Magvető, 1974), II, 602; hereafter cited as *From the Revolution in Art*.

26. Lajos Fülep to Georg Lukács, 28 December 1910, Lukács Archive; his italics.

27. Balázs, Diaries, spring 1912.

28. Béla Balázs to Georg Lukács, mid-June 1910, Akadémiai Levéltár.

29. Georg Lukács to Leo Popper, 9 November 1910, Lukács Archive.

30. Béla Balázs to Mihály Babits, 26 September 1910, Országos Széchényi Könyvtár, Kézirattár, Budapest.

31. Mannheim, *Lélek és kultúra*, p. 1.

32. Lajos Fülep, "Introduction," *A Szellem*, reprinted in *From the Revolution in Art*, II, 603.

33. Béla Fogarasi, *Zalai Béla: In Memoriam* (Budapest, 1916), p. 14.

34. Leo Popper, "Párizsi levél" (Letter from Paris), 1 February 1909, Lukács Archive.

35. Balázs, Diaries, 1915.

36. Lajos Fülep to Georg Lukács, early January 1911, Lukács Archive.

37. Karl Mannheim, "Ernst Bloch: *Geist der Utopie*," *Athenaeum*, 5, nos. 5–6 (1919), 208.

38. Balázs, Diaries, 23 December 1915.

39. Lukács' comment was reported in Balázs, Diaries, 1915.

40. Sándor Hevesi to Georg Lukács, 30 November 1910, Lukács Archive.

41. Paul Bourget, "Preface" (1885), in *Essais de psychologie contemporaine* (Essays in contemporary psychology) (Paris: Librairie Plon, 1912), I, xxi.

42. Leo Popper to Georg Lukács, 19 April 1909, Lukács Archive; his italics. This is a reference to Margaret Island, a pleasure park in the Danube between the Pest and Buda shores.

43. See Georg Simmel, "The Meaning of Culture," in P. A. Lawrence, ed., *Georg Simmel: Sociologist and European* (New York: Barnes and Noble Books, 1976).

44. Mannheim, *Lélek és kultúra*, p. 9.

45. Ibid., pp. 10, 27.

46. Ibid., p. 17.

47. Max Nordau, *Degeneration* (New York: Howard Fertig, 1968), p. 7.

48. Bourget, *Essais de psychologie contemporaine*, I, 26.

49. Béla Balázs to Georg Lukács, January 1911, Lukács Archive.

50. Béla Balázs, *Lehetetlen emberek* (Impossible people) (Budapest: Szépirodalmi Könyvkiadó, 1965), p. 142.

51. Mannheim, "Heidelbergi levelek," *Tűz*, 1–5 April 1922, pp. 91–95.

52. Anna Lesznai, "Reminiscences," in Karádi and Vezér, *A Vasárnapi kör*, p. 55.

53. Balázs, Diaries, 24 March 1916.

54. Georg Lukács to Paul Ernst, September 1911, Lukács Archive.

55. Anna Lesznai, Diaries, n.d., Petőfi Irodalmi Múzeum, Budapest.

56. Anna Lesznai, "Babonás észrevételek a mese és a tragédia lélektanához," (Superstitious insights into the psychology of the tragedy and the fairy tale), *Nyugat*, 14, nos. 13–24 (1918), 57–58; her italics.

57. Balázs, Diaries, 1907.

58. Karl Mannheim to Georg Lukács, 5 January 1912, Lukács Archive.

59. Balázs, Diaries, 1916.

60. Ibid.

61. Béla Balázs to Georg Lukács, 21 June 1915, Lukács Archive; his italics.

62. Béla Balázs to Georg Lukács, October 1916, Lukács Archive; his italics.

63. Balázs, Diaries, March 1917, Gyuri is the Hungarian form of George.
64. Georg Lukács, Diaries, 11 May 1910, Lukács Archive.
65. József Lukács to Georg Lukács, 23 August 1909, Lukács Archive.
66. Georg Lukács to Leo Popper, 9 November 1910, Lukács Archive.
67. Lukács, Diaries, 29 May 1910.
68. Lukács, Diaries, 26 June 1910.
69. Lukács, Diaries, 25 November 1911.
70. Georg Lukács to Leo Popper, 9 November 1910, Lukács Archive.
71. Ibid.
72. Georg Lukács to Leo Popper, December 1910, Lukács Archive.
73. Balázs, Diaries, 1913.
74. Hilda Bauer to Georg Lukács, 4 July 1912, Lukács Archive.
75. Balázs, Diaries, 28 May 1917.
76. Balázs, Diaries, 1918.
77. Arnold Hauser, "Reminiscences," in Karádi and Vezér, *A Vasárnapi kör*, p. 63.
78. Béla Balázs to Georg Lukács, October 1910, Lukács Archive.
79. Balázs, Diaries, 5 September 1905.
80. Balázs, Diaries, 7 September 1911.
81. Balázs, Diaries, 1915.
82. Balázs, Diaries, 28 May 1917.
83. Balázs, Diaries, February 1916.
84. Balázs, Diaries, September 1918.
85. Emma Ritoók, Diaries, courtesy of Erzébet Vezér.
86. Juliska Láng (1893–1955) was trained in both psychology and philosophy, receiving her doctorate from the University of Budapest in 1919. She married Mannheim after they had both emigrated from Hungary. After Mannheim's death in 1947, she practiced psychoanalysis and was associated with Anna Freud.
87. Edit Hajós (1889–1975) studied medicine in France and Switzerland and actually practiced medicine for a while in Hungary. In 1918 she went to Russia with a Red Cross team and remained behind to become a member of the Bolshevik party in Petrograd. After living in several countries, she finally settled in London. But her life of adventure was not yet over: in 1948, on the occasion of a brief visit to Hungary, she was jailed illegally and remained in solitary confinement for seven years. She described the experience under a pseudonym, Edith Bone, in *Seven Years Solitary* (New York: Harcourt, Brace, 1957).
88. Emma Ritoók (1868–1945) studied philosophy in Leipzig, Paris, and Berlin, where she was briefly associated with Simmel's seminar on the philosophy of culture. Unlike most of the other members of the Sunday Circle, she moved to the political right after the war.
89. Anna Lesznai (1885–1966) was closely associated with the literary journal *Nyugat* and also exhibited with the postimpressionist art-

ists known as "Nyolcak" (The Eight). In 1919 she briefly emigrated to Vienna, then returned to her native village, only to emigrate to New York permanently in 1939.

90. Anna Lesznai, *Kezdetben volt a kert* (In the beginning was the garden) (Budapest: Szépirodalmi Könyvkiadó, 1966), II, 149.

91. Balázs, Diaries, 22 November 1918.

92. Balázs, Diaries, February 1916.

93. Balázs, Diaries, 28 December 1915.

94. G. M. Young, *Victorian England: Portrait of an Age* (London: Oxford University Press, 1974), p. 91.

95. Georg Lukács to Lajos Fülep, May 1913, Lukács Archive.

96. Juliska Láng, "Mannheim Károly: *Lélek és kultúra. Előadások a szellemi tudományok köréből*" (Karl Mannheim: Soul and culture. Lectures from the course on humanistic studies), *Athenaeum*, 4, no. 3 (1918).

97. Balázs, Diaries, 28 December 1915.

98. Lajos Fülep to Imre Kner, n.d. [probably early 1920s], Akadémiai Levéltár, Budapest. Máli was Lesznai's nickname among her friends.

2. The Historical Formation of a Generation

1. Béla Balázs to Georg Lukács, 21 June 1915, Lukács Archive.

2. Karl Mannheim, "The Problem of Generations," in Paul Kecskeméti, ed., *Essays on the Sociology of Knowledge* (New York: Oxford University Press, 1952), pp. 276–321.

3. Georg Lukács, Béla Balázs, Lajos Fülep, and Anna Lesznai were all born in 1885, Friederich Antal in 1887, Edit Hajós in 1889, Béla Fogarasi in 1891, Arnold Hauser in 1892, and Karl Mannheim in 1893.

4. No attempt is made to argue here that only the assimilated Jewish middle classes were susceptible to the kind of social dislocation and cultural radicalism that characterized the Sunday Circle. Indeed, the greatest of the Hungarian modernists of this generation, the poet Endre Ady and the musician Béla Bartók, were not Jewish. What is being argued is that assimilated Jewish intellectuals were more likely to respond as a group to the political and social crises of the time because they were more vulnerable to marginalization than any other group in Hungary.

5. Lukács' grandfather had made his living producing and selling featherbeds and pillows.

6. The Lipótváros was an affluent, predominantly Jewish neighborhood in Budapest.

7. In an interview with Erzsébet Vezér and István Eörsi shortly before his death, Lukács recounted: "Our parents took us for a tour of Europe. We were in Paris and London, and everywhere they took us to art galleries. I considered this the height of pretentious-

ness . . . There was absolutely nothing in the art galleries that interested me; on the other hand, I knew that London had a first-class zoo. Why don't we go to the zoo? I looked down on my brother terribly because he accepted the art galleries and did not long for the zoo." On the same trip he was accidentally separated from his parents while touring the palace of Versailles. The parents finally found the child in front of a battle scene, surrounded by a large crowd to whom he was explaining the picture. In "Gelebtes Denken," Lukács Archive.

8. Marcell Benedek, a close childhood friend of Lukács', recounts in his diary that Lukács got the brilliant idea of founding a satirical magazine called *Ifjú Magyarország* (Young Hungary), which they planned to edit during the obligatory dance lessons held in the Lukács' apartment every week. "Besides Gyuri and myself, the rest of the contributors consisted of poetically inclined girls. Gyuri wrote articles of social satire, while I myself produced short stories and editorials on the occasion of national holidays such as March 15 . . . Unfortunately, the magazine did not have a long life. One of Gyuri's overly successful satirical pieces, which showed too close a likeness to some elegant Lipótváros ladies, brought down parental censorship." Marcell Benedek, *Naplómat olvasom* (Reading my journal) (Budapest: Szépirodalmi Könyvkiadó, 1965), p. 83.

9. Béla Balázs, *Álmodó ifjuság* (Dreams of youth) (Budapest: Magvetö és Szépirodalmi Könyvkiadó, 1976).

10. See Erzsébet Vezér, *Lesznai Anna élete* (The life of Anna Lesznai) (Budapest: Kossuth Könyvkiadó, 1979).

11. It seems that the feudal heritage of Alsókörtvélyes, where the Moskovitz estate was located, remained alive as late as the 1930s. On Lesznai's regular visits to Alsókörtvélyes, where she usually spent the summers, often in the company of literary friends from Budapest, she was received by the whole village as their mistress. Invited to a village wedding, she was welcomed with the following words of greeting in broken Hungarian: "We belong to your ladyship and your ladyship to us—since the days of your father and your grandfather we have lived together. This is how it is, and for this reason, partake of our food." In Vezér, *Lesznai Anna élete*, p. 124.

12. Quoted in Vezér, *Lesznai Anna élete*, pp. 13–14.

13. Georg Lukács, "Gelebtes Denken," Lukács Archive; his italics.

14. Béla Balázs, *Álmodó ifjuság*, p. 200.

15. Lukács, "Gelebtes Denken."

16. See Péter Hanák, ed., *Magyarország története, 1890–1918*, 2 vols. (The history of Hungary, 1890–1918) (Budapest: Akadémiai Kiadó, 1978).

17. Antal Csengery, *Csengery Antal összegyüjtött munkái* (The collected works of Antal Csengery) (Budapest: Kilian Frigyes, 1884), pp. 320–321.

18. See György Ránki and Iván Berend, *Economic Development in East-Central Europe in the 19th and 20th Centuries* (New York: Columbia University Press, 1974).

19. Anna Lesznai, Diaries, 1938, Petöfi Irodalmi Múzeum.

20. It was during this period that many Hungarian Jews went through the final stages of the assimilation process which had often started one or two generations earlier. The crucial phase of this transformation is brilliantly captured in Lajos Hatvany's semiautobiographical novel *Urak és emberek* (Men and gentlemen), which traces the family history of three generations of Hungarian Jews during the nineteenth century. The crucial confrontation in the novel occurs in the 1860s between the older Hermann Bondy, the successful Jewish entrepreneur of the 1830s, who still speaks German and remains aloof from Hungarian life, and his son Zsigmond, who, under the influence of his Hungarian tutor, begins to show unmistakable signs of Hungarian nationalism. In instructing the romantic young tutor to desist from his proselytizing efforts, Bondy summarizes admirably the attitude of his generation toward assimilation: "You must allow my son, Mr. Szalkay, to remain what he was born, a Jew. And if you must teach him something, then teach him to deal in business and how to make it profitable . . . Teach him to live here as if he were in a province where one goes merely to make a profit . . . Do you know what a *koved* is? It is the Yiddish word for a sinecure, an honorable post for which one gets no pay, or very little. I want no parliamentary representatives, judges, or professors in my family. My son should buy and sell here, but he should not sell himself, for no good will come of it . . . For have you ever seen a Jew who has gone after *koved* and has ended up well in this country?" The tutor's short answer, "But the child will have to live here. He will be Hungarian. He must love his nation," proved to be the more powerful position, and the one which, in the course of the 1860s and 1870s, would win out over the cautious pragmatism of the previous generation. See Lajos Hatvany, *Urak és emberek*, 2 vols. (Budapest: Szépirodalmi Könyvkiadó, 1963), I, 93–94.

21. Mihály Réz, "A választó jogról" (A few words about the right to vote), *Magyar Figyelő*, 2 (1912), 472.

22. Miklós Zay, "Zsidók a társadalomban" (Jews in society), *Huszadik Század*, 4, nos. 7–12 (1903), 948.

23. See Péter Hanák, "Polgárosodás és asszimiláció Magyarországon a XIX. században" (Urbanization and assimilation in Hungary during the nineteenth century), *Társadalmi Szemle*, 4 (1974), 513–536.

24. Zay, "Zsidók a társadalomban," pp. 954–955.

25. Endre Ady, "A sajtó és haragosai" (The press and its enemies), *Nagyváradi Napló*, 29 June 1901, reprinted in *Ady Endre összes prózai művei* (The collected prose works of Endre Ady), 11 vols., ed. Gyula Földessy and István Király (vols. 1–10) and Erzsébet Vezér and József

Láng (vol. 11) (Budapest: Akadémiai Kiadó, 1968–1977), I, 80; hereafter referred to as *AEÖPM*.

26. Endre Ady, "Glosszák" (Commentary), *A Hét*, 8 December 1907, in *AEÖPM*, II, 79.

27. Robert Musil, *The Man Without Qualities*, trans. and with an introduction by Eithene Wilkins and Ernst Kaiser (New York: Capricorn Books, 1965), p. 33.

28. The only exception to this might be the parliamentary crisis of 1905 over the language of command in the Hapsburg army, when the emperor had to appoint a government of his own after no Hungarian political group would accept the invitation to form a government. But even here, the conflict occurred not within parliament but rather between the Hungarian parliament and the emperor.

29. Géza Lengyel, "Az országház körül—Az osztály parlament lélektanához" (Around parliament: contributions to the psychological portrait of a class parliament), *Huszadik Század*, 9, nos. 7–12 (December 1908), 610.

30. See, for example, an article of János Arany, one of the leading Hungarian poets of the post-1848 generation, written in 1861: "In exchange for material well-being, modern Western techniques have undeniably already changed or destroyed much in our ancient traditions; and so long as the seed of our moral character remains sound, there is not much point in bewailing this tendency—or if we must, let it be only in poetry. There is nothing wrong, so long as the transformation takes place naturally, under the slow influence of time and circumstances; what would be wrong would be if the nation allowed itself to slip into a dull torpor, or if it violently tore from its being the traditions of the past." János Arany, "Visszatekintés" (Looking back), quoted in István Sötér, *Nemzet és haladás* (Budapest: Akadémiai Kiadó, 1963), p. 153.

31. For an excellent treatment of Hungarian new conservative tendencies, to which the present account is indebted, see Miklós Szabó, "Új vonások a századfordulói magyar konzervativ politikai gondolkodásban" (New elements in the political theory of Hungarian turn-of-the-century conservatism), *Történelmi Szemle*, 18, no. 3 (1974).

32. For a somewhat different interpretation of right-radical political thought, see Fritz Stern's pioneering study on the subject, *Politics of Cultural Despair: A Study in the Rise of the Germanic Ideology* (Berkeley: University of California Press, 1961).

33. See Carl E. Schorske, "Politics in a New Key: An Austrian Trio," in his *Fin de Siècle Vienna: Politics and Culture* (New York: Alfred A. Knopf, 1980).

34. Géza Petrassevich, *Magyarország és a zsidóság* (Hungary and Jewry), quoted in Szabó, "Új vonások," p. 63.

35. Within the Hungarian context a distinction is made between the

so-called traditional Hungarian middle classes, which consisted of the landowning nobility with medium-sized estates, who tended to be most active on the level of county politics, and the bourgeois middle classes, which were recruited mostly from the ranks of assimilated Germans and Jews and constituted a genuinely urban, commercial element in Hungary.

36. Hanák, *Magyarország története, 1890–1918*, I, 464.

37. Géza Petrassevich, *Magyarország és a zsidóság*, in Szabó, "Új vonások," p. 57.

38. See, for example, the remark of Péter Ágoston that "the general mood of anti-Semitism became evident [in Hungary] only from the second decade of this century," in *A zsidók útja* (The path of the Jews) (Nagyvárad: Nagyváradi Társadalom-Tudomány Társaság, 1917), p. 6.

39. Endre Ady, "Napló—Egy kényes téma" (Journal: a delicate subject), *Szabadság*, 3 January 1901, in *AEÖPM*, I, 408.

40. "Letter to the Editor," in *AEÖPM* I, 408.

41. Dezsö Szabó, "A magyar zsidóság organikus elhelyezkedése— Nyilt levél a *Múlt és Jövő* szerkesztőinek" (The organic assimilation of Hungarian Jewry: open letter to the editors of *Past and future*), *Huszadik Század*, 15, nos. 1–7 (1914), 341.

42. See "Zsidókérdés Magyarországon: A *Huszadik Század* körkérdése" (The Jewish question in Hungary: the questionnaire of *The twentieth century*), *Huszadik Század*, 18, nos. 7–12 (1917), 1–159.

43. Endre Ady, "Kecskeméthyék," *Nagyváradi Napló*, 16 November 1901, in *AEÖPM*, II, 281.

44. This account is based on Miklós Szabó, "Az 1091-es egyetemi 'keresztmozgalom' (Adalék a magyarországi szélsöjobboldal élettörténetéhez)" (The 1901 "cross movement" at the university: a chapter in the history of right radicalism in Hungary), *Történelmi Szemle* 4 (1970), 483–513, esp. p. 486.

45. Ibid., p. 495.

46. For an account of the "Pikler affair," see, besides Miklós Szabó's article, Zsigmond Kende, *A Galilei Kör megalakulása* (The founding of the Galilei circle) (Budapest: Akadémiai Kiadó, 1974); also Márta Tömöry, *Új vizeken járok* (On strange new seas) (Budapest: Gondolat, 1960).

47. In 1895 the students at the University of Budapest took to the streets in order to demonstrate in favor of the secularization laws separating church and state, which had just been passed by the liberal government.

48. Magister, "Az egyetemi ifjúság" (University students), *Magyar Figyelő*, I (1911), 36.

49. Marcell Benedek, *Naplómat olvasom* (Reading my journal) (Budapest: Szépirodalmi Könyvkiadó, 1965), p. 121.

50. Georg Lukács, "Thália Rediviva," *Huszadik Század*, 9, no. 11 (1908); reprinted in *Lukács György: Ifjúkori művek 1902–1918* (George Lukács:

early works), ed. Árpád Timár (Budapest: Magvető, 1977), p. 180, hereafter cited as *Lukács: Early Works.*

51. Ibid.
52. Benedek, *Naplómat olvasom,* p. 179.
53. Georg Lukács, "Gelebtes Denken."
54. Ibid.
55. Georg Lukács to Béla Balázs, 1940, Akadémiai Levéltár.
56. Lukács, "Gelebtes Denken."
57. Ibid.
58. Georg Lukács to Béla Balázs, 1940, Akadémiai Levéltár.
59. Lukács, "Gelebtes Denken."
60. Ibid.
61. Balázs, *Álmodó ifjúság,* p. 41.
62. Ibid., p. 29.
63. Anna Lesznai, *Kezdetben volt a kert* (In the beginning was the garden) (Budapest: Szépirodalmi Könyvkiadó, 1966), I, 217, 222.
64. Ibid., p. 222.
65. Anna Lesznai, Diaries, 1921, Petőfi Irodalmi Múzeum.
66. Lajos Fülep, "A Jövö nemzedék" (The coming generation), in *From the Revolution in Art,* I, 58.
67. See Fred Weinstein and Gerald M. Platt, *The Wish to Be Free* (Berkeley: University of California Press, 1969).
68. Balázs, *Álmodó ifjúság,* pp. 379–390.
69. Ibid., p. 86.
70. Ibid., pp. 84–85.
71. Béla Balázs to Georg Lukács, 25 June 1910, Lukács Archive.
72. In the December 1911 issue of *A Szellem,* Lukács wrote an article entitled "Jewish Mysticism," in which he reviewed appreciatively two Jewish mystical writings, "The Legend of Baalschem" and the "Story of Rabbi Nachmann," which had recently been translated and published by Martin Buber. A warm correspondence began between the two men in November 1911, when Lukács sent Buber a copy of his recently published book of essays, *Soul and Forms,* and thanked him for the experience of reading "Baalschem" and "Rabbi Nachmann."
73. Lesznai, Diaries.
74. Lajos Fülep to Ákos Dutka, n.d. [approximately 1904], Akadémiai Levéltár.
75. Lajos Fülep to Ákos Dutka, 7 March 1906, Akadémiai Levéltár.
76. Lukács was in fact the only member of the group who before 1918 thought seriously about emigrating. The idea of settling down permanently somewhere had already occurred to the restless young scholar as early as 1913, mostly, he wrote to Fülep, "because one can only travel properly if one is not living provisionally in a place. But where shall I settle? And when? I think that after all, I could not choose Italy, and Budapest is absolutely out of the question. These problems

cause a great many inner complications." Georg Lukács to Lajos Fülep, May 1913, Akadémiai Levéltár. Lukács eventually chose Heidelberg, which became his home between 1913 and 1917.
77. Balázs, *Álmodó ifjúság,* pp. 293–294.
78. Ibid., p. 418. The Tisza, one of the major rivers of Hungary, runs through Szeged, where Balázs was born.
79. Balázs, Diaries, 12 June 1916.
80. Lesznai, Diaries, 1927.
81. Lesznai, Diaries, 1930s.
82. Mannheim developed this concept into an important sociological category in *Ideology and Utopia* and also in the article "Conservative Thought," in Kurt H. Wolff, ed., *From Karl Manheim* (New York: Oxford University Press, 1971), pp. 132–222.
83. Karl Mannheim, *Lélek és kultúra* (Budapest: Franklin Társulat, 1918), p. 18.

3. Liberal Fathers and Postliberal Children

1. József Lukács to Georg Lukács, 23 August 1909, Lukács Archive.
2. Carl E. Schorske, "The Transformation of the Garden," in *Fin de Siècle Vienna: Politics and Culture* (New York: Alfred A. Knopf, 1980), p. 296.
3. József Lukács to Georg Lukács, 4 February 1911, Lukács Archive.
4. Béla Balázs to Georg Lukács, 4 May 1911, Lukács Archive.
5. József Lukács to Georg Lukács, 31 December 1911, Lukács Archive.
6. József Lukács to Georg Lukács, 2 July 1910, Lukács Archive.
7. Béla Balázs to Georg Lukács, 4 May 1911, Lukács Archive.
8. József Lukács to Georg Lukács, 11 April 1914, Lukács Archive.
9. *Athenaeum,* 5, nos. 5–6 (1919), 161.
10. The Kisfaludy Társaság was founded in the 1830s and became a semiofficial literary association which held monthly meetings, published a yearbook, and awarded prizes for scholarly and literary works.
11. Bernát Alexander to Georg Lukács, 21 January 1908, Lukács Archive.
12. Bernát Alexander to Lajos Fülep, 5 January 1911, Magyar Tudományos Akadémia Levéltára; hereafter referred to as MTA, Levéltára.
13. Bernát Alexander to Lajos Fülep, 27 October 1912, MTA, Levéltára.
14. Georg Lukács to Lajos Fülep, 20–22 December 1910, Lukács Archive.
15. Bernát Alexander to Lajos Fülep, 5 January 1911, MTA, Levéltára.
16. Schorske, "The Transformation of the Garden," p. 304.

17. "Beszélgetés Lukács Györgyel" (Conversation with Georg Lukács), in *Irodalmi Múzeum: Emlékezések* (Budapest: Petőfi Irodalmi Múzeum, 1967), p. 34.

18. Oszkár Jászi was born in 1875, and was twenty-five years old when *Twentieth Century* was founded. Rusztem Vámbéry was born in 1872, Bódog Somló and János Kégl in 1873, and Ödön Wildner and Péter Ágoston in 1874. The other leading figures—Ervin Szabó, Arnold Dániel, Ede Harkányi, Zsigmond Kunfi, József Madzsar, Aladár Székely, and Pál Szende—were all born between 1876 and 1879.

19. Oszkár Jászi to Bódog Somló, 8 October 1899, Országos Széchényi Könyvtár, Budapest.

20. Gusztáv Gratz, "A Társadalomtodományok Szabad Iskolája" (The Free School for Sociology), *Huszadik Század*, 7, nos. 1–6 (1906), 339.

21. Herbert Spencer, *Huszadik Század*, 1, nos. 1–6 (1900), 1.

22. Oszkár Jászi, "Tudományos publicisztika" (Scientific journalism), *Huszadik Század*, 1, nos. 1–6 (1900), 9.

23. See Zoltán Rónai, "A Társadalomtudományi Társaság fejlődése" (The development of the Sociological Society), *Huszadik Század*, 13, nos. 7–12 (1912), 471–478.

24. Jászi, "Tudományos publicisztika," p. 11.

25. Opening speech of Ágost Pulszky, first president of the Sociological Society, reprinted in *Huszadik Század*, 2, nos. 1–6 (1901).

26. Oszkár Jászi, "Társadalmi fejlődés és a gondolati szabadság" (Social evolution and freedom of thought), *Huszadik Század*, 4, nos. 1–6 (1903), 498.

27. Jászi, "Tudományos publicisztika," p. 11.

28. "Thália," *Huszadik Század*, 7, nos. 1–6 (1906), 172.

29. "Kortörténeti jegyzetek" (Notes about current events), *Huszadik Század*, 9, nos. 1–6 (1908), 398.

30. Oszkár Jászi, "Tiz év" (Ten years), *Huszadik Század*, 11, nos. 1–6 (1910), 2.

31. Oszkár Jászi, "Kultúrális elmaradottságunk okairól" (Causes of our cultural backwardness), *Huszadik Század*, 6, nos. 7–12 (1905), 2.

32. Ödön Wildner, "A XIX, század irodalmának pesszimizmusa" (Pessimism in nineteenth-century literature), *Huszadik Század*, 3, nos 1–6 (1902), 49.

33. Oszkár Jászi, "Van-e társadalmi haladás?" (Is there social evolution?), *Huszadik Század*, 13, nos. 7–12 (1912), 527.

34. Georg Lukács, "Introduction," in *Magyar irodalom-magyar kultúra* (Hungarian literature, Hungarian culture) (Budapest: Gondolat, 1970), p. 11.

35. Mihály Babits," A lélek és a formák" (Soul and forms), *Nyugat*, 3, nos. 13–24 (1910), 1563–1564.

36. Georg Lukács, "Arról a bizonyos homályosságról—Válasz Babits Mihálynak" (That so-called obscurity: answer to Mihály Babits), *Nyugat*, 3, nos. 13–24 (1910), 1749–1752.

37. Mihály Babits to Georg Lukács, 28 November 1910, Lukács Archive.

38. "Beszélgetés Lukács Györgyel," 33.

39. Anna Lesznai, Diaries, 1926, Petöfi Irodalmi Múzeum.

40. V. I. Lenin, *Materialism and Empirio-Criticism* (Peking: Foreign Language Press, 1972).

41. John Stuart Mill, *Autobiography* (New York: Columbia University Press, 1944), pp. 191–192.

42. Béla Balázs to Georg Lukács, 6 July 1911, Lukács Archive.

43. Béla Fogarasi, "Konzervativ és progressziv idealizmus" (Conservative and progressive idealism), *Huszadik Század*, 19, nos. 1–6 (1918), 193–206.

44. Lukács' comment on "Conservative and Progressive Idealism," reprinted in *Huszadik Század*, 19, nos. 1–6 (1918), 378–384.

45. In later years, Karl Mannheim was to pay eloquent tribute to Oszkár Jászi and the radicals for the ethical-political leadership they provided for the Lukács Circle. "My former veneration toward you," he wrote in a letter of 1933, "remains unaltered with time and the ethical example you set for my generation has been validated by history." Mannheim to Oszkár Jászi, 16 January 1933, Butler Library, Columbia University, New York City.

46. The radical sociologists were fully conscious of the peculiarly passive role played by Hungarian middle-class intellectuals in the political life of the nation. For an excellent analysis of the sociology of intellectuals in Hungary, see Zoltán Rónai, "A magyar intelligentsia" (The Hungarian intelligentsia), *Renaissance*, 8, no. 25 (1910), 715–721.

47. An approximate professional breakdown of membership in the Sociological Society: lawyers, 65; state and county officials, 55; university professors, 37; members of parliament, 13; doctors, 14; bankers, and industrialists, 4; editors, journalists, and writers, 6.

48. Rónai, "A Társadalomtudományi Társaság fejlödése," p. 471.

49. Bódog Somló, "A Társadalomtudomány Szabad iskolája" (The Free School for Sociological Studies), *Huszadik Század*, 8, nos. 1–6 (1907), 203.

50. Quoted in Ede Harkányi, "A középkor ujjáébredése Magyarországon" (The return of the Middle Ages in Hungary), *Huszadik Század*, 8, nos. 1–6 (1907), 172.

51. Oszkár Jászi to Bódog Somló, 2 April 1905, Országos Széchenyi Könyvtár, Budapest.

52. Oszkár Jászi to Bódog Somló, 21 November 1907, Országos Széchenyi Könyvtár, Budapest.

53. Jászi, "Tíz év," p. 7.

54. Rónai, "A Társadalomtudományi Társaság fejlödése," p. 475.
55. The Independence party was the major opposition party to the liberals. The two parties differed mostly on constitutional issues, the Independence party standing for greater Hungarian autonomy within the dualistic system.
56. Oszkár Jászi to Bódog Somló, 9 March 1910, Országos Széchenyi Könyvtár, Budapest.
57. Oszkár Jászi, "A polgárság ébredése" (The awakening of the bourgeoisie), *Világ*, 8 May 1910.
58. Jászi, "Tíz év," p. 4.
59. "Kortörténeti jegyzetek" (Notes about current events), *Huszadik Század*, 9, nos. 1–6 (1908), 192.
60. According to figures published by sociologists in 1909, the following elements made up the Hungarian middle classes: independent industrialists with five or more employees, 6,411; merchants with a taxable income of 20 to 21 kronen, 50,136; members of the free professions and state employees, 129,187. The total of 185,734 made up only 5 percent of the adult male population in 1909. David Pap, "A magyar polgárság az osztályharcban" (The Hungarian bourgeoisie in the class struggle), *Huszadik Század*, 10, nos. 1–6 (1909), 559.
61. Oszkár Jászi, "Politikai metamorfózisok" (Political metamorphosis), *Huszadik Század*, 13, nos. 1–6 (1912), 498.
62. Oszkár Jászi to Ervin Szabó, 23 October 1904, Párttörténeti Intézet. Sándor Csizmadia (1871–1929) was a Social Democratic leader, organizer, poet, and journalist.
63. One of the most interesting and powerful examples of this genre is Jászi's article entitled "Pócsi tanulság" (The lessons of Pócs), *Világ*, 17 September 1910: "Imagine to yourself a backward, poverty-stricken village at a distance of one or two days' travel from the nearest railway station. Traffic is constantly bogged down on the wretched roads, and during the winter months the village is virtually cut off from all communication with the outside world. Imagine to yourself a tumbledown schoolroom where a single teacher struggles to teach sometimes several hundred children. The district doctor does not visit the ailing for months on end. Lack of land and the growing population make earning a livelihood increasingly difficult, while taxes go up all the time. And this abandoned population, which hardly ever sees a teacher, a school, a doctor, is at the whim and mercy of the neighboring landowner, the county administration, and the gendarmerie. Their lot is to work; to pay taxes; . . . to serve in the army; to eat mush and drink alcohol; to fight with wolves on winter nights; to be grateful if the son can go to work for a few days' wages in the factory half a day and if the seduced daughter is thrown a few coins compensation; to beg at city banks for loans at 25 percent interest; . . . to be in constant terror at the receipt of every official notification, whose content, and often even language,

they do not understand; to await with chattering teeth the arrival, the sovereign orders, and lordly moods of his lordship the high judge . . . This is the life which millions of our people live day after day, week after week, month after month, year after year. They live like this without ever having even one ray of knowledge, enlightenment, economic prosperity penetrate their chimneyless, airless hovels, which they often share with their beasts in winter."

64. One of the best examples is Robert Braun's sociological analysis of the structure of village life, which appeared in serial form in *Huszadik Század*, beginning around 1910. It set the example for many similar works at the time. Braun's study consisted of questions to which answers were solicited from different layers of the village hierarchy, ranging from the teacher, the priest, and the merchant to the villagers themselves. Typical questions were: "What social divisions exist within the village?" "What groups stand outside?" "To whom do the villagers listen?" "Who are their leaders?" "Do villagers often leave peasant status to become servants, artisans, factory workers?" Robert Braun, "A falu lélektana" (The psychology of the village), *Huszadik Század*, 14, nos. 1–6 (1913), 545–571, 690–713.

65. Oszkár Jászi, *A nemzeti államok kialakulása és a nemzetiségi kérdés* (The development of the nation-state and the nationality question) (Budapest: Társadalomtudományi Könyvtár, 1912), p. 502.

66. *Magyar Figyelő*, 4, no. 1 (1914).

67. Oszkár Jászi to Pali Kéri, 1 March 1936, Butler Library, Columbia University, New York City.

68. Oszkár Jászi, "A radikális párt" (The Radical party), *Világ*, 7 June 1914.

69. Schorske, "The Transformation of the Garden," p. 304.

4. The Crisis of Aestheticism

1. Georg Lukács, "Gelebtes Denken," Lukács Archives; see also Georg Lukács, "Introduction," in *Magyar irodalom—Magyar kultúra* (Hungarian literature, Hungarian culture) (Budapest: Gondolat, 1970), pp. 6–7.

2. Several art critics and cultural commentators have argued that the decline of modernism can be dated to the beginning of its popularity in the interwar years. See Hilton Kramer, *The Age of the Avant-Garde: An Art Chronicle of 1956–1972* (New York: Farrar, Straus, and Giroux, 1973); Irving Howe, *Decline of the New* (New York: Harcourt, Brace, and World, 1963); Daniel Bell, *The Cultural Contradictions of Capitalism* (New York: Basic Books, 1976); Harry Levin, *Refractions: Essays in Contemporary Literature* (New York: Oxford University Press, 1966).

3. One of the most influential of these books was Georg Brandes, *Men of the Modern Breakthrough* (1883), which first introduced such au-

thors as Nietzsche and Ibsen to the young generation of Northern and Central Europe. In Germany the creed of the new generation was announced by Hermann Conradi and Karl Henckell in a collection, edited by Wilhelm Arendt, entitled *Moderne Dichtercharaktere* (1885), while in England the new cultural mood was first defined and interpreted by Havelock Ellis in *The New Spirit* (1892) and Arthur Symons in *The Symbolist Movement in Literature* (1890). See Malcom Bradbury and James McFarlane, "The Name and Nature of Modernism," in Bradbury and McFarlane, eds., *Modernism 1890–1930* (New York: Penguin Books, 1976).

4. Quoted in Helmut E. Gerber, "The Nineties: Beginning, End or Transition?" in Richard Ellmann, ed., *Edwardians and Late Victorians* (New York: Columbia University Press, 1960), p. 61.

5. Oscar Wilde, "The Decay of Lying," in Richard Ellmann and Charles Fiedelson, eds., *The Modern Tradition* (New York: Oxford University Press, 1965), p. 23.

6. Georg Lukács, "A kegyelemkenyér" (Bread of charity), in *Lukács: Early Works*, p. 11.

7. Georg Lukács, "John Ford: Egy modern drámaköltö Shakespeare korából" (John Ford: a modern dramatist from the age of Shakespeare), in *Lukács: Early Works*, p. 123.

8. Quoted in Ellen Moers, *The Dandy: Brummel to Beerbohm* (New York: Viking Press, 1960), p. 264.

9. Lewis Galatière, ed., *The Goncourt Journals, 1851–1870* (New York: Doubleday, Doran and Co., 1937), p. 23.

10. There exists a fairly large literature on the cultural and historical significance of late nineteenth-century decadence. See Osbert Burdett, *The Beardsley Period: An Essay in Perspective* (London: John Lane, The Bodley Head, 1925); Ian Fletcher, ed., *Decadence and the 1890s* (London: Edward Arnold, 1979); Richard Gilman, *Decadence: The Strange Life of an Epithet* (New York: Farrar, Straus, and Giroux, 1975); Matei Calinescu, *Faces of Modernity: Avant-Garde, Decadence, Kitsch* (Bloomington: Indiana University Press, 1977); Bernard Bergonzi, *The Turn of the Century: Essays on Victorian and Modern English Literature* (New York: Barnes and Noble, 1973); Graham Hough, *Image and Experience: Studies in a Literary Revolution* (London: Gerald Duckworth and Co., 1960); Richard Ellmann, ed., *Edwardians and Late Victorians* (New York: Columbia University Press, 1960); Janko Lavrin, *Aspects of Modernism: From Wilde to Pirandello* (Freeport, N.Y.: for Libraries Press, 1968).

11. Quoted in Bergonzi, *Turn of the Century*, p. 22.

12. Max Nordau, *Degeneration* (New York: Howard Fertig, 1968), p. 537.

13. Holbrook Jackson, *The Eighteen Nineties: A Review of Art and Ideas at the Close of the Nineteenth Century* (New York: Alfred A. Knopf, 1912), p. 7.

14. Lajos Fülep, "A müvészet útvesztöje" (The labyrinth of art), in *From the Revolution in Art*, I, 29.

15. Béla Bartók, "Magyar népzene és új magyar zene" (Hungarian folk songs and modern Hungarian music), in Béla Bartók, *Önéletrajz: Irások a zenéröi* (Autobiography and articles about music) (Budapest, 1946), p. 22.

16. Ibid., p. 6.

17. Ignotus [Hugo Veigelsberg], "Hadi készületek" (Preparations for war), *Nyugat*, 1, nos. 16–24 (1908), 451.

18. Dénes Görcsöni, "Nyugat," *Alkotmány*, 20 February 1908, in *Ady Endre összes prózai müvei* (Collected works of Endre Ady), 11 vols. (Budapest: Akadémiai Kiadó, 1968–1977), IX, 465.

19. Rusticus [István Tisza], "Levél a szerkesztöhöz" (Letter to the editor), *Magyar Figyelö*, September 1912, p. 406.

20. Ignotus, "Disputa," *Nyugat*, 5, nos. 1–12 (1912), 381.

21. Ignotus, "A *Nyugat* olvasóhoz" (To the reader of *Nyugat*), *Nyugat*, 5, nos. 13–24 (1912), 3.

22. Georg Lukács, "Berlin júliusban" (Berlin in July), in *Lukács: Early Works*, p. 16.

23. Lajos Fülep, "Még néhány müvészröl" (Concerning a few other artists), *Hazánk*, 26 April 1905, in *From the Revolution in Art*, I, 53.

24. Lajos Fülep, "A jövö nemzedék" (The future generation), *Hazánk*, 7 June 1905, in *From the Revolution in Art*, I, 57.

25. Arthur Symons, quoted in R. K. R. Thornton, " 'Decadence' in Late Nineteenth Century England," in Fletcher, ed., *Decadence and the 1890s*, p. 17.

26. Krisztina Passuth, *A Nyolcak festészete* (The art of "The Eight") (Budapest: Corvina, 1967), p. 73.

27. Bartók, *Önéletrajz*, p. 8.

28. Lajos Fülep, "Magyar festészet" (Hungarian painting), *Nyugat*, February 16, March 1, March 16, 1922, in *From the Revolution in Art*, I, 358–359.

29. Béla Balázs, Diaries, 11 January 1907, Akadémiai Levéltár, Budapest.

30. Arthur Symons, *The Symbolist Movement in Literature* (New York: E. P. Dutton and Co., 1958), p. 74.

31. Ibid., p. 4.

32. Hugo von Hofmannsthal, "The Letter of Lord Chandos," in *Selected Prose*, trans. Mary Hottinger and Tania and James Stern (New York: Pantheon Books, 1952), p. 134.

33. See Lavrin, *Aspects of Modernism*.

34. Lukács himself suggested these dates as signposts of his early development in his autobiographical sketch "Gelebtes Denken."

35. Mihály Babits, "A lélek és a formák" (Soul and forms), *Nyugat*, 3, nos. 13–24 (1910), 1563–1564.

36. Leo Popper to Georg Lukács, 7 June 1909, Lukács Archive.
37. So close were the ties between the essays and Irma Seidler's memory that Lukács at one point referred to the essays as expressions of the various stages and moods of their relationship. "The Philippe essay is ripening strangely. It seems this will be the most authentic Irma essay. The lyrical expression of my present state . . . With that, the main lyrical series will be complete: George, Beer-Hofmann, Kierkegaard, Philippe. Her connection with the others is somewhat looser; Novalis: the impressions of our first meeting; Kassner: Florence, Ravenna; Storm: the letters from Nagybánya. Even more distant; Stern: the sense of futility, the empty wintry mood after the break. Ernst: the hours of reckoning." Georg Lukács, Diaries, 20 May 1910, Lukács Archive.
38. Georg Lukács, "Rudolf Kassner," in *Soul and Forms*, in *Lukács: Early Works*, p. 144; henceforth, all references to Lukács' Soul and Forms essays will be from *Lukács: Early Works*.
39. Georg Lukács, "Levél a 'kisérletröl' " (Letter about the essay), in *Lukács: Early Works*, p. 321.
40. Georg Lukács, "Sören Kierkegaard és Regine Olsen," in *Lukács: Early Works*, p. 288.
41. Lukács, "Sören Kierkegaard és Regine Olsen," p. 295.
42. Georg Lukács, "Henrik Ibsen," in *Lukács: Early Works*, p. 103.
43. Georg Lukács to Leo Popper, 25 April 1909, Lukács Archive.
44. Georg Lukács to Sári Ferenczi, n.d. [around January 1909], Lukács Archive.
45. Ibid.
46. Ibid.
47. For a sensitive interpretation of the relationship between Lukács and Irma Seidler, see Ágnes Heller, "Georg Lukács and Irma Seidler," in Ágnes Heller, ed., *Lukács Reappraised* (New York: Columbia University Press, 1983).
48. Irma Seidler to Georg Lukács, 3 July 1908, Lukács Archive.
49. Irma Seidler to Georg Lukács, 25 October 1908, Lukács Archive.
50. Georg Lukács to Irma Seidler, November 1908, Lukács Archive.
51. Ibid.
52. Lukács, Diaries, 11 May 1910.
53. Lukács, "Sören Kierkegaard és Regine Olsen," p. 293.
54. Ibid.
55. Ferenc Baumgarten, one of Lukács' early friends.
56. Georg Lukács to Leo Popper, 25 April 1909, Lukács Archive.
57. Lukács, Diaries, 27–28 April 1910.
58. Lukács, Diaries, 8 May 1910.
59. Lukács, Diaries, 19 June 1910.
60. Lukács, Diaries, 26 June 1910.

61. Georg Lukács to Leo Popper, 9 November 1910, Lukács Archive.
62. Georg Lukács to Irma Seidler, 22 March 1910, Lukács Archive.
63. Lukács, Diaries, 11 February 1911.
64. Lukács, Diaries, 24 May 1911.
65. Georg Lukács to Leo Popper, 26 May 1911, Lukács Archive.
66. Lukács, "Gelebtes Denken."
67. Lukács, "Rudolf Kassner," p. 149.
68. Georg Lukács, "Az utak elváltak" (The parting of the roads), in *Lukács: Early Works*, p. 281.
69. Ibid., p. 282.
70. Georg Lukács, "Gaugin," in *Lukács: Early Works*, p. 115.
71. Georg Lukács, "Theodor Storm," in *Lukács: Early Works*, p. 325.
72. Paul Bourget, *Essais de psychologie contemporaine* (Paris: Librairie Plan, 1912), p. xxi.
73. Lukács, "Henrik Ibsen," p. 53.
74. Lukács, "Rudolf Kassner," p. 148.
75. Lukács, "Henrik Ibsen," pp. 91–92.
76. Georg Lukács, "Novalis," in *Lukács: Early Works*, p. 139.
77. Georg Lukács, "Richard Beer-Hofmann," in *Lukács: Early Works*, p. 204.
78. Georg Lukács, "Esztétikai kultúra" (Aesthetic culture), in *Lukács: Early Works*, p. 422.
79. Ibid., p. 425.
80. Lukács, Diaries, June 1910.
81. Lukács, "Richard Beer-Hofmann," p. 206.
82. Maurice Barrès, *Mes cahiers*, quoted in Zeev Sternhell, *Barrès et le nationalisme française* (Paris: A. Calin, 1972), p. 279.
83. See Fritz Stern, *Politics of Cultural Despair: A Study in the Rise of the Germanic Ideology* (Berkeley: University of California Press, 1961).
84. Barrès, *Mes cahiers*, p. 262.
85. Lajos Fülep, "Hangok a jövöböl" (Voices from the future), *Magyar Szemle*, 13 September 1906, in *From the Revolution in Art*, I, 477.
86. Béla Balázs, Diaries, date illegible [circa 1905], Akadémiai Levéltár.
87. Károly Kernstock, "A kutató müvészet" (The exploring art), speech delivered before the Galilei Circle on 9 February 1910, published in *Nyugat*, 2, no. 1 (1910), 96.
88. Ibid., p. 97.
89. Lukács, "Az utak elváltak," p. 284.
90. Fülep, "Magyar festészet," p. 376.
91. Lajos Fülep, "Európai müvészet és magyar müvészet" (European art and Hungarian art), in *From the Revolution in Art*, I, 273.
92. Lukács, "Esztétikai kultúra," p. 428.
93. Ibid.

94. Georg Lukács, "Új magyar líra" (The new Hungarian lyric), in *Lukács: Early Works*, p. 248.

95. Fülep, 'Magyar festészet," p. 371.

96. See Stephen Spender's eloquent characterization of the early modernists: "The significance of this early modern impulse is not just that it produced some masterpieces, not that it extended the boundaries of idioms, techniques and forms, but that in certain works a fragmented civilization was redeemed within the envisioned memory of the greatness of the past. To achieve these poignant states of remembering great unifying beliefs and art while confronting chaos and destruction, safe positions of sheltered certainty were avoided . . . the abandonment of metaphysical positions, the acceptance of moral and cultural voids, was the position which made possible the compressed epics of a fragmented culture. A vacuum of unbelief was filled with the incantation of an age of belief." Stephen Spender, *The Struggle of the Modern* (Berkeley: University of California Press, 1963), pp. 265–266.

5. Toward a New Metaphysics

1. Lajos Fülep, "Új müvészi stílus" (New artistic style), in *From the Revolution in Art*, I, 515.

2. Georg Lukács, "Esztétikai kultúra" (Aesthetic culture), in *Lukács: Early Works*, p. 431.

3. Ibid., p. 432.

4. Georg Lukács, "Válasz a *L'Effort libre* körkérdésére" (Answer to the questionnaire of *L'Effort libre*), in *Lukács: Early Works*, pp. 587–593.

5. Georg Lukács to Leo Popper, mid-October 1910, Lukács Archive.

6. Emile Boutraux, "Természet és szellem" (Nature and spirit), *A Szellem*, 1, no. 1 (March 1911), 19.

7. Thomas Willey, *Back to Kant: The Revival of Kantianism in German Social and Historical Thought* (Detroit: Wayne State University Press, 1978), p. 108.

8. Simmel seems to have been an object of criticism by other young thinkers of this generation, like José Ortega y Gasset, whose assessment of Simmel was uncannily similar to that of Lukács and his friends. "Simmel is a philosophic squirrel," he wrote, "leaping from bough to bough to show his virtuosity but merely nibbling the different nuts he encounters." Recounted in P. A. Lawrence, *Georg Simmel: Sociologist and European* (New York: Harper and Row, 1976), p. 18.

9. Georg Simmel to Georg Lukács, 25 May 1912, Lukács Archive.

10. Béla Balázs, Diaries, 28 November 1906, Akadémiai Levéltár.

11. Georg Lukács to Beatrice de Waard, 22 December 1910, Lukács Archive.

12. The reference was made in the context of a letter Paul Ernst

wrote to Lukács in 1916: "I believe that Simmel's problem, about which we have often spoken, constitutes the problem of the clever but passionless individual. He has no roots; thus, in his youth he has grown to surprising heights, but in maturity, when he should broaden his branches, he runs out of energy. I don't know if he himself feels it, but I consider him a tragic figure, and the truth is that I always regard him with the greatest pity." Paul Ernst to Georg Lukács, 23 March 1916, Lukács Archive.

13. Georg Lukács, "Georg Simmel," in *Lukács: Early Works*, p. 748.

14. Karl Mannehim, "Georg Simmel mint filozófus" (Georg Simmel as philosopher), *Huszadik Század*, 19, nos. 7–12 (1918), 194.

15. Georg Lukács, "Wilhelm Dilthey, 1833–1911," *A Szellem*, 1, no. 2 (December 1911), 253–254.

16. Lajos Fülep, "Nietzsche," in *From the Revolution in Art*, II, 598.

17. Ibid., p. 461.

18. Ibid., p. 463.

19. Georg Lukács, "Fülep Lajos Nietzschéről" (Lajos Fülep on Nietzsche), *Nyugat* 3, no. 14 (1910), 1014–1015.

20. Marianne Weber, *Max Weber: A Biography* (New York: John Wiley and Sons, 1975), p. 380.

21. Ibid., p. 466.

22. Georg Lukács, "Ariadne Naxosz Szigetén" (Ariadne on the island of Naxos), *Festschrift zum 50. Geburtstag von Paul Ernst, 1916*, in *Lukács: Early Works*, p. 660.

23. Balázs, Diaries, 1917.

24. Karl Mannheim, *Lélek és kultúra* (Soul and culture) (Budapest: Franklin Társulat, 1918), p. 8.

25. Anna Lesznai, Diaries, late 1920s, Petőfi Irodalmi Múzeum.

26. Georg Lukács, *A heidelbergi művészetfilozófia és esztétika* (The Heidelberg philosophy of art and aesthetics) (Budapest: Magvető, 1975), pp. 276–277.

27. Lesznai, Diaries, late 1920s.

28. Lesznai, Diaries, 1917–18.

29. Georg Lukács, "A vándor énekel: Balázs Béla költeményei" (The songs of the wanderer: the poetry of Béla Balázs), in *Lukács: Early Works*, p. 473.

30. Georg Lukács, "Tristán hajóján: Megjegyzések Balázs Béla új verseiről" (On the ship of Tristan: remarks about Béla Balázs' new poetry), in *Lukács: Early Works*, p. 648.

31. Georg Lukács, "Zsidó miszticizmus" (Jewish mysticism), *A Szellem*, 1, no. 2 (December 1911), 256.

32. Karl Mannheim to Georg Lukács, late December 1911 or early January 1912, Lukács Archive.

33. Karl Mannheim, "Ernst Bloch: *Geist der Utopie*," *Athenaeum*, 5, nos. 5–6 (1919), 208.

34. Quoted in Lesznai, Diaries, 1918.

35. Ibid.

36. Lesznai, Diaries, late 1920s.

37. Anna Lesznai, "Babonás észrevételek a mese és a tragédia lélektanához" (Superstitious remarks to the psychology of the fairy tale and the tragedy), *Nyugat*, 14, nos. 13–24 (1918), 60.

38. Quoted in Lesznai, Diaries, 1920s.

39. Mannheim, *Lélek és kultúra*, p. 9.

40. Lukács, "A vándor énekel," p. 474.

41. Lukács, "Esztétikai kultúra," p. 431.

42. Georg Lukács to Margaret Bendemann, 25 September 1912, Lukács Archive; his italics.

43. Béla Balázs to Georg Lukács, 21 June 1915, Lukács Archive; his italics.

44. Karl Mannheim to Georg Lukács, 13 March 1911, Lukács Archive.

45. Balázs, Diaries, July 1911.

46. Balázs, Diaries, 1917.

47. Quoted in Balázs, Diaries, February 1916.

48. Lukács, *A heidelbergi müvészetfilozófia és esztétika*, p. 150.

49. Georg Lukács, "Gelebtes Denken," Lukács Archive.

50. Lesznai, Diaries, n.d. [probably the autumn of 1912].

51. Balázs, Diaries, July 1913.

52. Lesznai, Diaries, n.d. [probably the autumn of 1912].

53. Wilhelm Worringer, *Abstraction and Empathy: A Contribution to the Psychology of Style* (New York: International Universities Press, 1953), pp. 45, 44.

54. Georg Lukács to Leo Popper, December 1910, Lukács Archive.

55. Lukács, "Gelebtes Denken."

56. Paul Hönigsheim, *On Max Weber* (New York: The Free Press, 1968), p. 27.

57. Max Weber to Georg Lukács, 10 March 1913, quoted in Marianne Weber, *Max Weber*, pp. 465–466.

58. Georg Lukács to Leo Popper, 20 December 1910, Lukács Archive.

59. Georg Lukács to Leo Popper, 15 June 1910, Lukács Archive.

60. Georg Lukács to Leo Popper, 20 December 1910, Lukács Archive.

61. Quoted in Balázs, Diaries, 1915.

62. Georg Lukács, "Leo Popper, 1886–1911: Nekrológ," in *Lukács: Early Works*, p. 560.

63. Georg Lukács, *A heidelbergi müvészetfilozófia és esztétika*, pp. 222–223, 211, 21.

64. Ibid., p. 23.

65. Ibid., pp. 86–87.

66. Ibid., pp. 33, 39.

67. Ibid., pp. 354, 143.

68. Lukács, "Gelebtes Denken."

69. Georg Lukács to Salamon Friedlaender, mid-July 1911, Lukács Archive.

70. Georg Lukács to Leo Popper, 20 December 1910, Lukács Archive.

71. Georg Lukács, "Leopold Ziegler," in *Lukács: Early Works*, p. 554.

72. Mannheim, *Lélek és kultúra*, p. 22.

73. Lukács, "Esztétikai kultúra," pp. 436–437.

74. Wassily Kandinsky, *Concerning the Spiritual in Art* (New York: Dover Publications, 1977), pp. 19, 14.

75. Hugo von Hofmannsthal, "Colors," in *Selected Prose*, trans. Mary Hottinger and Tania and James Stern (New York: Pantheon Books, 1952), p. 148.

76. Kandinsky, *Concerning the Spiritual in Art*, p. 14.

77. Stephen Spender, *The Struggle of the Modern* (Berkeley: University of California Press, 1963), p. 86.

78. Guillaume Apollinaire, *L'Esprit nouveau et les poètes* (The new spirit and the poets) (Paris: J. Haumont, 1946), pp. 24, 27.

79. Kandinsky, *Concerning the Spiritual in Art*, p. 20.

6. War and the Fragmentation of the Sunday Circle

1. Béla Balázs, Diaries, July 1914, Akadémiai Levéltár.

2. Georg Lukács, "Introduction," in *Utam Marxhoz: Válogatott filozófiai tanulmányok* (My road to Marxism: selected philosophical studies), 2 vols. (Budapest: Magvető, 1971).

3. Georg Lukács, "Gelebtes Denken," Lukács Archive.

4. Michael Löwy, *From Romanticism to Bolshevism*, trans. Patrick Camiller (London: New Library Books, 1979).

5. Lukács, "Gelebtes Denken."

6. Ervin Sinkó, *Az Optimistiák: Történelmi regény 1918/19-böl* (The optimists: historical novel from 1918–19), 2 vols. (Budapest: Forum Könyvkiadó, n.d.), I, 307.

7. Anna Lesznai, Diaries, 1920s, Petöfi Irodalmi Múzeum.

8. Balázs, Diaries, 12 August 1914.

9. Béla Balázs, *Lélek a háborúban* (The individual soul in the midst of war) (Gyoma: Kner Izidor Kiadása, 1916), pp. 53–54.

10. Balázs, Diaries, 12 August 1914.

11. Ibid.

12. Ibid.

13. Balázs, *Lélek a háborúban*, p. 91.

14. Béla Balázs to Georg Lukács, December 1914, Lukács Archive.

15. Georg Lukács, "A német értelmiség és a háború" (German intellectuals and the war), in *Lukács: Early Works*, pp. 830–836.

16. Béla Balázs to Georg Lukács, December 1914, Lukács Archive.

17. Georg Lukács, "Introduction" (1962), in *A regény elmélete* (The

theory of the novel), in *A heidelbergi müvészetfilozófia és esztétika—A regény elmélete* (The Heidelberg philosophy of art and aesthetics: the theory of the novel) (Budapest: Magvetö, 1975), p. 479; hereafter cited as *The Theory of the Novel*.

18. György Káldor, "Civilizáció és kultúra: Szabó Ervin emlékének" (Civilization and culture: in memory of Ervin Szabó), *A Probléma*, 1, no. 1 (1919).

19. Balázs, Diaries, 28 May 1917.

20. Quoted in Balázs, Diaries, May 1918.

21. Béla Balázs to Georg Lukács, March 1917, Lukács Archive.

22. The first semester began in the spring of 1917 and included the following lectures: Béla Balázs, "Dramaturgia" (Theory of the drama); Béla Fogarasi, "A filozófiai gondolkodás elmélete" (The theory of philosophical thinking); Lajos Fülep, "A nemzeti jelleg problémája a magyar képmüvészetben (The problem of national character in Hungarian art); Arnold Hauser, "A Kant utáni esztétika problémái" (The problems of post-Kantian aesthetics); Georg Lukács, "Etika" (Ethics); Karl Mannheim, "Ismeretelméleti és logikai problémák" (Epistemological and logical problems); and Emma Ritoók, "Az esztétikai hatás problémái" (The problems of aesthetic influence). The second semester of lectures, which began in February 1918, included Karl Mannheim, "Lélek és kultúra" (Soul and culture); Béla Balázs, "A lírai szenzibilitás" (Lyrical sensibility); Sándor Varjas, "Fenomenológiai kutatások" (Phenomenological research); Karl Mannheim, "Ismeretelméleti rendszerek szerkezeti elemzése" (Structural analysis of epistemological systems); Georg Lukács, "Esztétika" (Aesthetics); Béla Fogarasi, "A szellemtörténet módszerei" (Methods of intellectual history); Arnold Hauser, "A müvészi dilettantizmus" (Dilettantism in art); Antal Frigyes, "A modern festészet kompoziciójának és tartalmának kialakulása" (The development of the composition and content of modern art); Ervin Szabó, "A marxizmus végsö kérdéseiröl" (The ultimate implications of Marxism); Zoltán Kodály, "A magyar népdalról" (The Hungarian folk song); and Béla Bartók, "Népi zene és modern zene" (Folk music and modern music).

23. Karl Mannheim, *Lélek és kultúra* (Soul and culture) (Budapest: Franklin Társulat, 1918), p. 1.

24. Georg Lukács, "Introduction," in *Utam Marxhoz: Válogatott filozófiai tanulmányok* (My road to Marx: philosophical studies), 2 vols. (Budapest: Magvetö, 1971), I, 18.

25. Max Weber to Georg Lukács, 14 August 1916, Lukács Archive.

26. Lukács, *The Theory of the Novel*, p. 494.

27. Ibid., pp. 540, 593.

28. Ibid., p. 486.

29. Ibid., p. 512.

30. Ibid., p. 485.

31. Ibid., p. 593.

32. Georg Lukács to Max Weber, December 1915, Lukács Archive.

33. Georg Lukács to Leo Popper, 26 May 1911, Lukács Archive.

34. Georg Lukács, "A lelki szegénységröl" (Concerning the poor in spirit), in *Lukács: Early Works*, pp. 538, 540.

35. Ibid., p. 541.

36. Ibid., p. 543.

37. Georg Lukács to Leo Popper, August 1911, Lukács Archive.

38. Georg Lukács, Diaries, 22 October 1911, Lukács Archive.

39. Lukács, Diaries, 23 November 1911.

40. Lukács, Diaries, 25 November 1911.

41. Lukács, Diaries, 27 October 1911.

42. Lukács, Diaries, 15 December 1911.

43. Lukács, Diaries, 27 October 1911.

44. Georg Lukács, Notes for the Dostoevsky book, in Éva Karádi and Erzsébet Vezér eds., *A Vasárnapi Kör: Dokumentumok* (The Sunday Circle: documents) (Budapest: Gondolat, 1980), pp. 115–129.

45. Georg Lukács to Paul Ernst, March 1915, Lukács Archive.

46. Georg Lukács to Paul Ernst, 14 April 1915, Lukács Archive.

47. Georg Lukács to Paul Ernst, 4 May 1915, Lukács Archive.

48. Georg Lukács, "Megjegyzések az irodalomtörténet elméletéhez" (Remarks about the theory of the history of literature), in *Lukács: Early Works*, p. 398.

49. Béla Fogarasi, "A történeti materializmus kritikája" (A critique of historical materialism), *Athenaeum*, 2, no. 1 (1916), 65.

50. Georg Lukács, "Esztétikai kultúra" (Aesthetic culture), in *Lukács: Early Works*, p. 428.

51. Georg Lukács, "A kultúrszociológia lényegéröl és módszeréröl" (Concerning the goals and methods of the sociology of culture), in *Lukács: Early Works*, p. 618.

52. Rosa Luxemburg, *The Crisis of German Social Democracy* (New York: The Socialist Publication Society, 1918), p. 8.

53. Lukács, "Gelebtes Denken."

54. Georg Lukács to Paul Ernst, 5 September 1917, Lukács Archive.

55. Lukács, "Gelebtes Denken."

56. Balázs, Diaries, 29 November 1918.

57. Quoted in György Ránki, ed., *Magyarország Története, 1918–1919, 1919–1945* (History of Hungary) (Budapest: Akadémiai Kiadó, 1976), p. 71.

58. Michael Károlyi, *Hit illúziók nélkül* (Budapest: Magvetö, 1977), p. 160. (In English, *Memoirs of Michael Károlyi: Faith Without Illusion*, London: J. Cape, 1956.)

59. Balázs, Diaries, 29 November 1918.

60. Károlyi, *Hit illúziók nélkül*, p. 176.

61. Ibid., 191.

62. Ibid., p. 195.

63. "Osztályharcot" (Class struggle), *Vörös Ujság* (The red paper), 7 December 1918.

64. V. I. Lenin, *The Proletarian Revolution and the Renegade Kautsky* (Peking: Foreign Language Press, 1965), pp. 48–49.

65. Oszkár Jászi, "Proletárdiktatúra" (Dictatorship of the proletariat), *Szabadgondolat* (Freedom of thought) (December 1918).

66. Julien Benda, *The Treason of the Intellectuals* (New York: W. W. Norton, 1928).

67. Michael Polányi, "Új szkepticizmus" (New skepticism), *Szabadgondolat* (February 1919).

68. Miklós Sika, "A szocialista társadalom lélektani előfeltételei" (The psychological preconditions of a socialist society), *Szabadgonodolat* (February 1919).

69. Georg Lukács, "A bolsevizmus mint erkölcsi probléma" (Bolshevism as an ethical dilemma), *Szabadgondolat* (December 1918), reprinted in his *Történelem és osztálytudat* (History and class consciousness) (Budapest: Magvető, 1971), pp. 13, 16, 17.

70. Lukács, "A lelki szegénységről," p. 543.

71. Georg Lukács to Paul Ernst, 4 May 1915, Lukács Archive.

72. Georg Lukács "Taktika és etika" (Tactics and ethics), in *Utam Marxhoz*, II, 187, 189.

73. Ibid., 196.

74. Ibid., 197.

75. Emma Ritoók, Diaries, Courtesy of Erzsébet Vezér.

76. Anna Lesznai, Diaries, December 1918, Petőfi Irodalmi Múzeum.

77. Ibid.

78. Lesznai, Diaries, 1929.

79. Balázs, Diaries, 18 December 1919.

80. Balázs, Diaries, 17 August 1921.

81. For the cultural policies of the Kun regime, see Frank Eckelt, "The Internal Policies of the Hungarian Soviet Republic," in Iván Völgyes, ed., *Hungary in Revolution 1918–19: Nine Essays* (Lincoln: University of Nebraska Press, 1971).

82. "Lefoglalta a rendőrség Balázs Béla forradalmi naplóját: Korkép a Károlyi-bolsevizmusról" (The police have confiscated Béla Balázs' revolutionary diaries: pathological portrait of Károlyi-Bolshevism), *A Nap* (The sun), 29 November 1919.

83. Balázs, Diaries, December 1919.

84. Balázs, Diaries, 4 December 1919.

85. Balázs, Diaries, 16 May 1920.

86. Balázs, Diaries, 26 April 1921.

87. Quoted in Balázs, Diaries, 23 October 1920.

88. Balázs, Diaries, 12 July 1921.

89. Ibid.

90. Lajos Kassák, "Programme" (Program), *A Tett* (Action), 2, no. 10 (1916), 153.

91. Lajos Kassák, "Szintetikus irodalom" (Synthetic literature), *Ma* (Today), 1, no. 2 (1916), 20.

92. Milos Náray, "Bartók Béla," *Ma*, 3, no. 2 (1917), 20.

93. Balázs, Diaries, December 1915.

94. Ferenc Koszorú, "Balázs Béla: *Lélek a háborúban*" (Béla Balázs: *The individual soul in the midst of war*), *A Tett*, 2, no. 14 (1916), 246.

95. László Boross, "Balázs Béla: *Halálos fiatalság*" (Béla Balázs: *Fatal youth*), *Ma*, 3, no. 1 (1917), 14.

96. Lajos Kassák, "Aktivizmus" (Activism), *Ma*, 4, no. 4 (1919), 49.

97. Ibid., p. 48.

98. Lajos Kassák, "Levél Kun Bélához a müvészet nevében" (Letter to Béla Kun in the name of art), *Ma*, 4, no. 7 (1919), 148.

99. Sándor Barta, "A kultúrában forradalmasított ember" (The cultural revolutionary), *Ma*, 4, no. 6 (1919), 113.

100. The Kassák-Balázs debate of 1920 prefigures in important ways Lukács' own repudiation of expressionism in the 1930s. For a good account of Lukács' stand on expressionism, see Eugene Lunn, *Marxism and Modernism: A Historical Study of Lukács, Brecht, Benjamin and Adorno* (Berkeley: University of California Press, 1982).

101. Lajos Kassák, "Levél a müvészetröl" (Letter about aesthetics), *Bécsi Magyar Ujság* (Viennese Hungarian daily), 10 September 1920.

102. Béla Balázs, "Dada," *Bécsi Magyar Ujság*, 4 November 1920.

103. Balázs, Diaries, 16 October 1922.

104. Lajos Kassák, "Levél a müvészetröl" (Letter about aesthetics), *Bécsi Magyar Ujság*, 16 September 1920.

105. Karl Mannheim to Oszkár Jászi, 8 November 1936, Butler Library, Columbia University, New York City.

106. Anna Lesznai, Sketch for a novel (1954), Petöfi Irodalmi Múzeum.

107. Lesznai, Diaries, 1928.

108. Quoted in Lesznai, Diaries, 1927.

109. Lesznai, Diaries, n.d. [probably late 1920s].

110. Georg Lukács to Béla Balázs, 31 January 1940, Magyar Tudományos Akadémia, Kézirattár, Budapest.

111. Lajos Fülep to Imre Kner, 11 September 1932, Magyar Tudományos Akadémia, Kézirattár, Budapest.

112. Lajos Fülep to Imre Kner, 6 July 1942, Magyar Tudományos Akadémia, Kézirattár, Budapest.

INDEX

Index

DATE DUE